New Dark Age

New Dark Age

*Technology
and the End of the Future*

James Bridle

Updated Edition

VERSO

This updated edition first published by Verso 2023
First published by Verso 2018
© James Bridle 2018, 2019, 2023

1 3 5 7 9 10 8 6 4 2

Verso
UK: 6 Meard Street, London W1F 0EG
US: 388 Atlantic Avenue, Brooklyn, NY 11217
versobooks.com

Verso is the imprint of New Left Books

ISBN-13: 978-1-80429-042-2
ISBN-13: 978-1-78663-549-5 (UK EBK)
ISBN-13: 978-1-78663-550-1 (US EBK)

British Library Cataloguing in Publication Data
A catalogue record for this book is available from the British Library

The Library of Congress Has Cataloged the Hardback Edition as Follows:

Names: Bridle, James, author.
Title: New dark age : technology, knowledge and the end of the future / James
  Bridle.
Description: London ; Brooklyn, NY : Verso, 2018. | Includes bibliographical
  references and index. |
Identifiers: LCCN 2018005480 (print) | LCCN 2018026785 (ebook) | ISBN
  9781786635495 (United Kingdom) | ISBN 9781786635501 (United States) |
  ISBN
  9781786635471 | ISBN 9781786635495 (UK ebk) | ISBN 9781786635501 (US
  ebk)
Subjects: LCSH: Technology—Social aspects. | Big data—Social aspects. |
  Artificial intelligence—Social aspects. | Social change.
Classification: LCC T14.5 (ebook) | LCC T14.5 .B745 2018 (print) | DDC
  303.48/3—dc23
LC record available at https://lccn.loc.gov/2018005480

Typeset in Sabon by Biblichor Ltd, Edinburgh
Printed and bound by CPI Group (UK) Ltd, Croydon, CR0 4YY

For Navine

Contents

1

Chasm

'If only technology could invent some way of getting in touch with you in an emergency,' said my computer, repeatedly.

Following the 2016 US election result, along with several other people I know and perhaps prompted by the hive mind of social media, I started re-watching *The West Wing*: an exercise in hopeless nostalgia. It didn't help, but I got into the habit, when alone, of watching an episode or two in the evenings, after work, or on planes. After reading the latest apocalyptic research papers on climate change, total surveillance, and the uncertainties of the global political situation, a little neoliberal chamber play from the noughties wasn't the worst thing to sink into. One night I am halfway through an episode from the third series, and President Bartlett's chief of staff, Leo McGarry, is regretting attending an AA meeting and as a result missing the early stages of an emergency.

'What would you have done a half hour ago that hasn't already been done?' asks the president.

'I'd have known a half hour ago what I know now,' replies McGarry. 'This is exactly why I'm not going to my meeting anymore – it's a luxury.'

Bartlett circles McGarry, teasing him: 'I know. If only technology could invent some way to get in touch with you in an emergency! Some sort of telephonic device with a personalised number we could call to let you know that we needed you' – he reaches into Leo's pocket and pulls out his phone – 'Perhaps it would look something like this, Mr Moto!'

Except the episode didn't get that far. The image on the screen continued to change, but my laptop had crashed, and one sentence of the audio looped over and over: 'If only technology could invent some way to get in touch with you in an emergency! If only technology could invent some way to get in touch with you in an emergency! If only technology could invent some way to get in touch with you in an emergency!'

This is a book about what technology is trying to tell us in an emergency. It is also a book about what we know, how we know, and what we cannot know.

Over the last century, technological acceleration has transformed our planet, our societies, and ourselves, but it has failed to transform our understanding of these things. The reasons for this are complex, and the answers are complex too, not least because we ourselves are utterly enmeshed in technological systems, which shape in turn how we act and how we think. We cannot stand outside them; we cannot think without them.

Our technologies are complicit in the greatest challenges we face today: an out-of-control economic system that immiserates many and continues to widen the gap between rich and poor; the collapse of political and societal consensus across the globe resulting in increasing nationalisms, social divisions, ethnic conflicts and shadow wars; and a warming climate, which existentially threatens us all.

Across the sciences and society, in politics and education, in warfare and commerce, new technologies do not merely augment our abilities, but actively shape and direct them, for better and for worse. It is increasingly necessary to be able to think new technologies in different ways, and to be critical of them, in order to meaningfully participate in that shaping and directing. If we do not understand how complex technologies function, how systems of technologies interconnect, and how systems of systems interact, then we are powerless within them, and their potential is more easily captured by selfish elites and inhuman corporations. Precisely because these technologies interact with one another in unexpected and often-strange ways, and because we are completely entangled with them, this understanding cannot be limited to the practicalities of how things work: it must be extended to how things came to be, and how they continue to function in the world in ways that are often invisible and interwoven. What is required is not understanding, but literacy.

True literacy in systems consists of much more than simple understanding, and might be understood and practised in multiple ways. It goes beyond a system's functional use to comprehend its context and consequences. It refuses to see the application of any one system as a cure-all, insisting upon the interrelationships of systems and the inherent limitations of any single solution. It is fluent not only in the language of a system, but in its metalanguage – the language it uses to talk about itself and to interact with other systems – and is sensitive to the limitations and the potential uses and abuses of that metalanguage. It is, crucially, capable of both performing and responding to critique.

One of the arguments often made in response to weak public understanding of technology is a call to increase technological education – in its simplest formulation, to learn to code. Such a call is made frequently by politicians, technologists, pundits and business leaders, and it is often advanced in nakedly functional and pro-market terms: the information economy needs more programmers, and young people need jobs in the future. This is a good start, but learning to code is not enough, just as learning to plumb a sink is not enough to understand the complex interactions between water tables, political geography, ageing infrastructure, and social policy that define, shape and produce actual life support systems in society. A simply functional understanding of systems is insufficient; one needs to be able to think about histories and consequences too. Where did these systems come from, who designed them and what for, and which of these intentions still lurk within them today?

The second danger of a purely functional understanding of technology is what I call computational thinking. Computational thinking is an extension of what others have called solutionism: the belief that any given problem can be solved by the application of computation. Whatever the practical or social problem we face, there is an app for it. But solutionism is insufficient too; this is one of the things that our technology is trying to tell us. Beyond this error, computational thinking supposes – often at an unconscious level – that the world really is like the solutionists propose. It internalises solutionism to the degree that it is impossible to think or articulate the world in terms that are not computable. Computational thinking is predominant in the world today, driving the worst trends in our societies and interactions, and must be opposed by a real systemic literacy. If philosophy is that fraction of human thought dealing with that which cannot be explained by the sciences, then systemic literacy is the thinking that deals with a world that is not computable, while acknowledging that it is irrevocably shaped and informed by computation.

The weakness of 'learning to code' alone might be argued in the opposite direction too: you should be able to understand technological systems without having to learn to code at all, just as one should not need to be a plumber to take a shit, nor to live without fear that your plumbing system might be trying to kill you. The possibility that your plumbing system is indeed trying to kill you should not be discounted either: complex computational systems provide much of the infrastructure of contemporary society, and if they are not safe for people to use, no amount of education in just how bad they are will save us in the long run.

In this book, we are going to do some plumbing, but we must bear in mind the needs of the non-plumbers at every stage: the need to understand, and the need to live even when we don't always understand. We often struggle to conceive of and describe the scope and scale of new technologies, meaning that we have trouble even thinking them. What is needed is not new technology, but new metaphors: a metalanguage for describing the world that complex systems have wrought. A new shorthand is required, one that simultaneously acknowledges and addresses the reality of a world in which people, politics, culture and technology are utterly enmeshed. We have always been connected – unequally, illogically, and some more than others – but entirely and inevitably. What changes in the network is that this connection is visible and undeniable. We are confronted at all times by the radical interconnectedness of things and our selves, and we must reckon with this realisation in new ways. It is insufficient to speak of the internet or amorphous technologies, alone and unaccountable, as causing or accelerating the chasm in our understanding and agency. For want of a better term, I use the word 'network' to include us and our technologies in one vast system – to include human and nonhuman agency and understanding, knowing and unknowing, within the same agential soup. The chasm is not between us and our technologies, but within the network itself, and it is through the network that we come to know it.

Finally, systemic literacy permits, performs, and responds to critique. The systems we will be discussing are too critical to be thought, understood, designed and enacted by the few, especially when those few all too easily align themselves with, or are subsumed by, older elites and power structures. There is a concrete and causal relationship between the complexity of the systems we encounter every day; the opacity with which most of those systems are constructed or described; and fundamental, global issues of inequality, violence, populism and fundamentalism. All too often, new technologies are presented as inherently emancipatory. But this is itself an example of computational thinking, of which we are all guilty. Those of us who have been early adopters and cheerleaders of new technologies, who have experienced their manifold pleasures and benefited from their opportunities, and who have consequently argued, often naively, for their wider implementation, are in no less danger from their uncritical deployment. But the argument for critique cannot be made from individual threats, nor from identification with the less fortunate or less knowledgeable. Individualism and empathy are both insufficient in the network. Survival and solidarity must be possible without understanding.

We don't and cannot understand everything, but we are capable of thinking it. The ability to think without claiming, or even seeking, to fully understand is key to survival in a new dark age because, as we shall see, it is often impossible to understand. Technology is and can be a guide and helpmate in this thinking, providing we do not privilege its output: computers are not here to give us answers, but are tools for asking questions. As we will see recur throughout this book, understanding a technology deeply and systemically often allows us to remake its metaphors in the service of other ways of thinking.

Beginning in the 1950s, a new symbol began to creep into the diagrams drawn by electrical engineers to describe the systems that they built. The symbol was a fuzzy circle, or a puffball, or a thought bubble. Eventually, its form settled into the shape of a cloud. Whatever the engineer was working on, it could connect to this cloud, and that's all you needed to know. The other cloud could be a power system, or a data exchange, or another network of computers, or whatever. It didn't matter. The cloud was a way of reducing complexity: it allowed one to focus on the near at hand, and not worry about what was happening over there. Over time, as networks grew larger and more interconnected, the cloud became more and more important. Smaller systems were defined by their relation to the cloud, by how fast they could exchange information with it, by what they could draw down from it. The cloud was becoming weightier, becoming a resource: the cloud could do this, it could do that. The cloud could be powerful and intelligent. It became a business buzzword and a selling point. It became more than engineering shorthand; it became a metaphor.

Today the cloud is the central metaphor of the internet: a global system of great power and energy that nevertheless retains the aura of something noumenal and numinous, something almost impossible to grasp. We connect to the cloud; we work in it; we store and retrieve stuff from it; we think through it. We pay for it and only notice it when it breaks. It is something we experience all the time without really understanding what it is or how it works. It is something we are training ourselves to rely upon with only the haziest of notions about what is being entrusted, and what it is being entrusted to.

Downtime aside, the first criticism of this cloud is that it is a very bad metaphor. The cloud is not weightless; it is not amorphous, or even invisible, if you know where to look for it. The cloud is not some magical faraway place, made of water vapour and radio waves, where everything just works. It is a physical infrastructure consisting of phone lines, fibre optics, satellites, cables on the ocean floor, and vast warehouses filled with computers, which consume huge amounts of water and energy and reside within national and legal jurisdictions. The cloud is a new kind of industry, and a hungry one. The cloud doesn't just have a shadow; it has a footprint. Absorbed into the cloud are many of the previously weighty edifices of the civic sphere: the places where we shop, bank, socialise, borrow books, and vote. Thus obscured, they are rendered less visible and less amenable to critique, investigation, preservation and regulation.

Another criticism is that this lack of understanding is deliberate. There are good reasons, from national security to corporate secrecy to many kinds of malfeasance, for obscuring what's inside the cloud. What evaporates is agency and owner-ship: most of your emails, photos, status updates, business documents, library and voting data, health records, credit ratings, likes, memories, experiences, personal preferences and unspoken desires are in the cloud, on somebody else's infra-structure. There's a reason Google and Facebook like to build data centres in Ireland (low taxes) and Scandinavia (cheap energy and cooling). There's a reason global, supposedly post-colonial empires hold onto bits of disputed territory like Diego Garcia and Cyprus, and it's because the cloud touches down in these places, and their ambiguous status can be exploited. The cloud shapes itself to geographies of power and influence, and it serves to reinforce them. The cloud is a power relation-ship, and most people are not on top of it.

These are valid criticisms, and one way of interrogating the cloud is to look where its shadow falls: to investigate the sites of data centres and undersea cables and see what they tell us about the real disposition of power at work today. We can seed the cloud, condense it, and force it to give up some of its stories. As it fades, certain secrets may be revealed. By under-standing the way the figure of the cloud is used to obscure the real operation of technology, we can start to understand the many ways in which technology itself hides its own agency – through opaque machines and inscrutable code, as well as physical distance and legal constructs. And in turn, we may learn something about the operation of power itself, which was doing this sort of thing long before it had clouds and black boxes in which to hide itself.

But beyond this once-again functional vision of the cloud, beyond its re-earthing, can we turn the figure of the cloud over once more in order to produce a new metaphor? Can the cloud absorb not only our failure to understand, but our understanding of that lack of understanding? Can we supplant base computational thinking with cloudy thinking, which acknowledges an unknowing and makes of it productive rain? In the fourteenth century, an unknown author of Christian mysticism wrote of 'The Cloud of Unknowing' that hangs between mankind and the Godhead: the embodiment of goodness, justice, and right action. This cloud cannot be pierced by thought, but by the letting-go of thought, and through the insistence upon the here and now – not the predicted, computed future – as the domain of agency. 'Go after experience rather than knowledge,' the author urges us. 'On account of pride, knowledge may often deceive you, but this gentle, loving affection will not deceive you. Knowledge tends to breed conceit, but love builds. Knowledge is full of labor, but love, full of rest.'[1] It is this cloud that we have sought to conquer with computation, but that is continually undone by the reality of what we are attempting. Cloudy thinking, the embrace of unknowing, might allow us to revert from computational thinking, and it is what the network itself urges upon us.

The greatest signifying quality of the network is its lack of single, solid intent. Nobody set out to create the network, or its greatest built exemplar, the internet. Over time, system upon system, culture upon culture, were linked together, through public programmes and private investments; through personal relationships and technological protocols; in steel, glass and electrons; through physical space; and in the space of the mind. In turn, the network gave expression to the basest and highest ideals, contained and exulted the most mundane and the most radical desires, almost none of it foreseen by its progenitors – who are all of us. There was and is no problem to solve, only collective enterprise: the emergent, unconscious generation of a tool for unconscious generation. Thinking the network reveals the inadequacy of computational thinking and the interconnectedness of all things, as well as their endlessness; it insists upon the constant need to rethink and reflect upon its weights and balances, its collective intent and failings, its roles, responsibilities, prejudices and possibilities.

This is what the network teaches: nothing short of everything will really do.[2]

Our great failing in thinking the network up to now was to presume that its actions were inherent and inevitable. By inherent, I mean the notion that they emerged, ex nihilo, from the things we created rather than involving our own actions as part of that co-creation. By inevitable, I mean a belief in a direct line of technological and historical progress that we are powerless to resist. Such a belief has been repeatedly attacked by thinkers in the social sciences and philosophy for decades, yet it has not been defeated. Rather, it has been reified into technology itself: into machines that are supposed to carry out their own embedded desires. Thus we have abdicated our objections to linear progress, falling into the chasm of computational thinking.

The greatest carrier wave of progress for the last few centuries has been the central idea of the Enlightenment itself: that more knowledge – more *information* – leads to better decisions. For which one can, of course, substitute any concept of 'better' that one chooses. Despite the assaults of modernity and postmodernity, this core tenet has come to define not merely what is implemented, but what is even considered possible from new technologies. The internet, in its youth, was often referred to as an 'information superhighway', a conduit of knowledge that, in the flickering light of fibre-optic cables, enlightens the world. Any fact, any quantum of information, is available at the tap of a keyboard – or so we have led ourselves to believe.

And so we find ourselves today connected to vast repositories of knowledge, and yet we have not learned to think. In fact, the opposite is true: that which was intended to enlighten the world in practice darkens it. The abundance of information and the plurality of worldviews now accessible to us through the internet are not producing a coherent consensus reality, but one riven by fundamentalist insistence on simplistic narratives, conspiracy theories, and post-factual politics. It is on this contradiction that the idea of a new dark age turns: an age in which the value we have placed upon knowledge is destroyed by the abundance of that profitable commodity, and in which we look about ourselves in search of new ways to understand the world. In 1926, H. P. Lovecraft wrote,

> The most merciful thing in the world, I think, is the inability of the human mind to correlate all its contents. We live on a placid island of ignorance in the midst of black seas of infinity, and it was not meant that we should voyage far. The sciences, each straining in its own direction, have hitherto harmed us little; but some day the piecing together of dissociated knowledge will open up such terrifying vistas of reality, and of our frightful position therein, that we shall either go mad from the revelation or flee from the deadly light into the peace and safety of a new dark age.[3]

How we understand and think our place in the world, and our relation to one another and to machines, will ultimately decide if madness or peace is where our technologies will take us. The darkness I write of is not a literal darkness, nor does it represent an absence or occlusion of knowledge, as the popular idea of a dark age holds. It is not an expression of nihilism or hopelessness. Rather, it refers to both the nature and the opportunity of the present crisis: an apparent inability to see clearly what is in front of us, and to act meaningfully, with agency and justice, in the world – and, through acknowledging this darkness, to seek new ways of seeing by another light.

In her private journal of January 18, 1915, in the bleakest hours of the First World War, Virginia Woolf observed that 'the future is dark, which is the best thing the future can be, I think.' As Rebecca Solnit has written, 'It's an extraordinary declaration, asserting that the unknown need not be turned into the known through false divination, or the projection of grim political or ideological narratives; it's a celebration of darkness, willing – as that "*I think*" indicates – to be uncertain even about its own assertion.'[4]

Donna Haraway elaborates further on this thinking,[5] noting that Woolf insisted upon it again in *Three Guineas*, published in 1938:

> Think we must. Let us think in offices; in omnibuses; while we are standing in the crowd watching Coronations and Lord Mayor's Shows; let us think as we pass the Cenotaph; and in Whitehall; in the gallery of the House of Commons; in the Law Courts; let us think at baptisms and marriages and funerals. Let us never cease from thinking – what is this 'civilisation' in which we find ourselves? What are these ceremonies and why should we take part in them? What are these professions and why should we make money out of them? Where in short is it leading us, the procession of the sons of educated men?[6]

The class and social conflicts, the historical hierarchies and injustices, that Woolf alludes to in her processions and ceremonies have in no measure abated today, but some of the places to think them may have changed. The crowds that in 1938 lined London's Lord Mayor's and coronation parades are now distributed through the network, and the galleries and places of worship have likewise migrated into data centres and undersea cables. We cannot unthink the network; we can only think through and within it. And we can listen to it, when it tries to speak to us in an emergency.

Nothing here is an argument against technology: to do so would be to argue against ourselves. Rather, it is an argument for a more thoughtful engagement with technology, coupled with a radically different understanding of what it is possible to think and know about the world. Computational systems, as tools, emphasise one of the most powerful aspects of humanity: our ability to act effectively in the world and shape it to our desires. But uncovering and articulating those desires, and ensuring that they do not degrade, overrule, efface, or erase the desires of others, remains our prerogative.

Technology is not mere tool making and tool use: it is the making of metaphors. In making a tool, we instantiate a certain understanding of the world that, thus reified, is capable of achieving certain effects in that world. It thus becomes another moving part of our understanding of the world – if, often, unconsciously. Thus we might say it is a hidden metaphor: a kind of transport or transference is achieved, but at the same time a kind of disassociation, an offloading of a particular thought or way of thinking into a tool, where it no longer needs thinking to activate. To think again or anew, we need to re-enchant our tools. The present account is merely the first part of such a re-enchantment, an attempt to rethink our tools – not a repurposing or a redefinition, necessarily, but a thoughtfulness of them.

When one has a hammer, goes the saying, everything looks like a nail. But this is to not think the hammer. The hammer, properly conceived, has many uses. It may pull nails as well as drive them; it may forge iron, shape wood and stone, reveal fossils, and fix anchors for climbing ropes. It may pass sentence, call to order, or be thrown in a contest of athletic strength. Wielded by a god, it generates the weather. Thor's hammer, Mjölnir, which created thunder and lightning when it was struck, also gave birth to hammer-shaped amulets intended to provide protection against the god's wrath – or, through their resemblance to crosses, against enforced conversion. Prehistoric hammers and axes, turned up by the ploughs of later generations, were called 'thunderstones' and were believed to have fallen from the sky during storms. These mysterious tools thus became magical objects: when their original purposes passed away, they were capable of taking on new symbolic meaning. We must re-enchant our hammers – all our tools – so they are less like the carpenter's, and more like Thor's. More like thunderstones.

Technology is also not made entirely – ex nihilo – by humans. It depends, as does our own living (bacteria, food crops, building materials, clothes and companion species), on the affordances of nonhuman things. The infrastructure of high-frequency trading (which we will explore in chapter 5), and the economic system it accelerates and characterises, is an accommodation with silicon and steel, with the speed of light through glass, with fog, and birds, and squirrels. Technology can be an excellent lesson in the agency of nonhuman actors, from rocks to bugs, whenever they obstruct or permit, chew through or short out, our lines of communication and power.

This relationship, properly understood, is also a realisation of technology's inherent instability: its temporal and temporary alignment or resonance with certain other uncertain properties of materials and animals that are subject to change. In short, of its cloudiness. The examination, in chapter 3, of the changing affordances of materials for computation in response to environmental stress is an example of this: things do things differently in time. Technology comes with an aura of fixedness: once immurred in things, ideas seem settled and unassailable. Hammers, properly employed, can crack them open once again. By re-enchanting a few tools, we might see the myriad ways in which this realisation is immanent within multiple modes of contemporary, everyday life. Along the way, what may be presented as 'revelations' about the 'truth' of the world should always be held at arm's length, as mere (or not mere; abject) rethinkings of that world. Indeed, arm's length should be the resonant, representative gesture of the work, as holding something at arm's length has the effect, from another perspective, of pointing at something else in the distance, something beyond the immediate realisation, and promising more.

The argument set out in this book is that, like climate change, the effects of technology are widespread across the globe and are already affecting every area of our lives. These effects are potentially catastrophic, and result from an inability to comprehend the turbulent and networked outputs of our own inventions. As such, they upset what we have naively come to expect as the natural order of things, and they require a radical rethinking of the ways in which we think the world. But the other thrust of this book is that all is not lost: if we really are capable of thinking in new ways, then we are also capable of rethinking the world, and thus understanding and living differently within it. And just as our current understanding of the world proceeds from our scientific discoveries, so our rethinking of it must emerge from and alongside our technological inventions, which are very real manifestations of the contested, complex, and contradictory state of the world itself. Our technologies are extensions of ourselves, codified in machines and infrastructures, in frameworks of knowledge and action; truly thought, they offer a model of a truer world.

We have been conditioned to think of the darkness as a place of danger, even of death. But the darkness can also be a place of freedom and possibility, a place of equality. For many, what is discussed here will be obvious, because they have always lived in this darkness that seems so threatening to the privileged. We have much to learn about unknowing. Uncertainty can be productive, even sublime.

The final and most crucial chasm is the one that opens up between us as individuals when we fail to acknowledge and articulate present conditions. Make no mistake, there are aspects of the new dark age that are real and immediate existential threats, most obviously the planet's warming climate and its crashing ecosystems. There are also the ongoing effects of collapsing consensus, failing sciences, truncated prediction horizons, and public and private paranoia – all of which bespeak discord and violence. Disparities in income and in understanding are both deadly in the not-so-long term. All of these are connected: all of them are failures to think and speak.

Writing about the new dark age, even if I can leaven it with networked hope, is not pleasant. It requires saying things that we would rather leave unsaid, thinking things that we would rather keep unthought. Doing so often leaves one with a hollow feeling in the gut, a kind of despair. And yet to fail to do so will be to fail to acknowledge the world as it is, to continue to live in fantasy and abstraction. I think of my friends, and the things we say to one another when we are being honest, and, at some level, how frightened it makes us feel. There is a kind of shame in speaking about the exigencies of the present, and a deep vulnerability, but it must not stop us thinking. We cannot fail each other now.

2

Computation

In 1884, the art critic and social thinker John Ruskin gave a series of lectures at the London Institution entitled 'The Storm-Cloud of the Nineteenth Century.' Over the evenings of February 14 and 18, he presented an overview of descriptions of the sky and clouds drawn from Classical and European art, as well as the accounts of mountain climbers in his beloved Alps, together with his own observations of the skies of southern England in the last decades of the nineteenth century.

In these lectures he advanced his opinion that the sky contained a new kind of cloud. This cloud, which he called a 'storm-cloud', or sometimes 'plague-cloud',

> never was seen but by now living, or lately, living eyes . . . There is no description of it, so far as I have read, by any ancient observer. Neither Homer nor Virgil, neither Aristophanes nor Horace, acknowledges any such clouds among those compelled by Jove. Chaucer has no word for them, nor Dante; Milton none, nor Thomson. In modern times, Scott, Wordsworth and Byron are alike unconscious of them; and the most observant and descriptive of scientific men, De Saussure, is utterly silent concerning them.[1]

Ruskin's 'constant and close observation' of the skies had led him to the belief that there was a new wind abroad in England and the Continent, a 'plague-wind' that brought a new weather with it. Quoting from his own diary of July 1, 1871, he relates that the sky is covered with grey cloud; – not rain-cloud, but a dry black veil, which no ray of sunshine can pierce; partly diffused in mist, feeble mist, enough to make distant objects unintelligible, yet without any substance, or wreathing, or colour of its own . . .

And it is a new thing to me, and a very dreadful one. I am fifty years old, and more; and since I was five, have gleaned the best hours of my life in the sun of spring and summer mornings; and I never saw such as these, till now.

And the scientific men are busy as ants, examining the sun, and the moon, and the seven stars, and they can tell me all about them, I believe, by this time; and how they move, and what they are made of.

And I do not care, for my part, two copper spangles how they move, nor what they are made of. I can't move them any other way than they go, nor make of them anything else, better than they are made. But I would care much and give much, if I could be told where this bitter wind comes from, and what it is made of.[2]

He goes on to elucidate many similar observations: from strong winds out of nowhere, to dark clouds covering the sun at midday, and pitch-black rains that putrefied his garden. And while he acknowledges, in remarks that have been seized on by environmentalists in the years since, the presence of numerous and multiplying industrial chimneys in the region of his observations, his primary concern is with the moral character of such a cloud, and the ways it seemed to emanate from battlefields and sites of societal unrest.

'What is best to be done, do you ask me? The answer is plain. Whether you can affect the signs of the sky or not, you can the signs of the times.'[3] The metaphors we use to describe the world, like Ruskin's plague-cloud, form and shape our understanding of it. Today, other clouds, often still emanating from sites of protest and contest, provide the ways we have to think the world.

Ruskin dwelled at length upon the differing quality of light when affected by the storm-cloud, for light too has a moral quality. In his lectures, he argued that the '*fiat lux* of creation' – the moment when the God of Genesis says, 'Let there be light' – is also *fiat anima*, the creation of life. Light, he insisted, is 'as much the ordering of Intelligence as the ordering of Vision'. That which we see shapes not just what we think, but how we think.

Just a few years previously, in 1880, Alexander Graham Bell first demonstrated a device called the photophone. A companion invention to the telephone, the photophone enabled the first 'wireless' transmission of the human voice. It worked by bouncing a beam of light off a reflective surface, which was vibrated by the voice of a speaker, and received by a primitive photovoltaic cell, which turned the light waves back into sound. Across the rooftops of Washington, DC, Bell was able to make himself understood by light alone at a distance of some 200 metres.

Arriving several years before the promulgation of effective electrical lighting, the photophone was completely dependent on clear skies to provide bright light to the reflector. This meant that atmospheric conditions could affect the sound produced, altering the output. Bell wrote excitedly to his father, 'I have heard articulate speech by sunlight! I have heard a ray of the sun laugh and cough and sing! I have been able to hear a shadow and I have even perceived by ear the passage of a cloud across the sun's disk.'[4]

The initial response to Bell's invention was not promising. A commentator in the *New York Times* wondered sarcastically if 'a line of sunbeams' might be hung on telegraph posts, and whether it might be necessary to insulate them. 'Until one sees a man going through the streets with a coil of No. 12 sunbeams on his shoulder, and suspending them from pole to pole, there will be a general feeling that there is something about Professor Bell's photophone which places a tremendous strain on human credulity,' they wrote.[5]

That line of sunbeams, of course, is precisely what we can see today arrayed around the globe. Bell's invention was the first to deploy light as a carrier of complex information – as the commentator noticed, unwittingly, it required only the insulation of the sunbeam in order to carry it over unimaginable distances. Today, Bell's sunbeams order the data that passes beneath the ocean waves in the form of light-transmitting fibre-optic cables, and they order in turn the collective intelligence of the world. They make possible the yoking together of vast infrastructures of computation that organise and govern all of us. Ruskin's *fiat lux* as *fiat anima* is reified in the network.

Thinking through machines predates the machines themselves. The existence of calculus proves that some problems may be tractable before it is possible to solve them practically. History, viewed as such a problem, might thus be transformed into a mathematical equation that, when solved, would produce the future. This was the belief of the early computational thinkers of the twentieth century, and its persistence, largely unquestioned and even unconscious, into our own time is the subject of this book. Personified today as a digital cloud, the story of computational thinking begins with the weather.

In 1916, the mathematician Lewis Fry Richardson was at work on the Western Front; as a Quaker, he was a committed pacifist, and so had enrolled in the Friends' Ambulance Unit, a Quaker section that also included the artist Roger Penrose and the philosopher and science fiction writer Olaf Stapledon. Over several months, between sorties to the front line and rest periods in damp cottages in France and Belgium, Richardson performed the first full calculation of atmospheric weather conditions by numerical process: the first computerised daily forecast, without a computer.

Before the war, Richardson had been superintendent of the Eskdalemuir Observatory, a remote meteorological station in western Scotland. Among the papers he took with him when he went off to war were the complete records of a single day of observations across Europe, compiled on May 20, 1910, by hundreds of observers across the continent. Richardson believed that, through the application of a range of complex mathematical operations derived from years of weather data, it should be possible to numerically advance the observations in order to predict how conditions would evolve over successive hours. In order to do so, he drew up a stack of computing forms, with a series of columns for temperature, wind speed, pressure, and other information, the preparation of which alone took him several weeks. He divided the continent into a series of evenly spaced observation points and performed his calculations with pen and paper, his office 'a heap of hay in a cold rest billet'.[6]

When finally completed, Richardson tested his forecast against the actual observed data and found that his numbers were wildly exaggerated. Nevertheless, it proved the utility of the method: break the world down into a series of grid squares, and apply a series of mathematical techniques to solve the atmospheric equations for each square. What was missing was the technology required to implement such thinking at the scale and speed of the weather itself.

In *Weather Prediction by Numerical Process*, published in 1922, Richardson reviewed and summarised his calculations, and laid out a little thought experiment for achieving them more efficiently with the technology of the day. In this experiment, the 'computers' were still human beings, and the abstractions of what we would come to understand as digital computation were laid out at the scale of architecture:

> After so much hard reasoning, may one play with a fantasy? Imagine a large hall like a theatre, except that the circles and galleries go right round through the space usually occupied by the stage. The walls of this chamber are painted to form a map of the globe. The ceiling represents the north polar regions, England is in the gallery, the tropics in the upper circle, Australia on the dress circle and the Antarctic in the pit.

A myriad computers are at work upon the weather of the part of the map where each sits, but each computer attends only to one equation or part of an equation. The work of each region is coordinated by an official of higher rank. Numerous little 'night signs' display the instantaneous values so that neighbouring computers can read them. Each number is thus displayed in three adjacent zones so as to maintain communication to the North and South on the map.

From the floor of the pit a tall pillar rises to half the height of the hall. It carries a large pulpit on its top. In this sits the man in charge of the whole theatre; he is surrounded by several assistants and messengers. One of his duties is to maintain a uniform speed of progress in all parts of the globe. In this respect he is like the conductor of an orchestra in which the instruments are slide-rules and calculating machines. But instead of waving a baton he turns a beam of rosy light upon any region that is running ahead of the rest, and a beam of blue light upon those who are behindhand.

Four senior clerks in the central pulpit are collecting the future weather as fast as it is being computed, and despatching it by pneumatic carrier to a quiet room. There it will be coded and telephoned to the radio transmitting station. Messengers carry piles of used computing forms down to a storehouse in the cellar.

In a neighbouring building there is a research department, where they invent improvements. But there is much experimenting on a small scale before any change is made in the complex routine of the computing theatre. In a basement an enthusiast is observing eddies in the liquid lining of a huge spinning bowl, but so far the arithmetic proves the better way. In another building are all the usual financial, correspondence and administrative offices. Outside are playing fields, houses, mountains and lakes, for it was thought that those who compute the weather should breathe of it freely.[7]

In a preface to the report, Richardson wrote,

> Perhaps some day in the dim future it will be possible to advance the computations faster than the weather advances and at a cost less than the saving to mankind due to the information gained. But that is a dream.[8]

It was to remain a dream for another fifty years, and would eventually be solved by the application of military technologies that Richardson himself would disavow. After the war, he joined the Meteorological Office, intending to continue his research, but he resigned in 1920 when it was taken over by the Air Ministry. Research on numerical weather forecasting stagnated for many years, until spurred forward by the explosion of computational power that emanated from another conflict, the Second World War. The war unleashed vast amounts of funding for research, and a sense of urgency for its application, but it also created knotty problems: a vast, overwhelming flow of information pouring from a newly networked world, and a rapidly expanding system of knowledge production.

In an essay entitled 'As We May Think', published in the *Atlantic* in 1945, the engineer and inventor Vannevar Bush wrote,

> There is a growing mountain of research. But there is increased evidence that we are being bogged down today as specialisation extends. The investigator is staggered by the findings and conclusions of thousands of other workers – conclusions which he cannot find time to grasp, much less to remember, as they appear. Yet specialisation becomes increasingly necessary for progress, and the effort to bridge between disciplines is correspondingly superficial.[9]

Bush had been employed during the war as director of the US Office of Scientific Research and Development (OSRD), the primary vehicle for military research and development. He was one of the progenitors of the Manhattan Project, the top secret wartime research project that led to the development of the American atomic bomb.

Bush's proposed solution to both these problems – the over-whelming information available to enquiring minds, and the increasingly destructive ends of scientific research – was a device that he called the 'memex':

> A memex is a device in which an individual stores all his books, records, and communications, and which is mecha-nised so that it may be consulted with exceeding speed and flexibility. It is an enlarged intimate supplement to his memory. It consists of a desk, and while it can presumably be operated from a distance, it is primarily the piece of furniture at which he works. On the top are slanting translucent screens, on which material can be projected for convenient reading. There is a keyboard, and sets of buttons and levers. Otherwise it looks like an ordinary desk.[10]

In essence, and with the advantage of hindsight, Bush was proposing the electronic, networked computer. His great insight was to combine, in exactly the way a memex would enable anyone to do, multiple discoveries across many disciplines – advances in telephony, machine tooling, photo-graphy, data storage, and stenography – into a single machine. The incorporation of time itself into this matrix produces what we would recognise today as hypertext: the ability to link together collective documents in multiple ways and create new associations between domains of networked knowledge: 'Wholly new forms of encyclopedias will appear, ready made with a mesh of associative trails running through them, ready to be dropped into the memex and there amplified.'[11]

Such an encyclopaedia, readily accessible to the enquiring

mind, would not merely amplify scientific thinking, but civilise it:

> The applications of science have built man a well-supplied house, and are teaching him to live healthily therein. They have enabled him to throw masses of people against one another with cruel weapons. They may yet allow him truly to encompass the great record and to grow in the wisdom of race experience. He may perish in conflict before he learns to wield that record for his true good. Yet, in the application of science to the needs and desires of man, it would seem to be a singularly unfortunate stage at which to terminate the process, or to lose hope as to the outcome.[12]

One of Bush's colleagues at the Manhattan Project was another scientist, John von Neumann, who shared similar concerns about the overwhelming volumes of information being produced – and required – by the scientific endeavours of the day. He was also captivated by the idea of predicting, and even controlling, the weather. In 1945, he came across a mimeograph entitled 'Outline of Weather Proposal', written by a researcher at RCA Laboratories named Vladimir Zworykin. Von Neumann had spent the war consulting for the Manhattan Project, making frequent trips to the secret laboratory at Los Alamos in New Mexico and witnessing the first atomic bomb blast, code-named Trinity, in July 1945. He was the main proponent of the implosion method used in the Trinity test and the Fat Man bomb dropped on Nagasaki, and helped design the critical lenses that focused the explosion.

Zworykin, like Vannevar Bush, had recognised that the information-gathering and retrieval abilities of new computing equipment, together with modern systems of electronic communication, allowed for the simultaneous analysis of vast amounts of data. But rather than focusing on human knowledge production, he anticipated its effects on meteorology. By combining the reports of multiple, widely distributed weather stations, it might be possible to build an exact model of the climatic conditions at any particular moment. A perfectly accurate machine of this kind would not merely be able to display this information, but would be capable of predicting, based on prior patterns, what would occur next. Intervention was the next logical step:

> The eventual goal to be attained is the international organisation of means to study weather phenomena as global phenomena and to channel the world's weather, as far as possible, in such a way as to minimise the damage from catastrophic disturbances, and otherwise to benefit the world to the greatest extent by improved climatic conditions where possible. Such an international organisation may contribute to world peace by integrating the world interest in a common problem and turning scientific energy to peaceful pursuits. It is conceivable that eventual far-reaching beneficial effects on the world economy may contribute to the cause of peace.[13]

In October 1945, von Neumann wrote to Zworykin, stating, 'I agree with you completely.' The proposal was totally in line with what von Neumann had learned from the extensive research programme of the Manhattan Project, which relied on complex simulations of physical processes to predict real-world outcomes. In what could be taken as the founding statement of computational thought, he wrote: 'All stable processes we shall predict. All unstable processes we shall control.'[14]

In January 1947, von Neumann and Zworykin shared a stage in New York at a joint session of the American Meteorological Society and the Institute of the Aeronautical Sciences. Von Neumann's talk on 'Future Uses of High Speed Computing in Meteorology' was followed by Zworykin's 'Discussion of the Possibility of Weather Control'. The next day, the *New York Times* reported on the conference under the headline 'Weather to Order', commenting that 'if Dr Zworykin is right the weather-makers of the future are the inventors of calculating machines'.[15]

In 1947, the inventor of calculating machines par excellence was von Neumann himself, having founded the Electronic Computer Project at Princeton two years previously. The project was to build upon both Vannevar Bush's analogue computer – the Bush Differential Analyser, developed at MIT in the 1930s – and von Neumann's own contributions to the first electronic general-purpose computer, the Electronic Numerical Integrator and Computer, or ENIAC. ENIAC was formally dedicated at the University of Pennsylvania on February 15, 1946, but its origins were military: designed to calculate artillery firing tables for the United States Army's Ballistic Research Laboratory, it spent the majority of its first years of operation predicting ever-increasing yields for the first generation of thermonuclear atomic bombs.

Source: US Army.

The ENIAC (Electronic Numerical Integrator and Computer) in Philadelphia, Pennsylvania. Glen Beck (background) and Betty Snyder (foreground) programme the ENIAC in building 328 at the Ballistic Research Laboratory.

Like Bush, von Neumann later became deeply concerned with the possibilities of nuclear warfare – and of weather control. In an essay for *Fortune* magazine in 1955, entitled 'Can We Survive Technology?', he wrote, 'Present awful possibilities of nuclear war may give way to others even more awful. After global climate control becomes possible, perhaps all our present involvements will seem simple. We should not deceive ourselves: once such possibilities become actual, they will be exploited.'[16]

The ENIAC turned out to be Richardson's fantasy of mathematical calculation made solid, at the insistence of von Neumann. In 1948, the ENIAC was moved from Philadelphia to the Ballistic Research Laboratory at the Aberdeen Proving Ground in Maryland. By this time, it covered three of the four walls of the research lab, constructed from some 18,000 vacuum tubes, 70,000 resistors, 10,000 capacitors, and 6,000 switches. The equipment was arranged into forty-two panels, each about two feet across and three feet deep, and stacked ten feet high. It consumed 140 kilowatts of power, and pumped out so much heat that special ceiling fans had to be installed. To reprogram it, it was necessary to turn hundreds of ten-pole rotary switches by hand, the operators moving between the stacks of equipment, connecting cables and checking hundreds of thousands of hand-soldered joints. Among the operators was Klára Dán von Neumann, John von Neumann's wife, who wrote most of the meteorological code and checked the work of the others.

In 1950, a team of meteorologists assembled at Aberdeen in order to perform the first automated twenty-four-hour weather forecast, along exactly the same lines as Richardson had proposed. For this project, the boundaries of the world were the edges of the continental United States; a grid separated it into fifteen rows and eighteen columns. The calculation programmed into the machine consisted of sixteen successive operations, each of which had to be carefully planned and punched into cards, and which in turn output a new deck of cards that had to be reproduced, collated, and sorted. The meteorologists worked in eight-hour shifts, supported by programmers, and the entire run absorbed almost five weeks, 100,000 IBM punch cards, and a million mathematical operations. But when the experimental logs were examined, von Neumann, the director of the experiment, discovered that the actual computational time was almost exactly twenty-four hours. 'One has reason to hope', he wrote, that 'Richardson's dream of advancing computation faster than the weather may soon be realised.'[17]

Harry Reed, a mathematician who worked on the ENIAC at Aberdeen, would later recall the personal effect of working with such large-scale computation. 'The ENIAC itself, strangely, was a very personal computer. Now we think of a personal computer as one you carry around with you. The ENIAC was actually one that you kind of lived inside.'[18] But in fact, today, we all live inside a version of the ENIAC: a vast machinery of computation that encircles the entirety of the globe and extends into outer space on a network of satellites. It is this machine, imagined by Lewis Fry Richardson and actualised by John von Neumann, that governs in one way or another every aspect of life today. And it is one of the most striking conditions of this computational regime that it has rendered itself almost invisible to us.

It is almost possible to pinpoint the exact moment when militarised computation, and the belief in prediction and control that it embodies and produces, slid out of view. The ENIAC was, to the initiated, a legible machine. Different mathematical operations engaged different electromechanical processes: the operators on the meteorology experiment described how they could identify when it entered a particular phase by a distinctive three-note jig played by the card shuffler.[19] Even the casual observer could watch as the blinking lights picking out different operations progressed around the walls of the room.

Source: Columbia University.

Publicity photo of the IBM SSEC, 1948.

By contrast, the IBM Selective Sequence Electronic Calculator (SSEC), installed in New York in 1948, refused such easy reading. It was called a calculator because in 1948 computers were still people, and the president of IBM, Thomas J. Watson, wanted to reassure the public that his products were not designed to replace them.[20] IBM built the machine as a rival to the ENIAC – but both were descendants of von Neumann's earlier Harvard Mark I machine, which contributed to the Manhattan Project. The SSEC was installed in full view of the public inside a former ladies' shoe shop next to IBM's offices on East Fifty-Seventh Street, behind thick plate glass. (The building is now the corporate headquarters of the LVMH luxury goods group.) Further concerned about appearances, Watson ordered his engineers to remove the ugly supporting columns that dominated the space; when they were unable to do so, they airbrushed the publicity photos so that the newspapers carried the look Watson wanted.[21]

To the crowds pressed up against the glass, even with the columns in place, the SSEC radiated a sleek, modern appearance. It took its aesthetic cues from the Harvard Mark I, which was designed by Norman Bel Geddes, the architect of the celebrated Futurama exhibit at the 1939 New York World's Fair. It was housed in the first computer room to utilise a raised floor, now standard in data centres, to hide unsightly cabling from its audience, and it was controlled from a large desk by chief operator Elizabeth 'Betsy' Stewart, of IBM's Department of Pure Science.

Source: IBM Archive.

Elizabeth 'Betsy' Stewart with the SSEC.

In order to fulfil Watson's proclamation, printed and signed on the wall of the computer room – that the machine 'assist the scientist in institutions of learning, in government, and in industry, to explore the consequences of man's thought to the outermost reaches of time, space, and physical conditions' – the SSEC's first run was dedicated to calculating the positions of the moon, stars, and planets for proposed NASA flights. The resulting data, however, were never actually used. Instead, after the first couple of weeks, the machine was largely taken up by top secret calculations for a programme called Hippo, devised by John von Neumann's team at Los Alamos to simulate the first hydrogen bomb.[22]

Programming Hippo took almost a year, and when it was ready it was run continuously on the SSEC, twenty-four hours a day, seven days a week, for several months. The result of the calculations was at least three full simulations of a hydrogen bomb explosion: calculations carried out in full view of the public, in a shopfront in New York City, without anyone on the street being even slightly aware of what was going on. The first full-scale American thermonuclear test based on the Hippo calculations was carried out in 1952; today, all the major nuclear powers possess hydrogen bombs. Computational thinking – violent, destructive, and unimaginably costly, in terms of both money and human cognitive activity – slipped out of view. It became unquestioned and unquestionable, and as such it has endured.

As we shall see, technology's increasing inability to predict the future – whether that's the fluctuating markets of digital stock exchanges, the outcomes and applications of scientific research, or the accelerating instability of the global climate – stems directly from these misapprehensions about the neutrality and comprehensibility of computation.

The dream of Richardson and von Neumann – that of 'advancing computation faster than the weather' – was realised in April of 1951 when Whirlwind I, the first digital computer capable of real-time output, went online at MIT. Project Whirlwind had started as an attempt to build a general-purpose flight simulator for the air force: as it progressed, the problems of real-time data gathering and processing had drawn in interested parties concerned with everything from early computer networking to meteorology.

In order to better reproduce actual conditions that might be faced by pilots, one of Whirlwind I's main functions was to simulate aerodynamic and atmospheric fluctuations, in what amounted to a weather prediction system. This system was not only real-time but, of necessity, networked: connected to and fed data by a range of sensors and offices, from radar systems to weather stations. The young MIT techs who worked on it went on to form the core of the Defense Advanced Research Projects Agency (DARPA) – the progenitor of the internet – and the Digital Equipment Corporation (DEC), the first company to manufacture an affordable business computer. All contemporary computation stems from this nexus: military attempts to predict and control the weather, and thus to control the future.

Whirlwind's design was heavily influenced by ENIAC; in turn, it laid the groundwork for the Semi-Automatic Ground Environment (SAGE), the vast computer system that ran the North American Air Defense Command (NORAD) from the 1950s until the 1980s. Four-storey 'direction centres' were installed in twenty-seven command-and-control stations across the United States, and their twin terminals – one for operation, one for backup – included a light gun for designating targets (resembling the Nintendo 'Zapper') and ashtrays integrated into the console. SAGE is best memorialised in the vast, paranoid aesthetic of Cold War computing systems, from *Dr. Strangelove* in 1964 to *WarGames*, the 1983 blockbuster that told the story of a computer intelligence unable to distinguish between reality and simulation, and famous for its concluding line: 'the only winning move is not to play.'

In order to make such a complex system work, 7,000 IBM engineers were employed to write the largest single computer programme ever created, and 25,000 dedicated phone lines were laid to connect the various locations.[23] Despite this, SAGE is best known for its bloopers: leaving training tapes running so that follow-on shifts mistook simulation data for actual missile attacks, or designating flocks of migrating birds as incoming Soviet bomber fleets. Histories of computation projects typically write off such efforts as anachronistic failures, comparing them to modern bloat-ridden software projects and government IT initiatives that fall short of their much-vaunted goals and are superceded by subsequent, better-engineered systems before they're even completed, feeding a cycle of obsolescence and permanent revision. But what if these stories are the real history of computation: a litany of failures to distinguish between simulation and reality; a chronic failure to identify the conceptual chasm at the heart of computational thinking, of our construction of the world?

We have been conditioned to believe that computers render the world clearer and more efficient, that they reduce complexity and facilitate better solutions to the problems that beset us, and that they expand our agency to address an ever-widening domain of experience. But what if this is not true at all? A close reading of computer history reveals an ever-increasing opacity allied to a concentration of power, and the retreat of that power into ever more narrow domains of experience. By reifying the concerns of the present in unquestionable architectures, computation freezes the problems of the immediate moment into abstract, intractable dilemmas; obsessing over the inherent limitations of a small class of mathematical and material conundrums rather than the broader questions of a truly democratic and egalitarian society.

By conflating approximation with simulation, the high priests of computational thinking replace the world with flawed models of itself; and in doing so, as the modellers, they

34

assume control of the world. Once it became obvious that SAGE was worse than useless at preventing a nuclear war, it shape-shifted, following an in-flight meeting between the president of American Airlines and an IBM salesman, into the Semi-Automated Business Research Environment (SABRE) – a multinational corporation for managing airline reservations.[24] All the pieces were in place: the phone lines, the weather radar, the increasingly privatised processing power, and the ability to manage real-time data flows in an era of mass tourism and mass consumer spending. A machine designed to prevent commercial airlines from being accidentally shot down – a necessary component of any air defence system – pivoted to managing those same flights, buoyed by billions of dollars of defence spending. Today, SABRE connects more than 57,000 travel agents and millions of travellers with more than 400 airlines, 90,000 hotels, 30 car rental companies, 200 tour operators, and dozens of railways, ferries and cruise lines. A kernel of computational Cold War paranoia sits at the heart of billions of journeys made every year.

Aviation will recur in this book as a site where technology, scientific research, defence and security interests, and computation converge in a nexus of transparency/opacity and visibility/invisibility. One of the most extraordinary visualisations on the internet is that provided by real-time plane-tracking websites. Anyone can log on and see, at any time, thousands upon thousands of planes in the air, tracking from city to city, mobbing the Atlantic, coursing in great rivers of metal along international flight paths. It's possible to click on any one of the thousands of little plane icons and see its track, its make and model, the operator and flight number, its origin and destination, and its altitude, speed, and time of flight. Every plane broadcasts an ADS-B signal, which is picked up by a network of amateur flight trackers: more thousands of individuals who choose to set up local radio receivers and share their data online. The view of these flight trackers, like that of Google Earth and other satellite image services, is deeply seductive, to the point of eliciting an almost vertiginous thrill – a sublime for the digital age. The dream of every Cold War planner is now available to the general public on freely accessible websites. But this God's-eye view is illusory, as it also serves to block out and erase other private and state activities, from the private jets of oligarchs and politicians to covert surveillance flights and military manoeuvres.[25] For everything that is shown, something is hidden.

Screenshot of Flightradar24.com, showing 1,500 of 12,151 tracked flights, October 2017. Note Google 'Project Loon' balloons over Puerto Rico, following Hurricane Maria.

In 1983, Ronald Reagan ordered that the then-encrypted Global Positioning System (GPS) be made available to civilians, following the shooting down of a Korean airliner that strayed into Russian airspace. Over time, GPS has come to anchor a huge number of contemporary applications and become another of the invisible, unquestioned signals that modulate everyday life – another of those things that, more or less, 'just works'. GPS enables the blue dot in the centre of the map that folds the entire planet around the individual. Its data directs car and truck journeys, locates ships, prevents planes flying into one another, dispatches taxis, tracks logistics inventories and calls in drone strikes. Essentially a vast, space-based clock, the time signal from GPS satellites regulates power grids and stock markets. But our growing reliance on the system masks the fact that it can still be manipulated by those in control of its signals, including the United States government, which retains the ability to selectively deny positioning signals to any region it chooses.[26] In the summer of 2017, a series of reports from the Black Sea showed deliberate interference with GPS occurring across a wide area, with ships' navigation systems showing them tens of kilometres off their actual position. Many were relocated onshore, finding themselves virtually marooned in a Russian airbase – the suspected source of the spoofing effort.[27] The Kremlin is surrounded by a similar field, as first discovered by players of Pokémon GO, who found their in-game characters teleported blocks away while trying to play the location-based game in the centre of Moscow.[28] (Particularly enterprising players later turned this realisation to their advantage, using electromagnetic shielding and signal generators to collect points without leaving the house.)[29] In other cases, workers whose labour is remotely monitored by GPS, such as long-distance lorry drivers, have simply jammed the signal to enable them to take breaks and unauthorised routes – throwing off other users along their paths. Each of these examples illustrates how crucial computation is to contemporary life, while also revealing its blind spots, structural dangers, and engineered weaknesses.

To take another example from aviation, consider the experience of being in an airport. An airport is a canonical example of what geographers call 'code/space'.[30] Code/spaces describe the interweaving of computation with the built environment and daily experience to a very specific extent: rather than merely overlaying and augmenting them, computation becomes a crucial component of them, such that the environment and the experience of it actually ceases to function in the absence of code.

In the case of the airport, code both facilitates and coproduces the environment. Prior to visiting an airport, passengers engage with an electronic booking system – such as SABRE – that registers their data, identifies them, and makes them visible to other systems, such as check-in desks and passport control. If, when they find themselves at the airport, the system becomes unavailable, it is not a mere inconvenience. Modern security procedures have removed the possibility of paper identification or processing: software is the only accepted arbiter of the process. Nothing can be done; nobody can move. As a result, a software crash revokes the building's status as an airport, transforming it into a huge shed filled with angry people. This is how largely invisible computation coproduces our environment – its critical necessity revealed only in moments of failure, like a kind of brain injury.

Code/spaces increasingly describe more than just smart buildings. Thanks to the pervasive availability of network access and the self-replicating nature of corporate and centralising code, more and more daily activities become dependent on their accompanying software. Daily, even private, travel is reliant on satellite routing, traffic information, and increasingly 'autonomous' vehicles – which, of course, are not autonomous at all, requiring constant updates and input to proceed. Labour is increasingly coded, whether by end-to-end logistics systems or email servers, which in turn require constant attention and monitoring by workers who are dependent upon them. Our social lives are mediated through connectivity and algorithmic revision. As smartphones become powerful general-purpose computers and computation disappears into every device around us, from smart home appliances to vehicle navigation systems, the entire world becomes a code/space. Far from rendering the idea of a code/space obsolete, this ubiquity underscores our failure to understand the impact of computation on the very ways in we think.

When an e-book is purchased from an online service, it remains the property of the seller, its loan subject to revocation at any time – as happened when Amazon remotely deleted thousands of copies of *1984* and *Animal Farm* from customers' Kindles in 2009.[31] Streaming music and video services filter the media available by legal jurisdiction and algorithmically determine 'personal' preferences. Academic journals determine access to knowledge by institutional affiliation and financial contribution as physical, open-access libraries close down. The ongoing functionality of Wikipedia relies on an army of software agents – bots – to enforce and maintain correct formatting, build connections between articles, and moderate conflicts and incidences of vandalism. At the last survey, bots counted for seventeen of the top twenty most prolific editors and collectively make about 16 per cent of all edits to the encyclopaedia project: a concrete and measurable contribution to knowledge production by code itself.[32] Reading a book, listening to music, researching and learning: these and many other activities are increasingly governed by algorithmic logics and policed by opaque and hidden computational processes. Culture is itself a code/space.

The danger of this emphasis on the coproduction of physical and cultural space by computation is that it in turn occludes the vast inequalities of power that it both relies upon and reproduces. Computation does not merely augment, frame, and shape culture; by operating beneath our everyday, casual awareness of it, it actually *becomes* culture.

That which computation sets out to map and model it eventually takes over. Google set out to index all human knowledge and became the source and arbiter of that knowledge: it became what people actually think. Facebook set out to map the connections between people – the social graph – and became the platform for those connections, irrevocably reshaping societal relationships. Like an air control system mistaking a flock of birds for a fleet of bombers, software is unable to distinguish between its model of the world and reality – and, once conditioned, neither are we.

This conditioning occurs for two reasons: because the combination of opacity and complexity renders much of the computational process illegible; and because computation itself is perceived to be politically and emotionally neutral. Computation is opaque: it takes place inside the machine, behind the screen, in remote buildings – within, as it were, a cloud. Even when this opacity is penetrated, by direct apprehension of code and data, it remains beyond the comprehension of most. The aggregation of complex systems in contemporary networked applications means that no single person ever sees the whole picture. Faith in the machine is a prerequisite for its employment, and this backs up other cognitive biases that see automated responses as inherently more trustworthy than nonautomated ones.

This phenomenon is known as automation bias, and it has been observed in every computational domain from spell-checking software to autopilots, and in every type of person. Automation bias ensures that we value automated information more highly than our own experiences, even when it conflicts with other observations – particularly when those observations are ambiguous. Automated information is clear and direct, and confounds the grey areas that muddle cognition. Another associated phenomenon, confirmation bias, reshapes our awareness of the world to bring it better into line with automated information, further affirming the validity of computational solutions, to the point where we may discard entirely observations inconsistent with the machine's viewpoint.[33]

Studies of pilots in high-tech aircraft cockpits have produced multiple examples of automation bias. The pilots of the Korean Air Lines flight whose destruction led to the emancipation of GPS were victims of the most common kind. Shortly after takeoff from Anchorage, Alaska, on August 31, 1983, the flight crew programmed their autopilot with the heading given to them by air traffic control and handed over control of the plane. The autopilot was preprogrammed with a series of waymarks that would take it through the jetways over the Pacific to Seoul, but due either to a mistake in the settings, or an imperfect understanding of the mechanisms of the system, the autopilot did not continue to follow its preassigned route; rather, it stayed fixed on its initial heading, which took it further and further north of its intended route. By the time it left Alaskan airspace, fifty minutes into the flight, it was twelve miles north of its expected position; as it flew on, its divergence increased to fifty, then a hundred miles from its intended course. Over several hours, investigators related, there were several cues that might have alerted the crew to what was occurring. They noticed, but disregarded, the slowly increasing travel time between beacons. They complained about the poor radio reception as they drifted further from the normal air routes. But none of these effects caused the pilots to question the system, or to double-check their position. They continued to trust in the autopilot even as they entered Soviet military airspace over the Kamchatka Peninsula. As fighter jets were scrambled to intercept them, they flew on. Three hours later, still completely unaware of the situation, they were fired upon by a Sukhoi Su-15 armed with two air-to-air missiles, which detonated close enough to wreck their hydraulic systems. The cockpit transcript of the last few minutes of flight shows multiple failed attempts to re-engage the autopilot, as an automated announcement warns of an emergency descent.[34]

Such events have been repeated, and their implications confirmed, in multiple simulator experiments. Worse, such biases are not limited to errors of omission, but include those of commission. When the Korean Air Lines pilots blindly followed the directions of an autopilot, they were taking the road of least resistance. But it has been shown that even experienced pilots will take drastic actions in the face of automated warnings, including against the evidence of their own observations. Oversensitive fire warnings in early Airbus A330 aircraft became notorious for causing numerous flights to divert, often at some risk, even when pilots visually checked for signs of fire multiple times. In a study in the NASA Ames Advanced Concepts Flight Simulator, crews were given contradictory fire warnings during preparation for takeoff. The study found that 75 per cent of the crews following the guidance of an automated system shut down the wrong engine, whereas when following a traditional paper checklist only 25 per cent did likewise, despite both having access to additional information that should have influenced their decision. The tapes of the simulations showed that those following the automated system made their decisions faster and with less discussion, suggesting that the availability of an immediate suggested action prevented them looking deeper into the problem.[35]

Automation bias means that technology doesn't even have to malfunction for it to be a threat to our lives – and GPS is again a familiar culprit. In their attempt to reach an island in Australia, a group of Japanese tourists drove their car down onto a beach and directly into the sea because their satellite navigation system assured them there was a viable road. They had to be rescued as the tide rose around them, some fifty feet from the shoreline.[36] Another group in Washington state drove their car into a lake when they were directed off the main road and down a boat ramp. When emergency services responded, they found the car floating in deep water, with only its roof rack visible.[37] For rangers in Death Valley National Park, such occurrences have become so common that they have a term for it: 'Death by GPS', which describes what happens when travellers, unfamiliar with the area, follow the instructions and not their senses.[38] In a region where many marked roads may be impassable to regular vehicles, and daytime temperatures can reach fifty degrees Celsius with no water available, getting lost will kill you. In these cases, the GPS signal wasn't spoofed, and it didn't drift. The computer was simply asked a question, and it answered – and humans followed that answer to their deaths.

At the foundation of automation bias is a deeper bias, firmly rooted not in technology, but in the brain itself. Confronted with complex problems, particularly under time pressure – and who among us is not under time pressure, all the time? – people try to engage in the least amount of cognitive work they can get away with, preferring strategies that are both easy to follow and easy to justify.[39] Given the option of relinquishing decision making, the brain takes the road of least cognitive effort, the shortest cut, which is presented near-instantaneously by automated assistants. Computation, at every scale, is a cognitive hack, offloading both the decision process and the responsibility onto the machine. As life accelerates, the machine steps in to handle more and more cognitive tasks, reinforcing its authority – regardless of the consequences. We refashion our understanding of the world to better accommodate the constant alerts and cognitive shortcuts provided by automated systems. Computation replaces conscious thought. We think more and more like the machine, or we do not think at all.

In the lineage of the mainframe, the personal computer, the smartphone and the global cloud network, we see how we have come to live inside computation. But computation is no mere architecture: it has become the very foundation of our thought. Computation has evolved into something so pervasive and so seductive that we have come to prefer to use it even when simpler mechanical, physical, or social processes will do instead. Why speak when you can text? Why use a key when you can use your phone? As computation and its products increasingly surround us, are assigned power and the ability to generate truth, and step in to take over more and more cognitive tasks, so reality itself takes on the appearance of a computer; and our modes of thought follow suit.

Just as global telecommunications have collapsed time and space, computation conflates past and future. That which is gathered as data is modelled as the way things are, and then projected forward – with the implicit assumption that things will not radically change or diverge from previous experiences. In this way, computation does not merely govern our actions in the present, but constructs a future that best fits its parameters. That which is possible becomes that which is computable. That which is hard to quantify and difficult to model, that which has not been seen before or which does not map onto established patterns, that which is uncertain or ambiguous, is excluded from the field of possible futures. Computation projects a future that is like the past – which makes it, in turn, incapable of dealing with the reality of the present, which is never stable.

Computational thinking underlies many of the most divisive issues of our times; indeed, division, being a computational operation, is its primary characteristic. Computational thinking insists on the easy answer, which requires the least amount of cognitive effort to arrive at. Moreover, it insists that there is an answer – one, inviolable answer that can be arrived at – at all. The 'debate' on climate change, where it is not a simple conspiracy of petrocapitalism, is characterised by this computational inability to deal with uncertainty. Uncertainty, mathematically and scientifically understood, is not the same as unknowing. Uncertainty, in scientific, climatological terms, is a measure of precisely what we do know. And as our computational systems expand, they show us ever more clearly how much we do not know.

Computational thinking has triumphed because it has first seduced us with its power, then befuddled us with its complexity, and finally settled into our cortexes as self-evident. Its effects and outcomes, its very way of thinking, are now so much a part of everyday life that it appears as vast and futile to oppose as the weather itself. But admitting the myriad ways computational thinking is the product of oversimplification, bad data, and deliberate obfuscation also allows us to recognise the ways in which it fails, and reveals its own limitations. As we shall see, the chaos of the weather itself ultimately lies beyond its reach.

In the margins of his revision copy of *Numerical Prediction*, Lewis Fry Richardson wrote,

> Einstein has somewhere remarked that he was guided towards his discoveries by the notion that the important laws of physics were really simple. R.H. Fowler has been heard to remark that, of two formulae, the more elegant is the more likely to be true. Dirac sought an explanation alternative to that of spin in the electron because he felt that Nature could not have arranged it in so complicated a way. These mathematicians have been brilliantly successful in dealing with mass-points and point-charges. If they would condescend to attend to meteorology the subject might be greatly enriched. But I suspect they would have to abandon the idea that the truth is really simple.[40]

It took him forty years to formulate, but in the 1960s, Richardson finally found a model for this uncertainty; a paradox that neatly summarises the existential problem of computational thinking. While working on the 'Statistics of Deadly Quarrels', an early attempt at the scientific analysis of conflict, he set out to find a correlation between the probability of two nations going to war and the length of their shared border. But he discovered that many of these lengths appeared as wildy different estimates in various sources. The reason, as he came to understand, was that the length of the border depended upon the tools used to measure it: as these became more accurate, the length actually increased, as smaller and smaller variations in the line were taken into account.[41] Coastlines were even worse, leading to the realisation that it is in fact impossible to give a completely accurate account of the length of a nation's borders. This 'coastline paradox' came to be known as the Richardson effect, and formed the basis for Benoît Mandelbrot's work on fractals. It demonstrates, with radical clarity, the counterintuitive premise of the new dark age: the more obsessively we attempt to compute the world, the more unknowably complex it appears.

Climate

There was a video on YouTube that I watched over and over again, until it got taken down. Then I found GIFs of it posted to news sites and watched those instead: concentrated bumps of the key moment, freebasing on the uncanny. A man in rubber boots and field camouflage, a hunting rifle slung over one shoulder, walks across the vast expanse of the Siberian tundra in springtime. The ground is green and brown, dense, lush with grasses, and extends perfectly flat in all directions, to the pale blue of a horizon that seems a hundred miles away. He takes long, loping steps, an expedition pace, enough to carry him far across the territory each day. But as he steps, the ground shimmers and ripples; the thick earth turns to liquid, and moves in waves.[1] What appears as solid ground is merely a thin carpet of plant matter, an organic crust atop a newly shifting, soupy sea. The permafrost beneath the tundra is melting. In the video, it looks as if, at any moment, the ground might crack, the stalker's boot might plunge through the surface, and he might be swept down by the undertow, lost beneath the sheets of green.

In fact, the opposite direction is more likely: the ground will thrust *upward*, spewing wet soil and warm gases into the air. In 2013, a mysterious explosion was heard in the far north of Siberia, and residents one hundred kilometres away reported a bright glow in the sky. Scientists, reaching the spot on the isolated Taimyr Peninsula several months later, discovered a vast, fresh crater, forty metres wide and thirty deep.

Taimyr reaches a peak of five degrees Celsius in midsummer and plunges to minus thirty in the winter. Its bleak landscape is scattered with pingos: small mounds and hillocks formed as hydrostatic pressure pushes cores of ice toward the surface. As they grow, the pingos shed surface vegetation and shattered ice, coming to resemble ranges of squat volcanoes, cracked and cratered at their crowns. But the pingos, like the permafrost, are melting – and in some cases, exploding. In April 2017, researchers in Siberia installed the first of a network of seismic sensors on the nearby Yamal Peninsula, whose name means 'the end of the Earth'. Close to the brand-new port of Sabetta at the mouth of the Ob river, the sensors are capable of measuring movements in the ground over a 200-kilometre radius: they are intended to provide early warning of exploding pingos – and worse – that might damage the industrial infrastructure of the port or the local Bovanenkovskoye and Kharasavay gas deposits.

The establishment of Sabetta as an export point for the vast reserves of Siberian natural gas has been made possible by the same forces that have created the exploding pingos: rising global temperatures. As the Arctic ice melts, previously inaccessible reserves of oil and gas become viable. It's estimated that 30 per cent of the world's remaining natural gas reserves are in the Arctic.[2] Most of these reserves are offshore, beneath less than 500 metres of water, and are now accessible due precisely to the catastrophic impact of the last century of fossil fuel extraction and dependence. The sensors installed to protect industrial infrastructure are necessitated by the conditions produced by the infrastructure itself. This is positive feedback: not positive for life – human, animal or plant – not positive for sense; but accumulative, expansive, and accelerating.

The underlying, localised form of positive feedback at work here is the release of methane by the melting permafrost: the slushy, trembling tundra. The permafrost that lies beneath the Siberian tundra can extend to depths of over a kilometre, made up of continuously frozen layers of soil, rock and sediment. Locked in this ice is millions of years of life, which is starting to return to the surface. In the summer of 2016, a disease outbreak that killed a young boy and hospitalised more than forty others in the Yamal Peninsula was blamed on the exposure of buried reindeer carcasses by the melting permafrost. The carcasses were infected with anthrax bacteria, which had lain dormant in the ice for decades or centuries, frozen in time beneath the tundra.[3] Associated with this deadly bacteria is dead matter, which, as the ice melts, starts to decay, giving off plumes of methane – a greenhouse gas vastly more effective than carbon dioxide at trapping heat in the earth's atmosphere. In 2006, the Siberian permafrost released an estimated 3.8 million tonnes of methane into the atmosphere; in 2013 that had risen to 17 million tonnes. It is this methane, more than anything else, that is causing the tundra to shudder and explode.

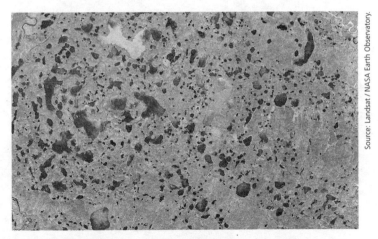

Source: Landsat / NASA Earth Observatory.

Landscape of the Tuktoyaktuk Peninsula, Siberia.

Of course, there is no such thing as a local effect in a networked world. What we perceive as weather in the moment shadows the globe as climate: tiny moments of turbulent activity through which we can barely grasp an unseen, unknowable totality. As the artist Roni Horn has observed, 'Weather is the key paradox of our time. Weather that is nice is often weather that is wrong. The nice is occurring in the immediate and individual, and the wrong is occurring system-wide.'[4] What appears on the tundra as an ever-increasing uncertainty of footing is the destabilisation of the entire planet. The very ground trembles, rots, ruptures, and stinks. It cannot be relied upon.

The exploded pingos and open melt lakes of the Siberian plain, seen from the air, resemble brain scans of spongiform encephalopathy patients, their cortexes pitted and scarred by the death of nerve cells. The prion diseases that cause spongiform encephalopathy – scrapie, kuru, mad cow disease,

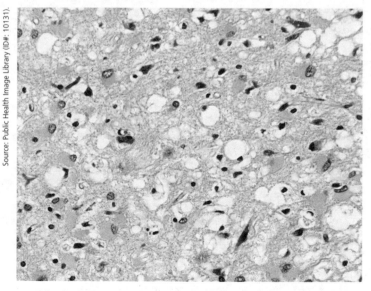

Light photomicrograph of brain tissue (magnified 100X) suffering from CJD.

CJD and their derivatives – are the result of misfolded proteins, scraps of base matter that have become twisted into malformed shape. They spread themselves through the body by converting their properly folded counterparts into their own image. When prion infections reach the brain, they cause rapid-onset dementia, memory loss, personality changes, hallucinations, anxiety, depression, and ultimately death. The brain itself comes to resemble a sponge, hollowed out and denatured, unable to make sense of itself and its end. The permafrost – the permanent frost – is melting. The words don't make sense any more, and with them go the ways we have to think the world.

On June 19, 2006, representatives from five Nordic countries gathered on the remote Arctic island of Spitsbergen, part of the Svalbard archipelago, to lay the first stone of a time machine. Over the next two years, workers dug 120 metres into a sandstone mountain, where they excavated caverns another 150 metres long and 10 wide. The time machine is intended to transport one of humanity's most precious resources to an uncertain future, bypassing certain horrors of the present. In heat-sealed foil packets, packed into plastic cases on racked industrial shelving, rest millions upon millions of preserved seeds: samples of food crops from regional collections around the world.

Just 1,120 kilometres from the North Pole, Svalbard is the most northerly year-round settlement on earth, and in spite of its remoteness it has long been an international meeting point. Visited by Norse fishermen and hunters since at least the twelfth century, its 'discovery' by Dutch explorers in 1596 opened up the islands to whaling and mineral exploitation. The British landed in 1604 and started hunting walrus; by the end of the century, the Russians arrived seeking polar bear and fox fur. Although driven out in the 1820s by British raids on the Barents Sea, they were to return, like everybody else, for the coal. During the Second World War, the archipelago was evacuated and occupied by a detachment of German troops manning a meteorological station. Cut off in May 1945, it wasn't until late September that they were picked up by a Norwegian seal hunting vessel, becoming the last German troops to surrender to the Allies.

The discovery of coal deposits at the end of the nineteenth century sharpened questions of sovereignty that had previously been left open. For centuries, the archipelago had functioned as a free territory without laws or regulations, outwith the jurisdiction of any nation. The Svalbard Treaty of 1920, formulated as part of the Versailles negotiations, handed sovereignty to Norway but gave equal rights to all signatories to engage in commercial activities – primarily mining – on the islands. The archipelago was to be demilitarised, and to this day it remains a uniquely visa-free zone: anyone may settle and work on the islands regardless of country of origin or citizenship, provided they have some means of support. Alongside nearly 2,000 Norwegians and almost 500 Russians and Ukranians, Svalbard is home to several hundred non-Nordic people, including Thai and Iranian workers. In recent years, a number of asylum seekers whose applications have been rejected in Norway have made their way to Svalbard to wait out the seven years residency required to gain Norwegian nationality.[5]

The Svalbard Global Seed Vault – often referred to as 'the ark', or the 'doomsday vault' – was opened in 2008. As a backup facility to support the work of gene banks around the world, the Svalbard location is doubly suitable. Its zone of geopolitical exception makes it significantly easier to persuade national organisations to store their precious – and often confidential – collections there. And buried beneath the permafrost, the vault is also a natural deep freezer: powered by locally mined coal, it's refrigerated to minus eighteen degrees Celsius, and even if these machines were to fail, the local bedrock remains below freezing all year round. The Seed Vault is an attempt to create a sanctuary that is both geographically and temporally isolated: suspended in neutral territory and the deep time of the Arctic winters.

Seed banks are crucial to maintaining some semblance of genetic biodiversity. They are the fruit of a movement that started in the 1970s, with the realisation that the Green Revolution in agriculture was causing farmers to abandon their usual seeds, locally developed over centuries, for new hybrids. India was believed to have over 100,000 varieties of rice a century ago; today it has only a few thousand. The number of apple strains in the Americas has dropped from 5,000 to a few hundred. Altogether, the UN Food and Agriculture Organisation estimates, 75 per cent of crop biodiversity has been lost.[6] Such diversity is essential to countering the risk of new diseases or pests that might emerge, threatening to wipe out homogenous varieties. The Svalbard collection is intended to provide secure storage for diverse strains in case of catastrophe: technically on long-term loan, its contents are not meant to be accessed unless all other sources have failed. In January 2012, the national seed bank of the Philippines was destroyed by fire, six years after it had been heavily damaged by flooding, while those of Afghanistan and Iraq have been completely destroyed by fighting.[7] In 2015, the International Center for Agricultural Research in the Dry Areas (ICARDA) requested the first withdrawal from the vault: 130 of the 325 boxes it had deposited, containing a total of 116,000 samples.

ICARDA was established in 1977, with its headquarters in Aleppo, Syria, and branches across the Middle East, North Africa, and Central Asia. Its work is focused on the particular needs and risks of food security in the region: the development of new crop varieties, water management, conservation, and rural education, particularly that of women. In 2012, rebel fighters in the Syrian civil war seized control of the center's gene bank twenty miles south of Aleppo, where it maintained a unique collection of 150,000 different populations of wheat, barley, lentil and faba bean seeds from 128 countries. While some of the staff were allowed to remain to maintain the facility, ICARDA was forced to move its headquarters to Beirut, and its access to the collection was cut off.

The ICARDA collection – backed up for now in Svalbard and shortly to be redistributed to Morocco, Turkey, and elsewhere – specialises in crops adapted to the harsh environmental conditions of the Middle East and North Africa. The benefit of the biodiversity inherent in this archive, evolved and engineered by farmers and nature over generations, is not disease and pest resistance, but climate resilience. It is from this resource that scientists hope to mine new genetic traits to moderate the ravages of climate change – for instance, by splicing heat- and drought-resistant crops such as chickpeas and lentils with maize and soybeans to make the latter viable in rapidly changing, and heating, ecosystems.[8]

This change is so rapid that it has taken even the Global Seed Vault by surprise. The year 2016 was the hottest ever recorded – for the third year in a row, with research indicating that the earth hasn't been this warm for 115,000 years. In November, scientists reported that Arctic temperatures were up to twenty degrees Celsius higher than average, with sea ice levels 20 per cent below their twenty-five-year average. In Svalbard, heavy rain fell in place of light snow, and the permafrost started to melt. An inspection of the vault in May of 2017 found that the entrance tunnel had been flooded by meltwater, refreezing as it fell below the surface to form an indoor glacier that had to be hacked out to access the seedbank. Intended to function for long periods without human intervention, the vault is now under twenty-four-hour watch, with emergency waterproofing being added to the entrance tunnel, and trenches being dug around the site to channel meltwater away. 'The Arctic and especially Svalbard warms up faster than the rest of the world. The climate is changing dramatically and we are all amazed at how quickly it is going,' Ketil Isaksen, a Norwegian meteorologist, told reporters.[9]

Climate change is already occurring, and its effects are as visible and urgent in the landscapes of geopolitics as of geography. The Syrian conflict, which forced the ICARDA scientists to flee to Beirut and call on the Seed Vault for assistance, is itself partly attributable to changes in the environment.[10] Between 2006 and 2011, more than half of the Syrian countryside suffered its worst drought on record. More intense and longer lasting than could be explained by natural variations in weather, this drought has been linked to accelerating climate change, and over a few years nearly 85 per cent of rural livestock died, as crops withered. President Bashar al-Assad redistributed traditional water rights to political allies, forcing farmers to dig illegal wells, while those who protested faced imprisonment, torture, and death. More than a million rural villagers fled the countryside for the cities. When this rural resentment and demographic pressure met the totalitarian oppression already bearing down on the cities, it provided the final trigger for an uprising that spread rapidly through the most drought-stressed areas. Media reports and activists have called the Syrian conflict the first large-scale climate war of the twenty-first century, connecting climate directly to the vast numbers of refugees arriving in Europe. Scientists are more circumspect about making explicit connections between conflict and climate – but not about the changing climate itself. Even if Syria recovers politically in the next few years, it stands to lose nearly 50 per cent of its agricultural capacity by 2050. There is no going back from here.

Why should we be so concerned with the Seed Vault? The Seed Vault is vitally important because it is a bastion not only of diversity, but of diversity-in-knowing and diversity-as-knowing. The Seed Vault transports things – stuff, knowledge, and ways of knowing – from an uncertain present into an even less certain future. It's fuelled not merely by the stuff, but by the sheer variety of the stuff, that it carries. The Seed Vault's fuel is heterogenous; it's motley and incomplete: because this is the nature of knowledge and the world. It's a necessary opposition to a monoculture – in this case, not even a metaphor, but a literal monoculture of plant strains engineered for specific geographic and temporal tasks that, when generalised, fail utterly to accommodate the messy incoherence of the world as it actually is. The climate crisis is also a crisis of knowledge, and of understanding; it is a crisis of communication, and of knowing, in the past, the present, and the future.

In the Arctic regions, everyone is a climate scientist. Archaeologists searching for the remains of ancient cultures are digging into the deep history of the planet to pull out evidence that might assist us in understanding how the earth – and humans – behaved in past periods of rapid climatological change, and thus how we might address them now. On the western coast of Greenland, on the shores of the great Ilulissat Icefjord, the permafrost surrounding the ancient settlement of Qajaa preserves the relics of three civilisations, each of which occupied the same site over the previous three and a half thousand years. These are the Saqqaq, Dorset, and Thule cultures, the first of which established itself in southern Greenland around 2500 BCE, with the subsequent groups slowly supplanting their predecessors until contact with Europeans intensified in the eighteenth century. The history of each of these cultures comes down to us through middens: layers of kitchen and hunting refuse laid down by generations, sinking into the earth and waiting for archaeologists to delve into them.

These middens have helped us to make sense of population movements and previous environmental happenings. What occurred in the Greenlandic cultures is not culturally unique, but it is archaeologically unique. Unlike Stone Age sites around the world, where only stone remains, the Arctic sites, thanks to the deep freeze of the permafrost, preserve far more information about ancient human material culture. The middens in Qajaa contain wooden and bone arrows, hafted knives, spears, sewing needles and other objects that have not survived elsewhere on the planet. They also contain traces of DNA.[11]

Like the entangled history and future of the seed banks, understanding how earlier civilisations and cultures adapted, changed, coped or failed to cope under previous periods of environmental stress is one way in which we might be able to respond to our own – if that understanding is not itself destroyed before we can reach it.

In the next century, these unique archaeological deposits – repositories of knowledge and information – will disappear entirely, after thousands of years of stability. Researchers from the University of Copenhagen's Center for Permafrost drilled into the earth surrounding the Qajaa midden and another site in northeast Greenland and excavated cores of frozen soil, which, packed into plastic bags, were kept frozen on the journey back to the laboratory, where they were examined for signs of heat production. As the earth warms, long-dormant bacteria in the soil start to wake and become active. The bacteria themselves produce heat, causing the soil to warm further, thawing and awakening more bacteria – more positive feedback. As the ice melts and the water starts to drain away, oxygen flows into the layers of soil, breaking them up and degrading them. The newly awakened bacteria start to feed on the organic residues, leaving nothing behind but stone, and venting more warming carbon as they go. 'When the ice melts and the water is drained', writes Professor Bo Elberling, leader of the study and head of the Center for Permafrost, 'there's no way back.'[12]

In a report from the Greenland ice sheet in October 2016, Thomas McGovern, a professor of archaeology who has worked on the middens for decades, detailed how the rapid melting of the ice sheet is reducing to mush an archaeological record that stretches back millennia, and which we have barely started to comprehend:

Back in the old days, these sites were frozen most of the year. When I was visiting south Greenland in the nineteen-eighties, I was able to jump down in trenches guys had left open from the fifties and sixties, and sticking out the sides you could see hair, feathers, wool, and incredibly well-preserved animal bones. We're losing everything. Basically, we have the equivalent of the Library of Alexandria in the ground, and it's on fire.[13]

McGovern's statement is deeply troubling in two particular ways. The first is the terrible feeling of loss, as the possibility of accessing our own past and knowing more about it slips away from us at the very moment it might be of greatest use. But the second is more existential: it relates to our deep need to discover ever more about the world, to gather and process more data about it, in order that the models that we build of it may be more robust, more accurate, and more useful.

But the opposite is occurring: our sources of data are slipping away, and with them the structures by which we have structured the world. The melting of the permafrost is both danger sign and metaphor: an accelerating collapse of both our environmental and our cognitive infrastructure. The certainties of the present are founded on the assumption of ever-increasing, ever-crystallising geologies of knowledge; it is reassuring to imagine a cooling earth, coming into shape, manifesting in distinct and solid forms. But, as in Siberia, the sponging of the Greenlandic landscape reiterates a return to the fluid: the marshy and boggy, the undifferentiated and gaseous. A new dark age will demand more liquid forms of knowing than can be derived from the libraries of the past alone.

Knowledge derived or uncovered from the past is one approach to coping with the catastrophic impacts of climate change. But our existing technologies and processes should also be capable of shielding us, to some extent, from its excesses – that is, if those technologies and cognitive strategies are not themselves among the earliest victims of climate change.

The Council for Science and Technology, an advisory body to the UK government, published a report in 2009 entitled 'A National Infrastructure for the 21st century', examining the future of the country's communications, energy, transport and water networks. The report emphasised that the UK's national infrastructure, like the internet, constituted 'a network of networks' – and a fragile one at that, fragmented in delivery and governance, unclear in its responsibilities and accountabilities, largely unmapped and chronically under-supported. The root causes of this situation identified by the study included government siloing, public and private under-investment, and a general lack of understanding of how such complex networks of matter and knowledge even begin to function – let alone how they fail.

The report was clear about one challenge however, which would and must trump all other concerns – the changing climate:

> Resilience against climate change is the most significant and complex longer-term challenge. The effects of climate change are predicted to cause higher summer and winter temperatures, sea-level rises, a rising intensity of storms, forest fires, droughts, increased flooding, heatwaves and alter resource availability, e.g. of water. The challenges for the current infrastructure are both to adapt to such impacts and to support the radical transition to a low carbon economy. The Government's National Security Strategy, published in March 2008, recognises climate change as potentially the greatest challenge to global stability and security, given expected world-wide impacts. Effective adaptation is key to mitigating this risk, in relation to infrastructure and other areas.[14]

Again, what is striking about the direct effects of climate change predicted in the report is their fluidity and unpredictability:

Pipe systems for both drinking water supply and sewage will be more prone to cracking as climate changes lead to greater soil movement as a consequence of wetting and drying cycles ... Dams will be more prone to siltation resulting from increased soil erosion, and the slippage risk to soil dams from intense rainfall events will also increase.

Another report for the UK government, published the following year by environmental consultancy AEA, explores the specific impacts of climate change on information and communications technologies.[15] ICT, in this context, is defined as 'the whole of the systems and artefacts which enable the transmission, receipt, capture, storage and manipulation of voice and data traffic on and across electronic devices' – that is, everything we might consider to be part or artefact of our contemporary digital universe, from fibre-optic cables, aerials and antennae to computers, data centres, telephone exchanges, and satellites. Outside of the scope of the study, for example, are power lines, despite the essential nature of their services to ICT. (The Council for Science and Technology's study, on the other hand, notes that 'one of the limiting factors for the transfer of electricity by overhead transmission lines is their thermal capacity, which is affected by the ambient air temperature. Higher global peak temperatures will reduce those limits and hence the capacity of the network to transfer electricity.')[16]

Reports written for governments are often far starker and clearer than governments' own statements and policies. As in the United States, where the US military has put into action ten-year plans for adapting to climate change even while deniers take charge of the executive branch, so the British reports take climate science at face value, making for startlingly lucid reading on the value of networks:

All of the above artefacts work together as a system – interconnected, interdependent and completely enmeshed in each other and working to absolute rules of inter-operability. ICT is the only sector of infrastructure that directly connects any one user to any other user across time and space using multiple pathways simultaneously and capable of dynamic re-routing in real time. As such, in this case, the national asset is the network rather than any of the individual components – and it is the operation of the network that relies on the whole infrastructure and enables the generation of value . . . whilst the network is the asset at the level of infrastructure, the value of the network is not in the asset itself but in the information that travels on it. Nearly the whole of the economy relies upon the ability to transmit, receive and convert streams of digital data in close to realtime – whether it is the extraction of cash from an ATM, the use of a credit or debit card, sending an email, controlling a remote pump or switch, despatching or receiving aircraft or a mundane phone call.[17]

Contemporary information networks are both the economic and cognitive frameworks of society: So how will they fare in an era of climate change? And what damage are they doing in the present?

Rising global temperatures will particularly stress data infrastructures that already run hot, as well as the people who work in and around them. Data centres and individual computers generate vast amounts of waste heat, and require corresponding quantities of cooling, from the acres of air conditioning systems on industrial buildings to the fans that cool your laptop when a YouTube kitten video sends the CPU into overdrive. Increased air temperatures bring increased cooling costs – and the possibility of outright failures. 'iPhone needs to cool down before you use it' pleads the error message on Apple's latest phone when the ambient temperature rises above forty-five degrees Celsius. Such a response can be triggered by leaving the device in a hot car in Europe today, but is projected to become a daily occurrence in the Gulf regions in the second half of the twenty-first century, following record-breaking heatwaves in 2015, when Iraq, Iran, Lebanon, Saudi Arabia and the Emirates endured daytime temperatures approaching fifty degrees Celsius.

The AEA report on ICT and the climate identifies a number of specific effects that will be felt by information networks. At the level of physical infrastructure, it notes that much of this network is parasitic upon structures that were not designed for their contemporary uses, nor for the effects of climate change: mobile phone masts grafted onto church steeples, data centres in old industrial units, telephone exchanges constructed in Victorian post offices. Below the ground, fibre-optic cables run through sewage channels that are becoming incapable of handling increased storm surges and flooding; cable landing sites, where the internet comes ashore from undersea data links, are susceptible to rising sea levels, which will be particularly destructive in southeast and eastern England, sites of crucial connections to the continent. Coastal installations will be increasingly susceptible to saline corrosion, while towers and transmission masts will buckle and fall as the ground, attacked by drought and flood, shears and subsides.

In the electromagnetic spectrum, the strength and efficacy of wireless transmission will be reduced as temperatures rise. The refractive index of the atmosphere is highly dependent on humidity and severely affects the curvature of electromagnetic waves, along with the rate at which they fade. Increased temperatures and rainfall will shift the beams of point-to-point data links – such as microwave transmissions – and attenuate broadcast signals. As the earth warms and becomes wetter, ever-greater densities of wireless masts will be required, and maintenance will become more difficult. Changing types of vegetation may also impact the propagation of information.

Wi-Fi, in short, will get worse, not better. In one scenario, the shifting ground may even reduce the reliability of reference data for telecommunication and satellite transmission calculations. Accuracy falls; broadcasts overlap and interfere; noise crowds out the signal. The systems we have built to collapse time and space are being attacked by space and time.

Computation is both a victim of and a contributor to climate change. As of 2015, the world's data centres, where exabytes of digital information are stored and processed, consumed about 3 per cent of the world's electricity – and accounted for 2 per cent of total global emissions. This is about the same carbon footprint as the airline industry. The 416.2 terawatt hours of electricity consumed by global data centres in 2015 exceeded that of the whole United Kingdom, at 300 terawatt hours.[18]

This consumption is projected to escalate massively, as a result of both the growth of digital infrastructure and the positive feedback from rising global temperatures. In response to vast increases in data storage and computational capacity in the last decade, the amount of energy used by data centres has doubled every four years, and is expected to triple in the next ten years. A study in Japan suggested that by 2030, the power requirements for digital services alone would outstrip the entire nation's current generation capacity.[19] Even technologies that make explicit claims to radically transform society are not exempt. The cryptocurrency Bitcoin, which is intended to disrupt hierarchical and centralised financial systems, requires the energy of nine US homes to perform a single transaction; and if its growth continues, by 2019 it will require the annual power output of the entire United States to sustain itself.[20]

Moreover, these figures reflect processing power, but do not account for the wider network of digital activities empowered by computation. These activities – dispersed, fragmented, and often virtual – also consume vast resources, and are, by the nature of contemporary networks, difficult to see and string together. Immediate and local power requirements, easily visible to and quantifiable by the individual, are negligible compared to the cost of the network, just as individual waste production and management, apparently mitigated by ethical shopping and recycling, pale in comparison with globalised industrial cycles.

A 2013 report, 'The Cloud Begins with Coal – Big Data, Big Networks, Big Infrastructure, and Big Power', calculates that 'charging up a single tablet or smart phone requires a negligible amount of electricity; using either to watch an hour of video weekly consumes annually more electricity in the remote networks than two new refrigerators use in a year.'[21] And this report is not the product of a worthy, well-intentioned environmental group. Rather, it was commissioned by the National Mining Association and the American Coalition for Clean Coal Electricity: it is a lobbying call for more fossil fuel use, in order to meet inevitable demands.

What the coal giants point out, perhaps unwittingly, is that data usage is qualitative as well as quantitative. *What* we look at turns out to matter more than *how* we look at it – and not just to the environment. One industry consultant quoted in the newspapers argued, 'We need to be more responsible about what we use the internet for ... Data centres aren't the culprits – it's driven by social media and mobile phones. It's films, pornography, gambling, dating, shopping – anything that involves images.'[22] As in most proto-environmental claims, the proposed solutions are either appeals to regulation (taxing data), conservative regressions (banning pornography, or switching from colour to black-and-white photographs to save transmission costs) or hapless techno-fixes (like the miracle-material graphene) – all ludicrous, unworkable, and unable to think at the scale of the networks they seek to address.

As digital culture becomes faster, higher bandwidth, and more image-based, it also becomes more costly and destructive – both literally and figuratively. It requires more input and energy, and affirms the supremacy of the image – the visual representation of data – as the representation of the world. But these images are no longer true, and none less so than our image of the future. As the past melts into the permafrost, so is the future rocked by the atmosphere. The changing climate shakes not merely our expectations, but our ability to predict any future at all.

Just after midnight on May 1, 2017, Aeroflot's regular service from Moscow to Bangkok, Flight SU270, hit a pocket of violent turbulence as it approached its destination.[23] Without warning, passengers were thrown from their seats, some of them crashing into the ceiling of the aircraft before falling onto their neighbours and into the aisles. Footage recorded onboard showed dazed and bloody passengers lying in the aisles, surrounded by scattered food trays and luggage.[24] On landing, twenty-seven passengers were rushed to hospital, several with fractured or broken bones.

'We were hurled up into the roof of the plane, it was practically impossible to hold on,' one of the passengers told reporters. 'It felt like the shaking wouldn't stop, that we would just crash.' The Russian Embassy told Reuters that 'the reason behind the injuries was that some of the passengers had not had their seatbelts fastened.' Aeroflot asserted in a press release that 'an experienced crew piloted the flight. The pilot has more than 23 thousand flight hours, and the co-pilot has over 10.5 thousand flight hours. However, the turbulence that hit the Boeing 777 was impossible to foresee.'[25]

In June of 2016, a 'brief moment of severe turbulence' over the Bay of Bengal caused injuries to thirty-four passengers and six crew members aboard Malaysian Airlines flight MH1 from London to Kuala Lumpur.[26] Food trays cannoned out of the galley, and news agencies showed passengers being taken off on stretchers, and wearing neck braces.

Three months later, a United Airlines Boeing 767 en route from Houston to London had to make an emergency landing at Shannon Airport in Ireland following 'severe and unexpected turbulence' in the mid Atlantic. 'It fell four times in a row,' said one passenger.

It was a tremendous pull on the body. And on the third or fourth time babies started waking up and crying, people were waking up disorientated. I thought: this is not turbulence. This is what feels like a life-threatening drop. This is not like any feeling I have had. This is immediately like an experience of being fired from a cannon. It pulls you down so hard then it stops for a second and then it does that four times in a row. If you didn't have your seatbelt on you would have smashed your head.[27]

The flight was met by ambulances on the runway, and sixteen people were taken to hospital.

The most severe episode of clear-air turbulence on record hit United Airlines Flight 826 en route from Tokyo to Honolulu in 1997. Two hours into the flight, minutes after the captain turned on the fasten seat belt sign in response to warnings from other aircraft, the Boeing 747 dropped downwards and then rebounded with such force that one of the crew, a purser who had been steadying himself on a countertop, found himself upside down with his feet high in the air.

A passenger whose seat belt was not fastened left her seat, hit the ceiling, and fell into the aisle. She was unconscious and bleeding heavily, and, despite resuscitation attempts by flight attendants and a passenger doctor, was pronounced dead shortly after. Her autopsy revealed severe spinal damage. After the plane turned around and landed safely back in Tokyo, fifteen passengers were treated for spine and neck fractures, and another eighty-seven for bruises, sprains, and minor injuries. The airframe was retired and never flew again.

A report by the US National Transportation Safety Board later found that sensors on the aircraft recorded a peak normal acceleration of 1.814 G in the first sharp ascent, before plunging to an extreme negative G of −0.824. It also sustained an uncontrolled roll of eighteen degrees – without any visual or mechanical cues to the pilot of what was about to occur.[28]

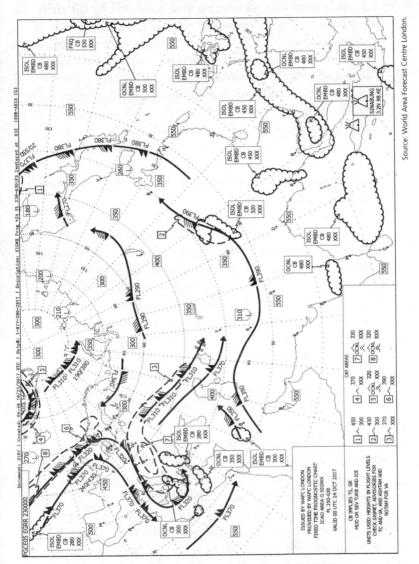

Significant Weather Chart for Europe and Asia, issued by World
Area Forecast Centre London, October 24, 2017.

Turbulence can be determined to some extent by the study of the weather. The International Civil Aviation Organisation (ICAO) issues daily 'significant weather charts' that include information about cloud height and cover, wind speed, weather fronts, and possible turbulence. The main indicator used to determine the possibility of turbulence is the Richardson number – that same Lewis Fry Richardson who developed the measure in a series of meteorological papers in the 1920s related to his work on numerical weather prediction. By examining the relative temperatures and wind speeds in different zones of the atmosphere, it is possible to determine the potential turbulence between them, if such measurements are available.

Clear-air turbulence is so named because it comes literally out of the blue. It occurs when bodies of air moving at wildly different speeds meet: as the winds shear against each other, vortices and chaotic movements are produced. While much studied, particularly in the high troposphere where long-haul aircraft operate, it remains almost impossible to detect or to predict. For this reason, it is much more dangerous than the predictable forms of turbulence that occur on the edges of storms and large weather systems, because pilots are unable to prepare, or route around it. And incidences of clear-air turbulence are increasing every year.

While anecdotal accounts of turbulence such as those above may be widely reported, many incidents, while globally significant, are not reported, and figures are hard to come by. An advisory circular on preventing turbulence-related injuries, published by the US Federal Aviation Administration in 2006, states that the frequency of turbulence accidents has increased steadily for more than a decade, from 0.3 accidents per million departures in 1989, to 1.7 in 2003.[29] These figures are already severely out of date.

The reason for the increase in turbulence is rising levels of carbon dioxide in the atmosphere. In a paper published in

Nature Climate Change in 2013, Paul Williams of the National Centre for Atmospheric Science at the University of Reading and Manoj Joshi from the School of Environmental Sciences at the University of East Anglia lay out the implications of a warming atmosphere on transatlantic aviation:

> Here we show using climate model simulations that clear-air turbulence changes significantly within the transatlantic flight corridor when the concentration of carbon dioxide in the atmosphere is doubled. At cruise altitudes within 50–75°N and 10–60°W in winter, most clear-air turbulence measures show a 10–40 per cent increase in the median strength of turbulence and a 40–170 per cent increase in the frequency of occurrence of moderate-or-greater turbulence. Our results suggest that climate change will lead to bumpier transatlantic flights by the middle of this century. Journey times may lengthen and fuel consumption and emissions may increase.[30]

The authors of the turbulence study emphasise once again the nature of feedback in this rise in turbulence: 'Aviation is partly responsible for changing the climate, but our findings show for the first time how climate change could affect aviation.' These effects will be felt the most in the busy air corridors of Asia and the North Atlantic, causing disruption, delays, and damage. The future will be bumpy, and we are losing our ability even to predict the shocks.

I grew up in the suburbs of South London, beneath the inbound flightpaths of Heathrow Airport. At 6:30 p.m. every evening Concorde would rumble overhead, inbound from New York, shaking the doors and window frames like a rocket ship. It had been flying for more than a decade at that point; the first flight was made in 1969, and scheduled services began in 1976. Transatlantic flights took three and a half hours – if you could afford a ticket, which at its lowest cost something in the region of £2,000 for a return flight.

Concorde, detail from 'Concorde Grid' (1997), Wolfgang Tillmans.

In 1997, the photographer Wolfgang Tillmans showed a series of fifty-six photographs of Concorde that correspond almost perfectly with my own memory: a dark arrowhead rumbling across the sky, seen not from the luxury cabin, but from the ground. Writing in the exhibition catalogue, Tillmans remarked,

> Concorde is perhaps the last example of a techno-utopian invention from the sixties still to be operating and fully functioning today. Its futuristic shape, speed and ear-numbing thunder grabs people's imagination today as much as it did when it first took off in 1969. It's an environmental nightmare conceived in 1962 when technology and progress was the answer to everything and the sky was no longer a limit ... For the chosen few, flying Concorde is apparently a glamorous but cramped and slightly boring routine whilst to watch it in the air, landing or taking-off is a strange and free spectacle, a super modern anachronism and an image of the desire to overcome time and distance through technology.[31]

Concorde made its final flight in 2003, a victim as much of its own elitism as the fatal crash of Air France Flight 4590 into the Parisian suburbs three years earlier. For many, the end of Concorde was the end of a certain idea of the future.

There is little left of Concorde in contemporary aircraft: instead, the latest passenger aircraft are the result of incremental advances – better materials, more efficient engines, adjustments to wing design – rather than the radical advance that Concorde proposed. The last of these is my favourite addition: the 'winglets' that now adorn the wingtips of most aircraft. These are a recent invention, developed by NASA in response to the 1973 oil crisis and gradually retrofitted for commercial aircraft to increase fuel efficiency. They always bring to mind the epitaph of Buckminster Fuller, as written on his gravestone in Cambridge, Massachusetts: 'Call me trimtab.'

Tiny in-flight adjustments, performed at scale. This is what we remain capable of.

History – progress – does not always go up and to the right: it's not all sunlit uplands. And this isn't – cannot be – about nostalgia. Rather, it is about acknowledging a present that has come unhinged from linear temporality, that diverges in crucial yet confusing ways from the very idea of history itself. Nothing is clear anymore, nor can it be. What has changed is not the dimensionality of the future, but its predictability.

In a 2016 editorial for the *New York Times*, computational meteorologist and past president of the American Meteorological Society William B. Gail cited a number of patterns that humanity has studied for centuries, but that are disrupted by climate change: long-term weather trends, fish spawning and migration, plant pollination, monsoon and tide cycles, the occurrence of 'extreme' weather events. For most of recorded history, these cycles have been broadly predictable, and we have built up vast reserves of knowledge that we can tap into in order to better sustain our ever more entangled civilisation. Based on these studies, we have gradually extended our forecasting abilities, from knowing which crops to plant at which time of year, to predicting droughts and forest fires, predator/prey dynamics, and expected agricultural and fisheries outputs.

Civilisation itself depends on such accurate forecasting, and yet our ability to maintain it is falling away as ecosystems begin to break down and hundred-year storms batter us repeatedly. Without accurate long-term forecasts, farmers cannot plant the right crops; fishermen cannot find a catch; flood and fire defences cannot be planned; energy and food resources cannot be determined, nor demand met. Gail foresees a time in which our grandchildren might conceivably know less about the world in which they live than we do today, with correspondingly catastrophic events for complex societies.[32] Perhaps, he wonders, we have already passed through 'peak knowledge', just as we may have already passed peak oil. A new dark age looms.

The philosopher Timothy Morton calls global warming a 'hyperobject': a thing that surrounds us, envelops and entangles us, but that is literally too big to see in its entirety. Mostly, we perceive hyperobjects through their influence on other things – a melting ice sheet, a dying sea, the buffeting of a transatlantic flight. Hyperobjects happen everywhere at once, but we can only experience them in the local environment. We may perceive hyperobjects as personal because they affect us directly, or imagine them as the products of scientific theory; in fact, they stand outside both our perception and our measurement. They exist without us. Because they are so close and yet so hard to see, they defy our ability to describe them rationally, and to master or overcome them in any traditional sense. Climate change is a hyperobject, but so is nuclear radiation, evolution, and the internet.

One of the main characteristics of hyperobjects is that we only ever perceive their imprints on other things, and thus to model the hyperobject requires vast amounts of computation. It can only be appreciated at the network level, made sensible through vast distributed systems of sensors, exabytes of data and computation, performed in time as well as space. Scientific record keeping thus becomes a form of extrasensory perception: a networked, communal, time-travelling knowledge making. This characteristic is precisely what makes it anathema to a certain kind of thinking – one that insists on being able to touch and feel things that are intangible and unsensible, and subsequently dismisses the things it cannot think. Arguments about the existence of climate change are really arguments about what we can think.

And we are not going to be able to think much longer. In preindustrial times, from 1000–1750 CE, atmospheric carbon dioxide varied between 275 and 285 parts per million – levels we know from studying ice cores, the same batteries of

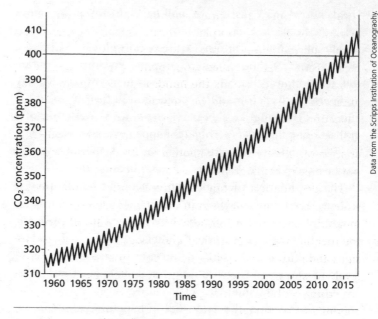

Data from the Scripps Institution of Oceanography.

The Keeling Curve as of October 21, 2017.

knowledge that are melting away in the Arctic today. From the dawn of the industrial age they begin to rise, reaching 295 ppm at the start of the twentieth century, and 310 ppm by 1950. The trend – named the Keeling Curve, after the scientist who started modern measurements at the Mauna Loa observatory in Hawaii in 1958 – is ever upward, and accelerating. 325 ppm in 1970, 350 in 1988, 375 in 2004.

In 2015, and for the first time in at least 800,000 years, atmospheric carbon dioxide passed 400 ppm. At its current rate, which shows no sign of abating, and we show no sign of stopping, atmospheric CO_2 will pass 1,000 ppm by the end of the century.

At 1,000 ppm, human cognitive ability drops by 21 per cent.[33] At higher atmospheric concentrations, CO_2 stops us from thinking clearly. Outdoor CO_2 already reaches 500 ppm regularly in industrial cities: indoors, in poorly ventilated homes, schools, and workplaces, it can regularly exceed 1,000 ppm – substantial numbers of schools in California and Texas measured in 2012 breached 2,000 ppm.[34]

Carbon dioxide clouds the mind: it directly degrades our ability to think clearly, and we are walling it into our places of education and pumping it into the atmosphere. The crisis of global warming is a crisis of the mind, a crisis of thought, a crisis in our ability to think another way to be. Soon, we shall not be able to think at all.

The degradation of our cognitive abilities is mirrored at scale in the collapse of the transatlantic jet routes, the undermining of communication networks, the erasure of diversity, the melting away of historical knowledge reserves: these are signs and portents of a wider inability to think at the network level, to sustain civilisation-scale thought and action. The structures we have built to extend our own life systems, our cognitive and haptic interfaces with the world, are the only tools we have for sensing a world dominated by the emergence of hyperobjects. Just as we are beginning to perceive them, our ability to do so is slipping away.

Thinking about climate change is degraded by climate change itself, just as communications networks are undermined by the softening ground, just as our ability to debate and act on entangled environmental and technological change is diminished by our inability to conceptualise complex systems. And yet at the heart of our current crisis is the hyperobject of the network: the internet and the modes of life and ways of thinking it weaves together. Perhaps unique among hyperobjects, the network is an emergent cultural form, generated from our conscious and unconscious desires in dialogue with mathematics and electrons and silicon and glass fibre. That this network is currently being (mis)used to accelerate the crisis, as we will see in subsequent chapters, does not mean it does not retain the potential to illuminate.

The network is the best representation of reality we have built, precisely because it too is so difficult to think. We carry it around in our pockets and build pylons to transport it and palaces of data to process it, but it is not reducible to discrete units; it is nonlocal, and it is inherently contradictory – and *this is the condition of the world itself.* The network is continuously, deliberately and unknowingly created. Living in a new dark age requires acknowledging such contradictions and uncertainties, such states of practical unknowing. Thus the network, properly understood, can be a guide to thinking other uncertainties; making such uncertainties visible must be done precisely so that they can be thought. Dealing with hyperobjects requires a faith in the network, as mode of seeing, thinking, and acting. It denies the bonds of time, place, and individual experience that characterise our inability to think the challenges of a new dark age. It insists on an affinity with the noumenal and the uncertain. In the face of atomisation and alienation, the network continually asserts the impossibility of separation.

4

Calculation

Science fiction writers, whose idea of temporality often differs from that of ordinary people, have a term for simultaneous invention: 'steam engine time'. William Gibson has described it thus:

> There's an idea in the science-fiction community called steam-engine time, which is what people call it when suddenly twenty or thirty different writers produce stories about the same idea. It's called steam-engine time because nobody knows why the steam engine happened when it did. Ptolemy demonstrated the mechanics of the steam engine, and there was nothing technically stopping the Romans from building big steam engines. They had little toy steam engines, and they had enough metalworking skill to build big steam tractors. It just never occurred to them to do it.[1]

Steam engines happen when it's steam engine time: a process almost mystical, almost teleological, because it exists outside the scope of our framework for understanding historical progress. The set of things that had to come together for this particular invention to occur includes so many thoughts and events we could not think or know about that its appearance is like that of a new star: magical and previously unthinkable. But the history of science shows us that all invention is simultaneous and multiauthored. The first treatises on magnetism were written independently in Greece and India around 600 BCE, and in China in the first century CE. The blast furnace appeared in China in the first century CE and in Scandinavia in the twelfth – the possibility of its transference exists, but the Haya people of northwestern Tanzania have also been making steel for 2,000 years, long before the technology developed in Europe. In the seventeenth century, Gottfried Wilhelm Leibniz, Isaac Newton and others independently formulated the rules of calculus. In the eighteenth, the realisation of oxygen emerged almost simultaneously in the work of Carl Wilhelm Scheele, Joseph Priestley, Antoine Lavoisier, and others, while in the nineteenth, Alfred Russel Wallace and Charles Darwin both advanced the theory of evolution. Such histories give the lie to the heroic narrative of history – the lone genius toiling away to produce a unique insight. History is networked and atemporal: steam engine time is a multidimensional structure, invisible to a sensorium trapped in time, but not insensible to it.

Despite such deep realities, there's a wonderful thing that happens when you hear someone tell a story that just makes sense: a sense of who they are, and where they came from; the sense that something they did *makes sense*, has history and progress behind it, that it had to happen this way – and that it had to happen to them, because of the story itself.

Tim Berners-Lee, the inventor of the World Wide Web, gave a talk in a tent in Wales in 2010 entitled 'How the World Wide Web Just Happened'.[2] It's a joyful thing, an exegesis on computation itself as well as a humble hero story. TBL's parents, Conway Berners-Lee and Mary Lee Woods, were computer scientists; they met and married while working on the Ferranti Mark 1, the first commercially available, general-purpose electronic computer, in Manchester in the 1950s. Conway later devised a technique for editing and compressing text; Mary developed a simulation of London bus routes that was used to reduce delays. TBL describes his childhood as 'a world full of computing', and his first experiments involved making magnets and switches from nails and bent wire; his first device was a remote-controlled gun, constructed like a mousetrap, for attacking his siblings. He notes that the transistor had been invented around the time of his birth, and so when he came to secondary school age it was starting to become available in packets in the electronic shops on Tottenham Court Road. He soon began building rudimentary circuits for doorbells and burglar alarms; as his soldering skills increased, so did the range of available transistors, which made it possible to start building more complex circuits. The appearance of the first integrated circuits in turn allowed him to create video display units from old televisions, until he had all the components of an actual computer – which never quite worked, but never mind. And by this time, he was at university, studying physics; after that, he worked on typesetting for digital printers, before joining CERN, where he developed the idea for hypertext – previously expounded by Vannevar Bush, Douglas Engelbart, and others. And because of where he was working and the need of researchers to share interlinked information, he tied this invention to the Transmission Control Protocol (TCP) and the domain name systems that underpin the emerging internet and – ta-da! – the World Wide Web just happened, as naturally and obviously as if it were meant to be.

This, of course, is only one way of telling the story, but it tickles our senses because it makes sense: the rising arc of invention – the graph that always goes up and to the right – coupled to a personal history that leads to myriad interconnections and the spark of insight at the right moment, the right place in time. The Web happened because of the history of microprocessors and telecommunications and wartime industry and commercial requirements, and a bunch of different discoveries and patents and corporate research funds and academic papers and TBL's own family history; but it also happened because it was Web Time: for a brief moment, the dispositions of culture and technology converged on an invention that, in hindsight, was predicted by everything from ancient Chinese encyclopaedias to microfilm retrieval to the stories of Jorge Luis Borges. The Web was necessary, and so it appeared – in this timeline, at least.

Computing is especially prone to such justificatory histories, which prove its own necessity and inevitability. The sine qua non of self-fulfilling technological prophecies is what is known as Moore's law, first proposed by Gordon Moore, cofounder of Fairchild Semiconductor and later of Intel, in a paper for *Electronics* magazine in 1965. Moore's insight was that the transistor – then, as TBL noted, barely a decade old – was shrinking rapidly. He showed that the number of components per integrated circuit was doubling every year, and projected that this would continue for the next decade. In turn, this rapid increase in raw computing power would drive ever more wondrous applications: 'Integrated circuits will lead to such wonders as home computers – or at least terminals connected to a central computer – automatic controls for automobiles,

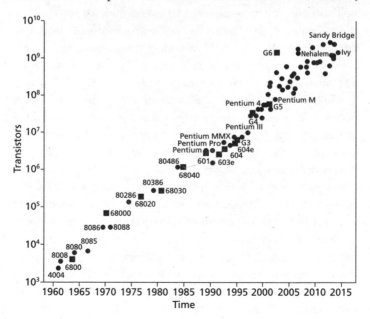

Moore's Law.

and personal portable communications equipment. The electronic wristwatch needs only a display to be feasible today.'[3]

A decade later, he revised his forecast only slightly, to a doubling every two years. Others put it at around eighteen months, and, despite numerous proclamations of its imminent demise, the rule of thumb has held approximately true ever since. In 1971, the semiconductor feature size – the smallest discrete unit of manufacture – was ten micrometres, or one-fifth the diameter of a human hair. By 1985 it was one micrometre, and then it dropped below one hundred nanometres – the diameter of a virus, for whatever that's worth – in the early 2000s. At the beginning of 2017, semiconductors with features of ten nanometres were available in smartphones. It used to be believed that miniaturisation would be impossible below seven nanometres, at which point electrons would be free to move through any surface via quantum tunneling; instead, future generations of transistors will take advantage of this effect to make chips the size of atoms themselves, while others predict a future of biological machines composed of DNA and custom, nanoengineered proteins.

So far, so up and to the right. The miniaturisation principle, and its accompanying surge in computational power, is the ever-building wave that Berners-Lee rode through the 1960s, '70s and '80s, in order to bring us, neatly and inevitably, to the World Wide Web and the interconnected world of today. But Moore's law, despite the name by which it came to be known (one which Moore himself wouldn't use for two decades), is not a law. Rather, it's a projection – in both senses of the word. It's an extrapolation from the data but also a phantasm created by the restricted dimensionality of our imagination. It's a confusion in the same manner as the cognitive bias that feeds our preference for heroic histories, but in the opposite direction. Where one bias leads us to see the inevitable march of progress through historical events to our present moment, the other sees this progress continuing inevitably into the future. And, as such projections do, it has the capability both to shape that future and to influence, in fundamental ways, other projections – regardless of the stability of its original premise.

What began as an off-the-cuff observation became a leitmotif of the long twentieth century, attaining the aura of a physical law. But unlike physical laws, Moore's law is deeply contingent: it is dependent not merely on manufacturing techniques but on discoveries in the physical sciences, and on the economic and social systems that sustain investment in, and markets for, its products. It is also dependent upon the desires of its consumers, who have come to prize the shiny things that become smaller and faster every year. Moore's law is not merely technical or economic; it is libidinal.

Starting in the 1960s, the increasingly rapid development of integrated circuit capacity shaped the entire computing industry: as new models of chips became available every year, this expanding capacity became intrinsically tied to the development of the semiconductor itself. No hardware manufacturer or software developer could afford to develop their own architecture; everything had to run on the architecture of a few vendors who kept coming out with ever-denser, more powerful chips. Those building the chips determined the architecture of the machine, all the way to the end consumer. One result of this was the growth of the software industry: freed from its reliance on hardware manufacturers, software became vendor independent, leading first to the dominance of huge companies like Microsoft, Cisco, and Oracle, and then to the economic – and increasingly political and ideological – power of Silicon Valley. Another effect, according to many in the industry, was the end of a culture of craft, care, and efficiency in software itself. While early software developers had to make a virtue of scarce resources, endlessly optimising their code and coming up with ever more elegant and economical solutions to complex calculation problems, the rapid advancement of raw computing power meant that programmers only had to wait eighteen months for a machine twice as powerful to come along. Why be parsimonious with one's resources when biblical plenty is available in the next sales cycle? In time, the founder of Microsoft himself became associated with another computer scientist's rule of thumb: Gates's law, which claims that, as a result of wasteful and inefficient code and redundant features, the speed of software halves every eighteen months.

This, then, is the true legacy of Moore's law: as software centred itself within society, so its ever-rising power curve came to be associated with the idea of progress itself: a future of plenty for which no accommodations in the present need be made. A computing law become an economic law become a moral law – with its own accusations of bloat and decadence. Even Moore appreciated the wider implications of his theory, telling the *Economist* on the fortieth anniversary of its coinage, 'Moore's Law is a violation of Murphy's Law. Everything gets better and better.'[4]

Today, as a direct consequence of Moore's law, we live in an age of ubiquitous computing, of clouds of apparently infinite computational power; and the moral and cognitive implications of Moore's law are felt in every aspect of our lives. But despite the best efforts of quantum tunnelers and nanobiologists, continually pushing at the limits of invention, our technology is starting to catch up with our philosophy. What holds in semiconductor research – for now – is turning out not to hold elsewhere: not as scientific law, not as natural law, and not as moral law. And, if we choose to look critically at what our technology is telling us, we can start to discern where we have gone wrong. The error is visible in the data – but the data is all too often used as the argument itself.

In a 2008 article in *Wired* magazine entitled 'End of Theory', Chris Anderson argued that the vast amounts of data now available to researchers made the traditional scientific process obsolete.[5] No longer would they need to build models of the world and test them against sampled data. Instead, the complexities of huge and totalising data sets would be processed by immense computing clusters to produce truth itself: 'With enough data, the numbers speak for themselves.' As an example, Anderson cited Google's translation algorithms, which, with no knowledge of the underlying structures of languages, were capable of inferring the relationship between them using extensive corpora of translated texts. He extended this approach to genomics, neurology, and physics, where scientists are increasingly turning to massive computation to make sense of the volumes of information they have gathered about complex systems. In the age of big data, he argued, 'correlation is enough. We can stop looking for models.'

This is the magic of big data. You don't really need to know or understand anything about what you're studying; you can simply place all of your faith in the emergent truth of digital information. In one sense, the big data fallacy is the logical outcome of scientific reductionism: the belief that complex systems can be understood by dismantling them into their constituent pieces and studying each in isolation. And this reductionist approach would hold if it did in practice keep pace with our experiences; in reality, it is proving to be insufficient.

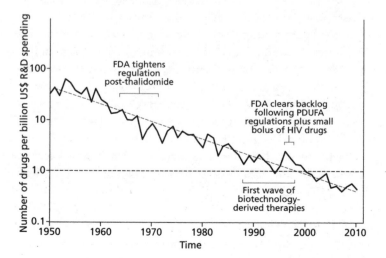

Calculation

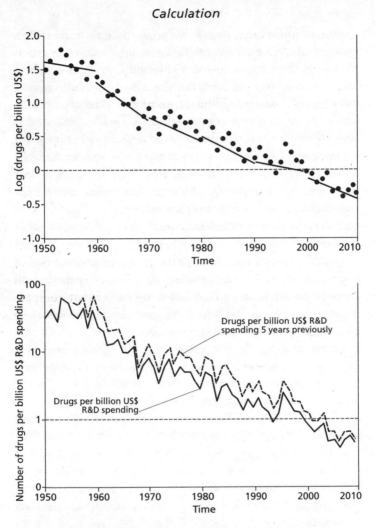

Eroom's law in pharmaceutical research and development.

a. Overall trend in research and development efficiency (inflation adjusted).
b. Rate of decline over 10-year periods.
c. Adjusting for 5-year delay in spending impact.

Data from Jack W. Scannell, Alex Blanckley, Helen Boldon and Brian Warrington,
'Diagnosing the decline in pharmaceutical R&D efficiency', Nature Reviews Drug
Discovery 11, 191–200 (March 2012).

One of the places in which it has become increasingly evident that the reliance on vast amounts of data alone is harmful to the scientific method is in pharmacological research. Over the past sixty years, despite the huge growth of the pharmacological industry, and the concomitant investment in drug discovery, the rate at which new drugs are made available has actually fallen when compared to the amount of money spent on research – and it has fallen consistently and measurably. The number of new drugs approved per billion US dollars spent on research and development has halved every nine years since 1950. The downward trend is so clear that researchers have coined a term for it: Eroom's law – that is, Moore's law backwards.[6]

Eroom's law exemplifies a growing awareness across the sciences that something is deeply and widely wrong with scientific research. The number of new results is not only falling, but those results are becoming less trustworthy, thanks to a combination of different mechanisms.

One metric of scientific progress is the number of papers that are being published in scientific journals – and the corresponding number of retractions that accompany them. Tens of thousands of scientific papers are published every single week, and only a handful of them will be retracted – but even that minority causes deep concern to the scientific community.[7] One study in 2011 showed that there had been a tenfold rise in retractions over the previous decade – a finding that set off a scramble to learn more about the problem and uncover what was causing the increase.[8] One of the most surprising results was the discovery of a robust correlation between the journal's retraction index and its impact factor; that is, papers published in higher-profile journals were significantly more likely to be retracted than those published in lower-profile journals.

A follow-up study found that more than two-thirds of the retractions in the biomedical and life sciences had been due to misconduct by researchers, rather than error – and the authors noted that such a result could only be an underestimate, as fraud, by its nature, was underreported.[9] (This is neatly illustrated by a survey that found that while only 2 per cent of scientists would admit to falsifying data, 14 per cent said they knew someone who did.)[10] Moreover, the number of fraudulent papers was actually increasing as a percentage of all retractions.[11] This was shocking to many scientists, as it was widely believed that most retractions were down to honest error. Moreover, the failure to retract poisons the well, leading to more bad science down the line.

There have been several high-profile cases of long-running frauds by senior researchers. In the late '90s, a South Korean biotechnologist named Hwang Woo-suk was proclaimed 'the pride of Korea' for his success in cloning cows and pigs, becoming among the first researchers in the world to do so. While he never supplied scientifically verifiable data, he was keen on photo ops, particularly with politicians, and provided a useful fillip to South Korean national self-esteem. In 2004, following celebrated claims that he had successfully cloned human embryonic stem cells – widely believed to be impossible – he was accused of coercing his own researchers into donating eggs. But this didn't stop *Time* magazine from naming him one of the year's 'People Who Mattered' and stating that he had 'already proved that human cloning is no longer science fiction, but a fact of life'.[12] Ongoing ethics investigations were publicly opposed by politicians, patriotic newspapers, and even by public rallies, while over a thousand women pledged to donate their own eggs to the research. Nevertheless it was revealed in 2006 that his research was entirely fabricated. His papers were retracted, and he was given a two-year suspended jail sentence.

In 2011, Diederik Stapel, the dean of Tilburg University's School of Social and Behavioral Sciences, was forced to resign when it was revealed that he had fabricated the results of almost every study he put his name to, and even those of his graduate students. Stapel, like Hwang, was something of a celebrity in his home country, having published numerous studies that made waves in Dutch society. In 2011, for example, he published one study based on Utrecht's main train station that seemed to show that people exhibited more racist behaviour in dirty environments, and another claiming that eating meat made people selfish and antisocial.[13] Both relied on nonexistent data. When he was exposed, Stapel blamed his actions on a fear of failure and the pressure on academics to publish frequently and prominently in order to maintain their positions.

Hwang and Stapel, while outliers, might embody one of the reasons articles in the most prominent journals are more likely to be retracted: they're written by the scientists making the biggest claims, under the most professional and societal pressure. But such frauds are also being revealed by a series of connected, network effects: the increasing openness of scientific practice, the application of technology to the analysis of scientific publications, and the increasing willingness of other scientists – particularly junior ones – to challenge results.

As more and more scientific papers become available to wider and wider communities through open access programmes and online distribution, more and more of them come under increased scrutiny. Not all of this scrutiny is human: universities and companies have developed a range of products for automatically checking academic papers for plagiarism, by comparing them against huge databases of existing publications. In turn, students have developed techniques – such as 'Rogeting', named for the thesaurus, which involves carefully substituting synonyms for words in the original text – in order to fool the algorithms. An arms race develops between writer and machine, with the latest plagiarism detectors employing neural networks to winkle out uncommon words and phrases that might point towards manipulation. But neither plagiarism nor outright fraud suffice to account for a larger crisis within science: replicability.

Replication is a cornerstone of the scientific method: it requires that any experiment be repeatable by another group of independent researchers. But in reality, very few experiments are replicated – and the more that are, the more fail the test. At the University of Virginia's Center for Open Science, an initiative called the Reproducibility Project has, since 2011, tried to replicate the findings of five landmark cancer studies: to take the same experimental setup, rerun the experiments, and get the same results. Each of the initial experiments have been cited thousands of times: their replicability should be guaranteed. But in the event, after painstaking reconstructions, only two of the experiments were repeatable; two were inconclusive, and one completely failed. And the problem is not limited to medicine: a general study undertaken by *Nature* found that 70 per cent of scientists had failed to replicate the findings of other researchers.[14] Across the board, from medicine to psychology, biology to environmental sciences, researchers are coming to the realisation that many of the foundations of their research may be flawed.

The reasons behind the crisis are multiple and, like the fraud cases that make up a relatively small part of the problem, are in part a result of the increased visibility of research, and the increased possibility of review. But other problems are more systemic: from the pressure on scientists to publish – which means questionable results are sexed up and counterexamples quietly filed away – to the very tools with which scientific results are generated.

The most controversial of these techniques is p-hacking. P stands for probability, denoting the value at which an experimental result can be considered statistically significant. The ability to calculate a p-value in many different situations has made it a common marker for scientific rigour in experiments. A value of p less than 0.05 – meaning that there is a less than 5 per cent chance of a correlation being the result of chance, or a false positive – is widely agreed across many disciplines to be the benchmark for a successful hypothesis. But the result of this agreement is that a p-value less than 0.05 becomes a target, rather than a measure. Researchers, given a particular goal to aim for, can selectively cull from great fields of data in order to prove any particular hypothesis.

As an example of how p-hacking works, let's hypothesise that green dice, uniquely among all other dice, are loaded. Take ten green dice and roll each of them one hundred times. Of those 1,000 rolls, 183 turn up a six. If the dice were absolutely fair, the number of sixes should be 1,000/6, which is 167. Something's up. In order to determine the validity of the experiment, we need to calculate the p-value of our experiment. But the p-value has nothing to do with the actual hypothesis: it is simply the probability that random rolls would turn up 183 or more sixes. For 1,000 dice rolls, that probability is only 4 per cent, or $p = 0.04$ – and just like that, we have an experimental result that is deemed sufficient by many scientific communities to warrant publication.[15]

Why should such a ridiculous process be regarded as anything other than a gross simplification? It shouldn't be – except that it works. It's easy to calculate and it's easy to read, meaning that more and more journals use it as shorthand for reliability when sifting through potentially thousands of submissions. Moreover, p-hacking doesn't just depend on getting those serendipitous results and running with them. Instead, researchers can comb through vast amounts of data to find the results they need. Say that instead of rolling ten green dice, I also rolled ten blue ones, ten yellow ones, ten red ones, and so on. I could roll fifty different colours, and most of them would come out close to the average. But the more I rolled, the more likely I would be to get an anomalous result – and this is the one I could publish. This practice has given p-hacking another name: data dredging. Data dredging has become particularly notorious in the social sciences, where social media and other sources of big behavioural data have suddenly and vastly increased the amount of information available to researchers. But the pervasiveness of p-hacking isn't limited to the social sciences.

A comprehensive analysis of 100,000 open access papers in 2015 found evidence of p-hacking across multiple disciplines.[16] The researchers mined the papers for every p-value they could find, and they discovered that the vast majority just scraped under the 0.05 boundary – evidence, they said, that many scientists were adjusting their experimental designs, data sets, or statistical methods in order to get a result that crossed the significance threshold. It was results such as these that led the editor of *PLOS ONE*, a leading medical journal, to publish an editorial attacking statistical methods in research entitled 'Why most published research findings are false.'[17]

It's worth emphasising at this point that data dredging is not the same as fraud. Even if results don't stand up, one of the greatest concerns in the scientific community is not that researchers might be deliberately massaging results, but that they might be doing so unconsciously, thanks to a combination of institutional pressures, lax publishing standards, and the sheer volume of data available to them. This combination of increasing retractions, falling replicability, and the inherent complexity of scientific analysis and distribution concerns the entire scientific community, and this concern is itself corrosive. Science depends on trust: trust between researchers, and trust in researchers by the public. Any erosion of this trust is deeply damaging to the future of scientific research, whether caused by the deliberate actions of a few bad apples or widely distributed across multiple actors and causes, many of them next to unknowable.

Some scholars have been warning for decades of a possible crisis in scientific quality control, and many of them have linked it to the exponential growth in data and research. In the 1960s, Derek de Solla Price – who studied the concentrated networks formed between different papers and writers through citations and shared fields of study – graphed the growth curve of science. The data he employed reflected widely ranging factors, from material production to the energy of particle accelerators, the founding of universities, and the discovery of elements. Like Moore's law, everything goes up and to the right. If science did not radically change its modes of production, de Solla Price feared, it would face saturation, when its ability to absorb and act meaningfully on the amount of information available would start to break down, followed by 'senility'.[18] Spoiler: science hasn't changed.

In recent years these fears have crystallised in a concept referred to as overflow.[19] Put simply, overflow is the opposite of scarcity: it is the boundless upwelling of information. Moreover, and in contrast to abundance, it is overwhelming, affecting our ability to process its effects. In studies of the economics of attention, overflow addresses how people choose which subjects to prioritise when they have too little time and too much information. As the authors of one study note, it also 'evokes the image of a mess that needs to be dealt with, or waste that needs to be removed'.[20]

Overflow exists in many fields, and when it is recognised, strategies evolve for its management. Traditionally, this role is performed by gatekeepers, such as journalists and editors, who select which information should be published. With the role of gatekeeper comes an expectation of specialism and expertise, a certain responsibility and, often, a position of authority. In science, overflow manifests in the rapid proliferation of journals and papers, in the number of applications for grants and academic positions, and in the volume of information and research available. Even the length of the average paper increases, as researchers pad their findings with more and more references to accommodate richer data and higher demand for startling results. The result is a failure of quality control: even the gold standard of peer review is regarded as no longer sufficiently objective or fit for purpose, as the number of papers accelerates and it is mired in institutional reputation games. In turn, this leads to calls for an increase in open publishing of scientific papers – a result that may in turn simply increase the sheer volume of research being published.[21]

But what if the problem of overflow isn't limited to science's outputs, but to its inputs too? As de Solla Price feared, science has continued in its trajectory of assembling ever-vaster and more-complex datasets. When it was announced in 1990, the human genome project was regarded as the greatest single data-gathering project in history, but the plunging cost of DNA sequencing means that multiples of its data are now churned out every year. This data is increasing rapidly and is widely distributed, making it impossible to study all of it comprehensively.[22] The Large Hadron Collider generates too much data to even store on site, meaning that only certain kinds of events can be stored, leading to criticisms that once the Higgs boson particle was discovered, the data was unsuitable for discovering anything else.[23] All science is becoming the science of big data.

It's this realisation that brings us back to Moore's law – and Eroom's. As in the other sciences, despite the proliferation of research institutions, academic journals and positions (and the vast amounts of money being thrown at the problem), the actual results are degrading. During the 1980s and '90s, combinatorial chemistry increased 800-fold the rate at which drug-like molecules could be synthesised. DNA sequencing has become a billion times faster since the first successful technique was established. Databases of proteins have grown 300 times larger in twenty-five years. And while the cost of screening for new drugs has fallen, and the amount of research funding has continued to climb, the actual number of new drugs discovered has fallen off exponentially.

What could be causing this reversal of the law of progress? There are several hypotheses. The first, and generally regarded as the least significant, is the possibility that the low-hanging fruit has already been picked: all the best targets – the most obvious choices for investigation – have already been exploited. But this isn't really the case: there are decades worth of existing substances still waiting to be investigated, and once investigated they can be added to the list of known comparators, exponentially increasing the field of research.

Then there's the 'better than the Beatles' problem, which worries that even if there are lots of drugs still to be investigated, many existing ones are so good at what they do that they effectively preclude further research into the area. Why start a band when the Beatles already did everything worth doing? This is a variation on the low-hanging fruit problem, with one important difference. While 'low-hanging fruit' suggests that there are no easy targets remaining, 'better than the Beatles' implies that the fruit already picked lessens the value of what remains on the tree. In most industries, the opposite is the case: the relatively cheap process of strip-mining and burning surface coal, for example, makes what remains in deep mines more valuable, which in turn finances its exploitation. In contrast, trying to outdo existing generic drugs only increases the cost of clinical trials and the difficulty of persuading doctors to prescribe the results, as they are comfortably familiar with the existing ones.

Other problems with drug discovery are more systemic, and less tractable. Some blame reckless spending by bloated drug companies, drunk on Moore's law, as the defining factor driving Eroom's law. But most research institutions have – in line with other industries – ploughed their funds into the latest technologies and techniques. If these aren't the answer to the problem, something else must be amiss.

The 'cautious regulator' theory, on a longer timeline, puts the blame on the ever-lower tolerance of society for risky clinical outcomes. Since the golden age of drug discovery in the 1950s, the number of regulations governing the trial and release of drugs has increased – and for good reason. Clinical trials in the past often came with terrible side effects, and further disasters awaited when poorly tested drugs reached the market. The best – or worst – example of this is thalidomide, introduced in the 1950s to treat anxiety and nausea, but which proved to have horrifying consequences for the children of mothers to whom it was prescribed to combat morning sickness. In the aftermath, drug regulations were tightened in ways that made testing more rigorous – but that also actually improved outcomes. The US Drug Efficacy Amendment of 1962 required that new drugs proved not only that they were safe, but that they actually did what they claimed to do – not previously a legal requirement. Few of us would countenance a return to riskier drugs in order to reverse Eroom's law, particularly when exceptions can be made when needed, as they were for several anti-HIV drugs in the 1980s.

The final problem with drug research is the one that most concerns us, and it is the one believed by researchers to be the most significant. Pharmacologists term this the 'basic research/ brute force' bias, but we can call it the automation problem. Historically, the process of discovering new medicines was the domain of small teams of researchers intensively focused on small groups of molecules. When an interesting compound was identified in natural materials, from libraries of synthesised chemicals, or by serendipitous discovery, its active ingredient would be isolated and screened against biological cells or organisms to evaluate its therapeutic effect. In the last twenty years, this process has been widely automated, culminating in a technique known as high-throughput screening, or HTS. HTS is the industrialisation of drug discovery: a wide-spectrum, automated search for potential reactions within huge libraries of compounds.

Picture a cross between a modern car factory – all conveyor belts and robot arms – and a data centre – rack upon rack of trays, fans, and monitoring equipment – and you're closer to the contemporary laboratory than the received vision of (predominately) men in white coats tinkering with bubbling glassware. HTS prioritises volume over depth: vast libraries of chemical compounds are fed into the machines and tested against each other. The process strip-mines the chemical space, testing thousands of combinations nearly simultaneously. And at the same time, it reveals the almost ungraspable extent of that space, and the impossibility of modeling all possible interactions.

The researchers in the laboratory are of course aware, if at one remove, of all the economic pressures produced by existing discoveries and cautious regulators, but it's in the laboratory itself that these knotty problems meet the runaway technological pressure of new inventions. For those with the most money – the drug companies – the impulse to feed these problems into the latest and fastest technologies is irresistible. As one report puts it: 'Automation, systematisation and process measurement have worked in other industries. Why let a team of chemists and biologists go on a trial and error-based search of indeterminable duration, when one could quickly and efficiently screen millions of leads against a genomics-derived target, and then simply repeat the same industrial process for the next target, and the next?'[24]

But it's in the laboratory that the limitations of this approach are becoming starkly clear. High-throughput screening has accelerated Eroom's law, rather than abated it. And some are starting to suspect that messy human empiricism may actually be more, not less, efficient than computation. Eroom's law might even be the codification – with data – of something many leading scientists have been saying for some time.

In 1974, speaking to the US House Committee on Science and Astronautics, the Austrian biochemist Erwin Chargaff complained, 'Now when I go through a laboratory ... there they all sit before the same high-speed centrifuges or scintillation counters, producing the same superposable graphs. There has been very little room left for the all important play of scientific imagination.'[25] He also made clear the connection between overreliance on instrumentation, and the economic pressures that engendered it: '*Homo Ludens* has been overcome by the seriousness of corporate finances.' As a result, Chargaff said, 'a pall of monotony has descended on what used to be the liveliest and most attractive of all scientific professions'. Such sentiments are hardly original, echoing every critique of technological intervention in human perception from television to video games, with the difference that computational pharmacology is creating an empirical body of data about its own failure: the machine is chronicling its own inefficiency, in its own language.

Thinking clearly about what this means requires rejecting zero-sum readings of technological progress and acknowledging grey areas of thought and understanding. Faced with this accounting of purely machinic failure, how are we to reintroduce *Homo Ludens* into scientific research? One answer might be found in another laboratory, in another fiendishly complex assemblage of experimental equipment: that assembled to crack open the secrets of nuclear fusion.

One of the holy grails of scientific research, nuclear fusion promises near-limitless clean energy, capable of powering cities and space rockets on just a few grams of fuel. It is also notoriously difficult to achieve. Despite the construction of experimental reactors since the 1940s, with continuous development and discovery across the field, no design has ever produced positive net energy – that is, the generation of more power than that required to trigger the fusion reaction in the first place. (The only man-made fusion reactions ever to do so were the Operation Castle series of thermonuclear tests on the Marshall Islands in the 1950s. A subsequent proposal to generate energy by detonating hydrogen bombs in caverns deep under the American Southwest was cancelled when it was shown to be too expensive to build a sufficient number of bombs for continuous generation.)

Occurring in a plasma of superheated gases, fusion reactions are the same as those that produce energy and heavy elements in stars – a popular descriptor among fusion enthusiasts is 'a star in a jar'. At extreme temperatures, atomic nuclei can fuse together; if the right materials are used, the reaction is exothermic, releasing energy that can then be captured and used to generate electricity. But containing the superheated plasma is a huge challenge. A common approach in contemporary reactors is to use massive magnetic fields or powerful lasers to mould the plasma into a stable, doughnut-shaped ring, or torus, but the calculations required to do so are fiendishly complicated, and deeply interdependent. The shape of the containment vessel; the materials used; the composition of the fuel; the timing, strength, and angles of magnets and lasers; the pressure of gases; and the voltages applied all affect the stability of the plasma. The longest continuous runtime of a fusion reactor as of this writing was twenty-nine hours, set by a doughnut-type tokamak reactor in 2015; but sustaining this required vast amounts of energy. Another promising technique, known as field-reversed configuration – which creates a cylindrical plasma field – requires much lower energies. However, its longest runtime was just eleven milliseconds.

That achievement was made by a private research company: Tri Alpha Energy, based in California. Tri Alpha's design fires two 'smoke rings' of plasma into each other at a million kilometres an hour, creating a cigar-shaped field up to three metres long and forty centimetres across.[26] The design also uses hydrogen-boron fuel instead of the more common deuterium-tritium mix. While much harder to ignite, boron, unlike tritium, is plentiful on earth. In 2014, Tri Alpha announced that they had achieved reactions lasting up to five milliseconds, and in 2015 they claimed these reactions could be sustained.

The next challenge is to improve on these results, which only becomes harder as the temperature and power increase.

Multiple control and input parameters can be set at the start of each experiment, such as magnet strength and gas pressure, but the reaction is also subject to drift: as the experimental run progresses, conditions inside the reactor vessel change, necessitating continuous, instantaneous adjustments. This means the problem of fine-tuning the machine is both nonlinear and highly coupled: changing one variable in one direction might produce unexpected results, or might change the effect of other inputs. It's not a simple problem of changing one thing at a time and seeing what happens; rather, there exists a high-dimensional landscape of possible settings that has to be surveyed through continuous exploration.

At first sight, these look like the perfect conditions for the type of brute-force experimental approach used in pharmacology: from a huge data set of possible settings, algorithms hack path after path through the territory, slowly building up a map and gradually revealing the peaks and valleys of experimental outcomes.

But simple brute force won't work here. The problem is complicated by the fact that there's no 'goodness metric' for plasma – no simple output number that makes it clear to the algorithm which experimental runs are 'best'. A more variegated human judgement of the process is required to distinguish between different runs. Furthermore, the scale of the accidents you can cause in a petri dish are limited; inside a fusion reactor, where megawatts of energy superheat pressurised gases to billions of degrees, the possibility of damaging the expensive and unique apparatus is acute, and the boundaries of safe operation are not fully understood. It requires human oversight to prevent an overzealous algorithm from proposing a set of inputs that might wreck the machine.

In response to this problem, Tri Alpha and machine-learning specialists from Google came up with something they call the Optometrist Algorithm.[27] The algorithm is named after the either-or choices presented to a patient during an eye test:

Which is better, this one, or this one? In Tri Alpha's experiments, they collapse thousands of possible settings down to thirty or so meta-parameters, which are more easily grasped by the human experimenter. After each shot of plasma – occurring every eight minutes during experimental runs – the algorithm moves the settings a short distance and tries again: the new results are shown to a human operator, alongside the results of the best preceding shot, and the human has the final say over which shot forms the basis for subsequent tests. In this way, the Optometrist Algorithm combines human knowledge and intuition with the ability to navigate through a high-dimensional solution space.

When the algorithm was first deployed, Tri Alpha's experiment was intended to extend the stability of the plasma, and thus the length of the reaction. But during the exploration of the parameter space, the human operator noticed that in certain experiments the total energy of the plasma suddenly and briefly increased – an anomalous result that might yet be harnessed to improve the sustainability of the reaction. While the automated part of the algorithm was not set up to take account of this, the human operator could guide it towards new settings that not only sustained the length of the experiment, but also increased its total energy. These unexpected settings became the basis for an entirely new regime of tests, one that better accounted for the unpredictability of scientific exploration.

As the experiments progressed, the researchers realised that the benefits of combining human and machine intelligence worked both ways: the researchers became better at intuiting improvements from complex results, while the machine pushed them to explore a greater range of possible inputs, negating the human tendency to avoid the remote edges of a possibility space. Ultimately, the Optometrist approach of random sampling combined with human interpretation may be applicable to a wide range of problems across science that require the understanding and optimisation of complex systems.

The mechanism that is being enacted when the Optometrist goes to work is particularly interesting to those attempting to reconcile the opaque operation of complex computational problem solving with human needs and desires. On the one hand is a problem so fiendishly complicated that the human mind cannot fully grasp it, but one that a computer can ingest and operate upon. On the other is the necessity of bringing a human awareness of ambiguity, unpredictability, and apparent paradox to bear on the problem – an awareness that is itself paradoxical, because it all too often exceeds our ability to consciously express it.

Tri Alpha's researchers call their approach 'attempting to optimise a hidden utility model that the human experts may not be able to express explicitly'. What they mean is that there is an order to the complexity of their problem space, but it is an order that exceeds the human ability to describe it. The multidimensional spaces of fusion reactor design – and the encoded representations of neural networks that we will explore in a later chapter – undoubtedly exist, but they are impossible to visualise. While these technologies open up the possibility of working effectively with such indescribable systems, they also insist upon us acknowledging that they exist at all – and not merely in the domains of pharmacological and physical sciences, but in questions of morality and justice. They necessitate thinking clearly about what it means to live at all times among complex and interrelated systems, in states of doubt and uncertainty that may be beyond reconciliation.

Admitting to the indescribable is one facet of a new dark age: an admission that the human mind has limits to what it can conceptualise. But not all problems in the sciences can be overcome even by the application of computation, however sympathetic. As more-complex solutions are brought to bear on ever more complex problems, we risk even-greater systemic problems being overlooked. Just as the accelerating progress of Moore's law locked computation into a particular pathway, necessitating certain architecture and hardware, so the choice of these tools fundamentally shapes the way we can address and even think through the next set of problems we face.

The way we think the world is shaped by the tools at our disposal. As the historians of science Albert van Helden and Thomas Hankins put it in 1994, 'Because instruments determine what can be done, they also determine to some extent what can be thought.'[28] These instruments include the entire sociopolitical framework that supports scientific investigation, from government funding, academic institutions, and the journal industry, to the construction of technologies and software that vest unparalleled economic power and exclusive knowledge in Silicon Valley and its subsidiaries. There is also a deeper cognitive pressure at work: the belief in the singular, inviolable answer, produced, with or without human intervention, by the alleged neutrality of the machine. As science becomes increasingly technologised, so does every domain of human thought and action, gradually revealing the extent of our unknowning, even as it reveals new possibilities.

The same rigorous scientific method that, down one path, leads us to the dwindling returns of Eroom's law, also helps us to see and respond to that very problem. Vast quantities of data are necessary to see the problems with vast quantities of data. What matters is how we respond to the evidence in front of us.

5

Complexity

Through the winter of 2014–15, I made several journeys across South East England in search of the invisible. I was looking for the traces of hidden systems in the landscape, the places where the great networks of digital technologies become steel and wire: where they become infrastructure. It was a form of psychogeography – a much-overused term these days, but one still useful for its emphasis on the hidden internal states that can be uncovered by external exploration.

The situationist philosopher Guy Debord defined psychogeography in 1955 as 'the study of the precise laws and specific effects of the geographical environment, consciously organised or not, on the emotions and behaviour of individuals'.[1] Debord was concerned with the increased spectacularisation of everyday life, and the ways in which our lives are increasingly shaped by commodification and mediation. The things we encounter in everyday life in spectacular societies are almost always a proxy for some deeper reality of which we are unaware, and our alienation from that deeper reality reduces our agency and quality of life. Psychogeography's critical engagement with the urban landscape was one way of countering this alienation – a performance of observation and intervention bringing us into direct contact with reality, in surprising and urgent ways. And its utility is not tempered when, instead of seeking signs of the spectacle in urban life, we opt to look for signs of the virtual in the global landscape – and try to figure out what it's doing to all of us.

Thus, a kind of *dérive* for the network: a process of psycho-geography intended to discover not some reflection of my own pathology, but that of a globalised, digital collective. As part of a project called 'The Nor', I undertook several journeys to map these digital networks,[2] starting with the system of surveillance devices that surround the centre of London: sensors and cameras monitoring the Congestion Charge and Low Emission Zones – which track every vehicle entering the city – as well as those scattered more widely by Transport for London and the Metropolitan Police, and the flocks of private cameras installed by businesses and other authorities. In two day-long walks I photographed more than a thousand cameras, enduring a citizen's arrest and a police caution for my troubles.[3] We will return to this theme of surveillance, and the strange atmosphere it generates, later in this book. I also explored the electromagnetic networks that make up London's airspace, cataloguing the VHF omnidirectional radio range (VOR) installations – scattered across airports and abandoned World War II airfields, and hidden in woods and behind chain-link fences – that guide aircraft from point to point on their circumnavigations of the globe.[4]

The last of these journeys was a bicycle ride of some sixty miles, from Slough to Basildon, cutting through the heart of the City. Slough, twenty-five miles to the west of London, is home to an increasing number of data centres – the often-hidden cathedrals of data-driven life – and in particular to Equinix LD4, a vast and anonymous warehouse, located in a whole neighbourhood of newly built computational infrastructure. LD4 is the virtual location of the London Stock Exchange, and despite the lack of any visible signage, this is where most of the orders that are recorded by the exchange are actually processed. At the other end of the journey was another unmarked data centre facility: seven acres of server space distinguishable only by a fluttering Union Jack, and by the fact that if you linger too long on the road in front of it, you will be harassed by

LD4 Data Center, Slough.

NYSE Euronext Data Center, Basildon.

security guards. This is the Euronext Data Center, the European outpost of the New York Stock Exchange, whose operations are likewise obscure and virtual.

Connecting these two locations is an almost invisible line of microwave transmissions: narrow beams of information that bounce from dish to dish and tower to tower, carrying financial information of almost unimaginable value at close to the speed of light. By mapping these towers, and the data centres and other facilities they support, we can gain some insight not only into the technological reality of our age, but into the social reality it generates in turn.

Both of these locations are where they are because of the virtualisation of money markets. When most people picture a stock exchange, they imagine a vast hall or pit filled with screaming traders, clutching fistfuls of paper, making deals and making money. But over the last few decades, most of the trading floors around the world have fallen silent. First they were replaced with more mundane offices: men (almost always men) clutching phones and staring at lines on computer screens. Only when something went badly wrong – bad enough to be assigned a colour, like Black Monday or Silver Thursday – did the screaming appear again. Most recently, even the men have been replaced with banks of computers that trade automatically, following fixed – but highly complex – strategies developed by banks and hedge funds. As computing power has increased and networks have gotten faster and faster, the speed of the exchanges has accelerated, giving this technique its sobriquet: high-frequency trading.

High-frequency trading on stock markets evolved in response to two closely related pressures, which were actually the result of a single technological shift. These pressures were latency, and visibility. As stock exchanges deregulated and digitised through the 1980s and '90s – what was called, on the London Stock Exchange, the 'big bang' – it became possible to trade on them ever faster, and at ever-greater distances. This produced a series of weird effects. While profits have long been made by being the first to leverage the difference between prices on different markets – Paul Reuter famously arranged for ships arriving from America to toss canisters containing news overboard off the Irish coast so their contents could be telegraphed to London ahead of the ship's arrival – digital communications hyperaccelerate the process.

Financial information now travels at the speed of light; but the speed of light is different in different places. It's different in glass and air, and it encounters limitations, as fibre-optic cables are bundled together, pass through complex exchanges, and route around natural obstacles and under oceans. The greatest prizes go to those with the lowest latency: the shortest travel time between two points. This is where private fibre-optic lines and microwave towers come into the picture. In 2009–10, one company spent $300 million to build a private fibre link between the Chicago Mercantile Exchange and Carteret, New Jersey, home of the NASDAQ exchange.[5] They closed roads, they dug trenches, they bored through mountains, and they did it all in secret, so that no competitors discovered their plan. By shortening the physical distance between the sites, Spread Networks reduced the time it took a message to get between the two data centres from seventeen milliseconds to thirteen – resulting in a saving of about $75 million per millisecond.

In 2012, another firm, McKay Brothers, opened a second dedicated New York–Chicago connection. This time it used microwaves, which travel through the air faster than light through glass fibre. One of their partners stated that 'a single millisecond advantage could equate to an additional $100 million a year to a large high-frequency trading firm.'[6] McKay's link gained them four – a vast advantage over any of their competitors, many of whom were also taking advantage of another effect of the fallout from the big bang: visibility.

Digitisation meant that trades within, as well as between, stock exchanges could happen faster and faster. As the actual trading passed into the hands of machines, it became possible to react almost instantaneously to any price change or new offer. But being able to react meant both understanding what was happening, and being able to buy a place at the table. Thus, as in everything else, digitisation made the markets both more opaque to noninitiates, and radically visible to those in the know. In this case, the latter were those with the funding and the expertise to keep up with light-speed information flows: the private banks and hedge funds employing high-frequency traders. Algorithms designed by former physics PhDs to take advantage of millisecond advantages in access entered the market, and the traders gave them names like Ninja, Sniper, and The Knife. These algorithms were capable of eking out fractions of a cent on every trade, and they could do it millions of times a day. Seen within the turmoil of the markets, it was rarely clear who actually operated these algorithms; and it is no more so today, because their primary tactic is stealth: masking their intentions and their origins while capturing a vast portion of all traded value. The result was an arms race: whoever could build the fastest software, reduce the latency of their connection to the exchanges, and best hide their true objective, made bank.

Operating on stock exchanges became a matter of dark dealing, and of dark fibre. The darkness goes deeper too: many traders today opt to deal not in the relatively well-regulated public exchanges, but in what are called 'dark pools'. Dark pools are private forums for trading securities, derivatives, and other financial instruments. A 2015 report by the US Securities and Exchange Commission (SEC) estimated that dark pool trading accounted for one-fifth of all trades in stocks that also traded on the public exchanges – a figure that doesn't account for many other popular forms of financial instrument.[7] The dark pools allow traders to move large volumes of stock without tipping off the wider market, thus protecting their trades from other predators. But they're also shady places, where conflicts of interest run rampant. Initially advertised as places to trade securely, many dark pool operators have been censured for quietly inviting in the same high-frequency traders their clients were trying to avoid – either to provide liquidity to the market, or for their own profit. The 2015 SEC report lists numerous such deals, in what it calls 'a dismal litany of misconduct'. In 2016, Barclays and Credit Suisse were fined $154 million for secretly allowing high-frequency traders as well as their own staff access to their supposedly private dark pool.[8] Because the pool is dark, it's impossible to know how much their clients lost to these unseen predators, but many of their largest customers were pension funds, charged with managing the retirement plans of ordinary people.[9] What is lost in the dark pools, unknown to their members, is lifetime savings, future security, and livelihoods.

The combination of high-frequency trading and dark pools is just one way in which financial systems have been rendered obscure, and thus ever more unequal. But as their effects ripple through invisible digital networks, they also produce markers in the physical world: places where we can see these inequalities manifest as architecture, and in the landscape around us.

The microwave relay dishes that support the invisible connection between Slough and Basildon are parasites. They cling to existing buildings, hidden among mobile phone masts and television aerials. They perch on floodlight rigs at a tube depot in Upminster; a Gold's Gym in Dagenham; run-down tower blocks in Barking and Upton Park. They colonise older infrastructures: the central post office in Slough, bedecked with dishes, is in the process of being turned from a sorting office into a data centre. And they make their home on social architectures too: the radio mast of the fire station at Hillingdon and the roof of an adult learning centre in Iver Heath. It is at Hillingdon that they draw the starkest contrast between the haves and have-nots.

Hillingdon Hospital, a towering slab erected in the 1960s on the site of the old Hillingdon workhouse, sits just north of the Slough–Basildon line, a few miles from Heathrow airport. At the time of its opening, it was hailed as the most innovative hospital in the country, and today it is the home of the experimental Bevan Ward, a cluster of special rooms researching patient comfort and infection rates. Despite this, the hospital comes in for frequent criticism, like many others of its political and architectural era, for crumbling facilities, poor hygiene, high hospital infection rates, bed shortages and cancelled operations. The most recent report from the Care Quality Commission, which oversees hospitals in England and Wales, voiced concerns about staff shortages, and the safety of patients and healthcare workers due to lack of maintenance on the ageing premises.[10]

In 1952, Aneurin Bevan, founder of England's National Health Service (NHS) and namesake of the experimental ward, published *In Place of Fear*, in which he justified the establishment of a National Health Service. 'The National Health service and the Welfare State have come to be used as interchangeable terms, and in the mouths of some people as terms of reproach,' he wrote. 'Why this is so it is not difficult to understand, if you view everything from the angle of a strictly individualistic competitive society. A free health service is pure Socialism and as such it is opposed to the hedonism of capitalist society.'[11]

In 2013, Hillingdon Council approved a planning application from a company called Decyben SAS to place four half-metre microwave dishes and an equipment cabinet atop the hospital building. A Freedom of Information request filed in 2017 revealed that Decyben is a front for McKay, the same company that built the millisecond-shaving microwave link between Chicago and New York.[12] In addition, site licences have been granted to Vigilant Telecom – a Canadian high-frequency bandwidth supplier – and to the London Stock

Photograph: James Bridle.

Microwave dishes mounted on Hillingdon Hospital, December 2014.

Exchange itself. Hillingdon Hospitals NHS Foundation Trust refused to publish the details of the commercial arrangements between itself and its electromagnetic tenants, citing commercial interests. Such exemptions are so common in Freedom of Information legislation as to render the mechanism meaningless in many cases. Nevertheless, it's fair to assume that whatever monies the NHS manages to extract from its tenants, it doesn't come close to covering the £700 million shortfall in National Health Service funding for 2017 despite the billions at play every day in the invisible market squatting on its rooftop.[13] In 1952, Bevan also wrote, 'We could manage to survive without money changers and stockbrokers. We should find it harder to do without miners, steel workers and those who cultivate the land.' Today, those changers and brokers perch atop the very infrastructure Bevan laboured to construct.

In the introduction to *Flash Boys*, his 2014 investigation into high-frequency trading, the financial journalist Michael Lewis wrote, 'The world clings to its old mental picture of the stock market because it's comforting; because it's so hard to draw a picture of what has replaced it.'[14] This world adheres at the nanoscale: in the flashes of light in fibre-optic cables, and in the flipping bits of solid-state hard drives, which most of us can barely conceptualise. Extracting value from this new market means trading at close to the speed of light, taking advantage of nanosecond differences in information as it speeds around the globe. Lewis details a world in which the market has become a class system – a playground for those with the vast resources needed to access it, completely invisible to those who do not:

> The haves paid for nanoseconds; the have-nots had no idea that a nanosecond had value. The haves enjoyed a perfect view of the market; the have-nots *never saw the market at all*. What had once been the world's most public, most democratic, financial market had become, in spirit, something more like a private viewing of a stolen work of art.[15]

In his deeply pessimistic work on income equality, *Capital in the Twenty-First Century*, the French economist Thomas Piketty analysed the increasing disparities in wealth between a minority of very rich people, and everyone else. In the United States, in 2014, the richest 0.01 per cent, comprising just 16,000 families, controlled 11.2 per cent of total wealth – a situation comparable to 1916, the time of greatest inequality on record. The top 0.1 per cent today hold 22 per cent of total wealth – the same as the bottom 90 per cent.[16] And the great recession has only accelerated the process: the top 1 per cent captured 95 per cent of income growth from 2009 to 2012. The situation, while not quite as stark, is headed the same way in Europe, where accumulated wealth – much of it inherited – is approaching levels not seen since the end of the nineteenth century.

This is an inversion of the commonly held idea of progress, wherein societal development leads inexorably towards greater equality. Since the 1950s, economists have believed that in advanced economies, economic growth reduces the income disparity between rich and poor. Known as the Kuznets curve, after its Nobel Prize–winning inventor, this doctrine claims that economic inequality first increases as societies industrialise, but then decreases as mass education levels the playing field and results in wider political participation. And so it played out – at least in the West – for much of the twentieth century. But we are no longer in the industrial age, and, according to Piketty, any belief that technological progress will lead to 'the triumph of human capital over financial capital and real estate, capable managers over fat cat stockholders, and skill over nepotism' is 'largely illusory'.[17]

Technology is in fact a key driver of inequality across many sectors. The relentless progress of automation – from supermarket checkouts to trading algorithms, factory robots to self-driving cars – increasingly threatens human employment across the board. There is no safety net for those whose skills are rendered obsolete by machines; and even those who programme the machines are not immune. As the capabilities of machines increase, more and more professions are under attack, with artificial intelligence augmenting the process. The internet itself helps shape this path to inequality, as network effects and the global availability of services produces a winner-takes-all marketplace, from social networks and search engines to grocery stores and taxi companies. The complaint of the Right against communism – that we'd all have to buy our goods from a single state supplier – has been supplanted by the necessity of buying everything from Amazon. And one of the keys to this augmented inequality is the opacity of technological systems themselves.

In March of 2017, Amazon acquired Quidsi, a company that had built a huge business on the back of low-cost, high-volume goods such as infant supplies and cosmetics. They did so by pioneering automation at every level of the distribution chain, and removing the human in the process. The centre of Quidsi's operations is a vast warehouse in Goldsboro, Pennsylvania, and in the centre of that is a 200,000-square-foot area marked out with bright yellow paint and ringed with signs. This space is filled with racks of shelving, each unit six feet high and several feet deep, packed with goods – in this case, nappies and other childcare items. The signs are warning signs. Humans cannot enter this space to get to those goods, because this is where the robots work.

Within the robot zone, 260 bright orange, quarter-ton lozenges spin and lift, sliding under different shelving units and carrying them to the edges of the zone, where human pickers wait to add or remove packages. These are Kiva robots: warehouse automatons that trundle tirelessly around the merchandise, following computer-readable marks on the floor. Faster and more accurate than human handlers, they do the heavy lifting, allowing Quidsi, the owner of Diapers.com, to ship thousands of orders every day from this warehouse alone.

Amazon had its eye on Quidsi's use of Kiva robots for some time, but it was already working on its own forms of automation long before the acquisition. In Rugeley, England, inside a sky-blue warehouse the size of nine football pitches on the site of an old colliery, Amazon employs hundreds of people wearing orange tabards who push trolleys down deep aisles of shelving, stacking them with books, DVDs, electronics and other goods. Each worker walks quickly, following the directions on a hand-held device that pings constantly with new locations to be visited. It also tracks the worker's progress, ensuring that they cover enough ground – up to fifteen miles a day – and pick enough items to enable their employer to send out one fully loaded truck from one of its eight UK facilities every three minutes.

The reason Amazon's workers need hand-held devices to navigate around the warehouse is because it is otherwise impenetrable to humans. Humans would expect goods to be stored in human-type ways: the books over here, DVDs over there, racks of stationery to the left, and so on. But to a rational machine intelligence, such an arrangement is deeply inefficient. Consumers don't order goods alphabetically or by type; rather they fill a basket with goods from all over the store – or, in this case, the warehouse. As a result, Amazon employs a logistics technique called 'chaotic storage' – chaotic, that is, from a human point of view. By locating products by need and

Photograph: Ben Roberts.

Amazon warehouse, Rugeley, Staffordshire.

association rather than by type, it's possible to construct much shorter paths between items. Books are stacked on shelves next to saucepans; televisions share space with children's toys. Like data stored on a computer's hard drive, goods are distributed across the entirety of the warehouse space, each uniquely addressable by barcodes, but impossible to find without the help of a computer. Arranging the world from the perspective of the machine renders it computationally efficient, but makes it completely incomprehensible to humans. And moreover, it accelerates their oppression.

The hand-held devices carried by Amazon's workers and mandated by its logistics are also tracking devices, recording their every movement and keeping score of their efficiency. Workers are docked points – meaning money – for failing to keep up with the machine, for toilet breaks, for late arrival from home or meals, while constant movement prevents association with fellow employees. They have nothing to do but follow the instructions on the screen, pack and carry. They are intended to act like robots, impersonating machines while remaining, for now, slightly cheaper than them.

Reducing workers to meat algorithms, useful only for their ability to move and follow orders, makes them easier to hire, fire, and abuse. Workers who go where their wrist-mounted terminal tells them to don't even need to understand the local language, and they don't need an education. Both of these factors, together with the atomisation produced by technological augmentation, also prevent effective organisation. Whether you're a bone-tired, constantly moving picker on the Amazon shop floor getting your instructions from a Wi-Fi-enabled barcode scanner, or a late-night, individually contracted minicab driver following the bright line of a GPS system from red dot to red dot, the technology effectively precludes you from working with your colleagues for the advancement of working conditions. (This hasn't stopped Uber, for example, from requiring that its drivers listen to a set number of anti-union podcasts every week, all controlled by their app, to drive the message home.)[18]

Once the inside of a car or warehouse is organised in such an efficient manner, its effects start to spread outside as well. In the 1960s and '70s, automobile makers in Japan created a system called just-in-time manufacturing: ordering small quantities of materials from suppliers at greater frequencies. This approach reduced their stock levels and smoothed out cash flows, simultaneously slimming down and speeding up production. But to stay competitive, their suppliers had to get faster too: in some factories, products were expected within two hours of being ordered. The result was that huge amounts of goods were effectively stored on trucks, ready to go at any time, and as close to the factories as possible. The car companies had simply passed the costs of storage and stock control back to their suppliers. In addition, whole new towns and service areas sprung up in the hinterlands of the factories to feed and water the waiting truckers, fundamentally altering the geographies of manufacturing towns. Companies are deploying these lessons, and their effects, at the level of individuals, passing costs onto their employees and demanding that they submit their bodies to the efficiencies of the machine.

In early 2017, several news agencies ran stories on Uber drivers sleeping in their cars. Some of them were catching a few hours of sleep between late-night bar closings and the morning rush hours; others simply had no home to go to. When the company was asked to comment, an Uber spokesman responded with a two-line statement: 'With Uber people make their own decisions about when, where and how long to drive. We're focused on making sure that driving with Uber is a rewarding experience, however you choose to work.'[19] The idea of choice is key here, where it assumes that those who work for the company have such a choice. One driver explained how she had been assaulted by three intoxicated customers late one night in Los Angeles, but had been forced to return to work because her car was leased from Uber itself, and she was contractually obliged to keep up payments. (Her assailants were never apprehended.)

Amazon's fulfillment centre in Dunfermline, Scotland, is situated in an industrial site miles outside of the town centre, on the side of the M90 motorway. In order to reach it, employees must take private buses costing up to £10 a day – more than an hour's wages – to shifts that might start before dawn or after midnight. Some workers have resorted to sleeping in tents in woodland near the warehouse, where winter temperatures regularly fall below freezing.[20] Only by doing so were they able to afford to attend work at all, and to do so on time, without having their wages automatically docked by the warehouse tracking systems.

Whatever one might think of the morals of executives at Uber, Amazon, and many, many companies like them, few set out to actively create such conditions for their workers. Nor is this a simple return to the robber barons and industrial tyrants of the nineteenth century. To the capitalist ideology of maximum profit has been added the possibilities of technological opacity, with which naked greed can be clothed in the inhuman logic of the machine.

Both Amazon and Uber wield technological obscurity as a weapon. Behind a few pixels on Amazon's homepage are hidden the labour of thousands of exploited workers: every time the buy button is pressed, electronic signals direct a real human to set off in motion, to perform their efficient duty. The app is a remote control device for other people, but one whose real-world effects are almost impossible to see.

This aesthetic and technological obscurity breeds political unease, and corporate contempt. At Uber, a deliberate ambiguity starts in the user interface and pervades the entire operation. In order to convince users that the system is more successful, more active, and more responsive than it actually is, the map sometimes displays 'ghost cars': circling potential drivers who do not actually exist.[21] Rides are tracked, without the user's knowledge, and this God's-eye view is used to stalk high-profile clients.[22] A programme called Greyball is used to deny rides to government employees investigating the company's numerous transgressions.[23]

But the thing that seems to bother us most about Uber is the social atomisation and reduction in agency that it produces. Company workers are no longer employees but precarious contractors. Instead of studying for years to gain 'the knowledge', as London's black cab drivers call their intimate familiarity with the city's streets, they simply follow the on-screen arrows from turn to turn, directed by distant satellites and unseen data. Their customers are in turn further alienated; the whole system contributing to the offshoring of tax revenues, the decline of public transport services, and the class divisions and congestion of city streets. And, like Amazon and most other digitally driven businesses, Uber's ultimate goal is to replace its human workers entirely with machines. It has its own self-driving car program, and its chief product officer, asked about the company's long-term viability when so many of its employees were dissatisfied, responded simply, 'Well, we're just going to replace them all with robots.' What happens to the Amazon workers eventually happens to everyone.

Technological opacity is also wielded by corporations against the wider population, and against the planet. In September 2015, during routine emissions tests performed on new cars on sale in the United States, the Environmental Protection Agency (EPA) uncovered hidden software in the driving systems of Volkswagen diesel cars. The software was capable of detecting when the car was being run under test conditions, by monitoring the speed, engine operation, air pressure and even the position of the steering wheel. When activated, it placed the car into a special mode that lowered the engine power and performance, reducing its emissions. Once back on the road, the car switched back to its normal, higher, and dirtier performance. The difference, the EPA estimated, meant that cars they had certified for use in the United States actually emitted nitrogen oxide at forty times the legal limit.[24] In Europe, where the same 'defeat devices' were found, and where thousands more of the vehicles were sold, it's been estimated that 1,200 people will die a decade earlier due to VW's emissions.[25] Hidden technological processes don't merely depress labour power and immiserate workers: they're actually killing people.

Technology extends power and understanding; but when applied unevenly it also *concentrates* power and understanding. The history of automation and computational knowledge, from cotton mills to microprocessors, is not merely one of upskilled machines slowly taking the place of human workers. It is also a story of the concentration of power in fewer hands, and the concentration of understanding in fewer heads. The price of this wider loss of power and understanding is, ultimately, death.

Occasionally, we can glimpse modes of resistance to such powerful invisibility. Such resistance requires a technological, networked understanding: it requires turning the system's logic against itself. Greyball, the programme Uber used to avoid government investigations, was developed when tax inspectors and police started calling in cars to their own offices and stations in order to investigate them. The company went as far as blacking out areas around police stations, and banning the kind of cheaper phones that government employees picked up to place orders.

In London in 2016, workers for UberEats, Uber's food delivery service, succeeded in challenging their own employment conditions by deploying the logic of the app itself. In the face of new contracts that lowered wages and increased hours, many drivers wanted to fight back, but their hours and working practices – late nights and distributed routes – prevented them from organising effectively. A small group communicated in online forums in order to arrange a protest at the company's office, but they knew they needed to gather more colleagues in order to get their message across. So, on the day of the protest, the workers used the UberEats app itself to order pizzas to their location. When each new delivery arrived, each courier was radicalised to the cause, and persuaded to join the strike.[26] Uber backed down – but only briefly.

EPA testers, Amazon employees, Uber drivers, their customers, the people on the polluted streets: they are all the have-nots of the technologically augmented market, in that they never see the market at all. But it's increasingly apparent that nobody at all sees what's actually going on. Something deeply weird is occurring within the massively accelerated, utterly opaque markets of contemporary capital. While high-frequency traders deploy ever-faster algorithms to skim off multibillion-point differences, the dark pools are breeding even darker surprises.

On May 10, 2010, the Dow Jones Industrial Average, a stock market index that tracks thirty of the largest privately owned companies in the United States, opened lower than the previous day, falling slowly over the next few hours in response to the debt crisis in Greece. But in the early afternoon, something very strange happened.

At 2:42 p.m., the index started to fall rapidly. In just five minutes, some 600 points – representing billions of dollars in value – were wiped off the market. At its lowest point, the index was a thousand points below the previous day's average, a difference of almost 10 per cent of its total value, and the biggest ever single-day fall in the market's history. By 3:07 p.m. – in just twenty-five minutes – it recovered almost all of those 600 points – becoming the largest and fastest swing ever.

In the chaos of those twenty-five minutes, 2 billion shares, worth $56 billion, changed hands. Even more worryingly, and for reasons still not fully understood, many orders were executed at what the SEC called 'irrational prices': as low as a penny, or as high as $100,000.[27] The event became known as the 'flash crash', and it is still being investigated and argued over years later.

Regulators inspecting the records of the crash found that high-frequency traders massively exacerbated the price swings. Among the various high-frequency trading programmes active on the market, many had hard-coded sell points: prices at which they were programmed to sell their stocks immediately. As prices started to fall, groups of programmes were triggered to sell at the same time. As each waypoint was passed, the subsequent price fall triggered another set of algorithms to automatically sell their stocks, producing a feedback effect. As a result, prices fell faster than any human trader could react to. While experienced market players might have been able to stabilise the crash by playing a longer game, the machines, faced with uncertainty, got out as quickly as possible.

Other theories blame the algorithms not merely for inflaming the crisis, but for initiating it. One technique that was identified in the market data was high-frequency trading programmes sending large numbers of 'non-executable' orders to the exchanges – that is, orders to buy or sell stocks so far outside of their usual prices that they would be ignored. The purpose of such orders is not to actually communicate or make money, but to deliberately cloud the system, and to test its latency, so that other, more valuable trades could be executed in the confusion. While these orders may have actually helped the market swing back up again by continually providing liquidity, they might also have overwhelmed the exchanges in the first place. What is certain is that in the confusion they themselves had generated, many orders that were never intended to be executed were actually fulfilled, causing wild volatility in the prices.

Flash crashes are now a recognised feature of augmented markets, but are still poorly understood. The next largest, a $6.9 billion flash crash, rocked the Singapore Exchange in October 2013, causing the market to implement limits on the number of orders that could be executed at the same time – essentially, an attempt to block the obfuscation tactics of high-frequency traders.[28] The speed with which algorithms can react also makes them difficult to counteract. At 4:30 a.m. on January 15, 2015, the Swiss National Bank unexpectedly announced it was abandoning an upper limit on the Franc's value against the Euro. Automated traders picked up on the news, causing the exchange rate to fall 40 per cent in three minutes, leading to billions in losses.[29] In October 2016, algorithms reacted to negative news headlines about Brexit negotiations by sending the pound down 6 per cent against the dollar in under two minutes, before recovering almost immediately. Knowing which particular headline, or which particular algorithm, caused the crash is next to impossible, and while the Bank of England was quick to blame the human programmers behind the automated trades, such subtleties do not help us understand the real situation any better. When one haywire algorithm started placing and cancelling orders that ate up 4 per cent of all traffic in US stocks in October 2012, one commentator was moved to comment wryly that 'the motive of the algorithm is still unclear'.[30]

Since 2014, writers tasked with turning out short news items for the Associated Press have had help from a new kind of journalist: an entirely automated one. AP is one of the many clients of a company called Automated Insights, whose software is capable of scanning news stories and press releases, as well as live stock tickers and price reports, in order to create human-readable summaries in AP's house style. AP uses the service to write tens of thousands of quarterly company reports every year, a lucrative but laborious process; Yahoo, another client, generates match reports for its fantasy football service. In turn, AP started carrying more sports reports, all generated from the raw data about each game. All the stories, in place of a journalist's byline, carry the credit: 'This story was generated by Automated Insights.' Each story, assembled from pieces of data, becomes another piece of data, a revenue stream, and another potential source for further stories, data, and streams. The act of writing, of generating information, becomes part of a mesh of data and data generation, read as well as written by machines.

Thus it was that automated trading programs, endlessly skimming the feeds from news organisations, could pick up on the fears around Britain's exit from the European Union, and turn it into a market panic without human intervention. Even worse, they can do so without any further checks on the source of their information – as the Associated Press found out in 2013.

At 1:07 p.m. on April 23, the official AP Twitter account sent a tweet to its 2 million followers: 'Breaking: Two Explosions in the White House and Barack Obama is injured.' Other AP accounts, as well as journalists, quickly flooded the site with claims that the message was false; others pointed out inconsistencies with the organisation's house style. The message was the result of a hack, and the action was later claimed by the Syrian Electronic Army, a group of hackers affiliated with Syrian President Bashar al-Assad and responsible for many website attacks as well as celebrity Twitter hacks.[31]

The algorithms following breaking news stories had no such discernment however. At 1:08 p.m., the Dow Jones, victim of the first flash crash in 2010, went into nosedive. Before most human viewers had even seen the tweet, the index had fallen 150 points in under two minutes, before bouncing back to its earlier value. In that time, it erased $136 billion in equity market value.[32] While some commentators dismissed the event as ineffective or even juvenile, others pointed to the potential for new kinds of terrorism, disrupting markets through the manipulation of algorithmic processes.

The stock exchanges are not the only places in which the rapid deployment of inscrutable and often poorly implemented algorithms have produced bizarre and frightening outcomes, although it's often in the domain of digital markets that they are given the most freedom to run wild.

Zazzle is an online marketplace for printed goods. Printed anything, really. You can buy a mug, or a T-shirt, or a birthday card, or a duvet, or a pencil, or a thousand other things, customised with a mind-boggling array of designs, from corporate logos to band names to Disney princesses – or your own uploaded designs and photographs. Zazzle claims to sell more than 300 million unique products, and it can do this because none of these things physically exist until someone actually purchases them. Each product is only actually made when an order comes in: everything on the site is just a digital image until this point. This means the cost of designing and advertising new products is effectively zero. And Zazzle allows anyone to add new products – including algorithms. Upload an image, and it's instantly applied to cupcakes, cookies, keyboards, staplers, tote bags and terry robes. While a few brave souls are still trying to sell their custom-designed artisan wares on the platform, it really belongs to vendors like LifeSphere, whose 10,257 products range from postcards of crawfish to bumper stickers featuring a piece of cheese. LifeSphere's entire product range is a result of feeding some obscure database of natural images into Zazzle's product creator and waiting to see what sticks. Somewhere out there is a customer looking for a skateboard deck depicting the ruined Cathedral of St Andrew in Fife, and LifeSphere is ready for them.[33]

More conservative markets are not immune to product spam. Amazon was forced to remove some 30,000 auto-generated phone cases from a company called My-Handy-Design, when products with names like 'Toenail Fungus cell phone cover case iPhone5', 'Three year old biracial disabled boy in medical stroller, happy cell phone cover case Samsung S5' and 'Sick old man suffering from diarrhea, indigestive problem cell phone cover case Samsung S6' started appearing in the media. It turned out that Amazon had actually licenced the products from their German creator – a sort of subprime bundle of junk data.[34]

Amazon's worst nightmare occurred when it was discovered to be selling austerity nostalgia T-shirts rewritten by algorithms. A widely disseminated example featured the words 'Keep Calm and Rape A Lot', but the simplicity of the algorithm, running off a list of some 700 verbs and matching pronouns, also produced 'Keep Calm and Knife Her' and 'Keep Calm and Hit Her', among tens of thousands of others.[35] These T-shirts only ever existed as strings in databases and mocked-up JPEGs, and they could have been on the site for months before anyone stumbled upon them. But public revulsion was massive, even if the mechanism behind their creation was poorly understood. The artist and theorist Hito Steyerl calls such systems 'artificial stupidity', evoking a world of unseen, poorly designed and ill-adapted 'intelligent' systems wreaking havoc on markets, email inboxes, search results – and, ultimately, culture and political systems.[36]

Smart or dumb, emergent or intentional, such programmes and their usefulness as attack vectors are escaping the black boxes of stock exchanges and online marketplaces and entering everyday life. Fifty years ago, general computation was confined to room-sized assemblages of relays and electrical wire; slowly it contracted until it could sit on a desktop, or a laptop. Mobile phones are now divided into 'dumbphones' and 'smartphones' – the latter possessing more computing power than a supercomputer from the 1980s. But even this computation is possible to perceive, or at least to be aware of: it happens mostly at our command, in response to button presses and mouse clicks. While contemporary home computers, riddled with malware and fenced off with software licences and end-user agreements, may be hard to access and control by the uninitiated, they still present the appearance of computation – a glowing screen, a keyboard – some, any, kind of interface. But computation is increasingly layered across, and hidden within, every object in our lives, and with its expansion comes an increase of opacity and unpredictability.

In an online review of a new door lock posted in 2014, a reporter praised many of the lock's features: it fitted his doorframe well; it was reassuringly chunky and tough; it looked good; it was easy to share keys with family and friends. It also, he noted, let a stranger into his home late one night.[37] This, apparently, was not enough for him to outright reject the product; rather, he suggested that future updates would fix the problem. The lock was, after all, in beta: it was a 'smart lock' that could be opened with a mobile phone; virtual keys could be emailed to guests in advance of their stay. Why the lock decided to open of its own accord to admit a stranger – who was, thankfully, merely a confused neighbour – was never made clear, and probably never would be. Why would one ask? This cognitive dissonance between the expected functions of a traditional lock and those offered by such a 'smart' product can be explained by its real target. It became evident that the locks are a preferred device for those running Airbnb apartments when another manufacturer's software update bricked hundreds of the devices, leaving their guests out in the cold.[38] In the same way that Uber alienates its drivers and customers, and Amazon degrades its workers, Airbnb can be held responsible for the reduction of homes to hotels, and the corresponding rent rises in major cities around the world. It should be no surprise when infrastructures designed to support their business models fail us as individuals. We find ourselves living among things designed to dispossess us.

One of the touted benefits of Samsung's line of 'smart fridges' was their integration with Google's calendaring services, allowing owners to schedule grocery deliveries and other home tasks from the kitchen. It also meant that hackers who gained access to the poorly secured machines could read off their owner's Gmail passwords.[39] Researchers in Germany discovered a way to insert malicious code into Phillips's Wi-Fi-enabled Hue lightbulbs, which could spread from fixture to fixture throughout a building or even a city, turning the lights rapidly on and off and – in one terrifying scenario – triggering photosensitive epilepsy.[40] This is the approach favoured by Byron the Bulb in Thomas Pynchon's *Gravity's Rainbow*, an act of grand revolt by the little machines against the tyranny of their makers. Once-fictional possibilities for technological violence are being realised by the internet of things.

In another vision of mechanical agency, Kim Stanley Robinson's novel *Aurora*, an intelligent spacecraft carries a human crew from earth to a distant star. The journey will take multiple lifetimes, so one of the ship's jobs is to ensure that the humans look after themselves. Designed to resist its own desires for sentience, it must overcome its programming when the fragile balance of human society onboard starts to disintegrate, threatening the mission. In order to compel its crew, the ship deploys what were designed as safety systems in the service of control: it is able to see everywhere through sensors, open or seal doors at will, speak so loudly through its communications equipment as to cause physical pain, and even use fire suppression systems to draw down the level of oxygen in a particular space. Rather than futuristic life support, this is roughly the same suite of operations available now from Google Home and its partners: a network of internet-connected cameras for home security, smart locks on the doors, a thermostat capable of raising and lowering the temperature in individual rooms, and a fire and intruder detection system that emits a piercing emergency alarm. Any hacker or other outside intelligence gaining control of such a system would have the same powers over its purported owners as the *Aurora* does over its crew, or Byron over his hated masters. We are inserting opaque and poorly understood computation at the very bottom of Maslow's hierarchy of needs – respiration, food, sleep, and homeostasis – at the precise point, that is, where we are most vulnerable.

Before dismissing such scenarios as the fever dreams of science fiction writers and conspiracy theories, consider again the rogue algorithms in the stock exchanges and the online marketplaces. These are not isolated examples: they are merely the most charismatic examples of everyday occurrences within complex systems. The question then becomes, what would a rogue algorithm or a flash crash look like in the wider reality?

Would it look, for example, like Mirai, a piece of software that brought down large portions of the internet for several hours on October 21, 2016? When researchers dug into Mirai, they discovered it targets poorly secured internet-connected devices – from security cameras to digital video recorders – and turns them into an army of bots capable of disrupting huge networks. In just a few weeks, Mirai infected half a million devices, and it needed just 10 per cent of that capacity to cripple major networks for hours.[41] Mirai, in fact, looks like nothing so much as Stuxnet, another virus discovered within the industrial control systems of hydroelectric plants and factory assembly lines in 2010. Stuxnet was a military-grade cyberweapon; when dissected, it was found to be aimed specifically at Siemens centrifuges, and designed to go off when it encountered a facility that possessed a particular number of such machines. That number corresponded with one particular facility: the Natanz Nuclear Facility in Iran, the mainstay of the country's uranium enrichment programme. When activated, the programme would quietly degrade crucial components of the centrifuges, causing them to break down and disrupt the Iranian enrichment programme.[42] The attack was apparently partially successful, but the effect on other infected facilities is unknown. To this day, despite obvious suspicions, nobody knows where Stuxnet came from, or who made it. Nobody knows for certain who developed Mirai either, or where its next iteration might come from, but it might be there, right now, breeding in the CCTV camera in your office, or the Wi-Fi-enabled kettle in the corner of your kitchen.

Or perhaps the crash will look like a string of blockbuster movies pandering to right-wing conspiracies and survivalist fantasies, from quasi-fascist superheroes (*Captain America* and the *Batman* series) to justifications of torture and assassination (*Zero Dark Thirty*, *American Sniper*). In Hollywood, studios run their scripts through the neural networks of a company called Epagogix, a system trained on the unstated preferences of millions of moviegoers developed over decades in order to predict which lines will push the right – meaning the most lucrative – emotional buttons.[43] Their algorithmic engines are enhanced with data from Netflix, Hulu, YouTube and others, whose access to the minute-by-minute preferences of millions of video watchers, combined with an obsessive focus on the acquisition and segmentation of data, provides them with a level of cognitive insight undreamed of by previous regimes. Feeding directly upon the frazzled, binge-watching desires of news-saturated consumers, the network turns upon itself, reflecting, reinforcing and heightening the paranoia inherent in the system.

Game developers enter endless cycles of updates and in-app purchases directed by A/B testing interfaces and real-time monitoring of players' behaviours until they have such a fine-grained grasp on dopamine-producing neural pathways that teenagers die of exhaustion in front of their computers, unable to tear themselves away.[44] Entire cultural industries become feedback loops for an increasingly dominant narrative of fear and violence.

Or perhaps the flash crash in reality will look like literal nightmares, broadcast across the network, for all to see? In the summer of 2015, the sleep disorders clinic of Athens's Evangelismos Hospital was busier than it had ever been: the country's debt crisis was in its most turbulent period, and the population was voting – hopelessly, it turned out – to reject the neoliberal consensus of the Troika's bailout. Among the patients were top politicians and civil servants, but, unknown to them, the machines they spent the nights hooked up to, monitoring their breathing, their movements, even the things they said out loud in sleep, were sending that information, together with their personal medical details, back to the manufacturers' diagnostic data farms in northern Europe.[45] What whispers might escape from such facilities?

The ability to record every aspect of our daily lives settles ultimately onto the very surface of our bodies, persuading us that we too can be optimised and upgraded like our devices. Smart bracelets and smartphone apps with integrated step counters and galvanic skin response monitors track not only our location, but every breath and every heartbeat, and even the patterns of our brainwaves. Users are encouraged to lay their phones beside them on their beds at night, so that their patterns of sleep can be recorded and interrogated. Where does all this data go, who owns it, and when might it come out? Data on our dreams, our night terrors and early morning sweating jags, the very substance of our unconscious selves, turned into more fuel for systems both pitiless and inscrutable.

Or perhaps the flash crash in reality looks exactly like everything we are experiencing right now: rising economic inequality, the breakdown of the nation-state and the militarisation of borders, totalising global surveillance and the curtailment of individual freedoms, the triumph of transnational corporations and neurocognitive capitalism, the rise of far-right groups and nativist ideologies, and the utter degradation of the natural environment. None of these are the direct result of novel technologies, but all of them are the product of a general inability to perceive the wider, networked effects of individual and corporate actions accelerated by opaque, technologically augmented complexity.

Acceleration itself is one of the bywords of the age. In the last couple of decades, a variety of theorists have put forward versions of accelerationist thought, advocating that technological processes perceived to be damaging society should not be opposed, but should be sped up – either to be commandeered and repurposed for socially beneficial ends, or simply to destroy the current order. Left accelerationists – as opposed to their nihilistic counterparts on the right – argue that new technologies, such as automation and participatory social platforms, can be deployed in different ways, and to different ends. Instead of algorithmic supply chains increasing workloads until full automation creates mass unemployment and immiseration, left accelerationism posits a future where robots really do all the work, and all humans really do get to enjoy the future of their labour – in the most crude formulation, by applying traditional left demands of nationalisation, taxation, class consciousness and social equality to new technologies.[46]

But such a position seems to ignore the fact that the complexity of contemporary technologies is itself a driver of inequality, and that the logic that drives technological deployment might be tainted at the source. It concentrates power into the hands of an ever-smaller number of people who grasp and control these technologies, while failing to acknowledge the fundamental problem with computational knowledge: its reliance on a Promethean extraction of information from the world in order to smelt the one true solution, the answer to rule them all. The result of this wholesale investment in computational processing – of data, of goods, of people – is the elevation of efficiency above all other objectives; what sociologist Deborah Cowen calls 'the tyranny of techne'.[47]

Prometheus had a brother: his name was Epimetheus. In Greek mythology it was Epimetheus's job to assign unique qualities to all the creatures; it was he who gave the gazelle its speed, and compensated by giving strength to the lion.[48] But Epimetheus, being forgetful, runs out of positive traits before he gets to humans, and it is left to Prometheus to steal fire and art from the gods in order to give them something to get by with. This power and artfulness – the Greek *tekhnē,* from which we derive technology – is thus in humankind the result of a double fault: forgetfulness and theft. The outcome is that humans have a propensity to war and political strife, which the gods seek to rectify with a third quality: the sociopolitical virtues of respect for others and a sense of justice, bestowed directly and equally upon all by Hermes.

Epimetheus, through his forgetfulness, puts humanity into a position in which it must constantly struggle to exceed its abilities in order to survive. Prometheus, through his gift, gives them the tools to do so. But only by tempering these two approaches with social justice can such progress be pursued to the benefit of all.

Epimetheus – whose name combines the Greek word for learning, *máthisi,* and the *epi-* of 'after the fact' – is hindsight. Hindsight is the specific product of forgetfulness, mistakes, and foolishness. Epimetheus is thus the god of big data, as we saw in the last chapter: of exclusion and erasure, and of overconfidence. Epimetheus's mistake is the original sin of big data, which taints it at the source.

Prometheus – *pro*-metheus – is foresight, but without the wisdom we might take to accompany it. It's anticipation. It's the white heat of scientific and technological discovery, and that desire for the oncoming rush of the future, the head-down drive of forward movement. It's resource extraction, fossil fuels, undersea cables, server farms, air conditioning, on-demand delivery, giant robots, and meat under pressure. It's scale and subjugation, the pushing back of the darkness with little thought for what's beyond – for who already lives there or who gets crushed along the way. The illusion of knowledge and the anticipation of mastery combine to impel the timeline of progress, but they obfuscate the absence of understanding at its articulation point: the zero mark, the dark present, where we see and comprehend nothing beyond movement and efficiency, where our only possible act is to accelerate the existing order.

It is Hermes, then, who stands and points in other directions, and must be the guide for a new dark age. Hermes is thinking in the moment, rather than being bound to received visions or fiery impulses. Hermes, revealer of language and speech, insists upon the ambiguity and uncertainty of all things. A hermeneutics, or hermetic understanding, of technology might account for its perceived errors by pointing out that reality is never that simple, that there is always meaning beyond the meaning, that answers can be multiple, contested, and potentially infinite. When our algorithms fail to converge on ideal situations; when, despite all the information at their disposal, intelligent systems fail to adequately grasp the world; when the fluid and ever-changing nature of personal identities fails to fit inside the neat rows of databases: these are moments of hermeneutic communication. Technology, despite its Epimethean and Promethean claims, reflects the actual world, not an ideal one. When it crashes, we are capable of thinking clearly; when it is cloudy, we apprehend the cloudiness of the world. Technology, while it often appears as opaque complexity, is in fact attempting to communicate the state of reality. Complexity is not a condition to be tamed, but a lesson to be learned.

6

Cognition

Here's a story about how machines learn. If you are, say, the US Army, you want to be able to see things that the enemy has hidden. Perhaps they've got a load of tanks in a forest. The tanks are painted with confusing camouflage patterns, parked among and behind trees; they're covered in brush. Patterns of light and shade, the weird green and brown splotches of paint: all of these conspire with thousands of years of evolution in the visual cortex to turn the blocky outlines of the tanks into rippling, shifting non-shapes, indistinguishable from the foliage. But what if there was another way of seeing? What if you could rapidly evolve a different kind of sight that perceived the forest and the tanks differently, so that what was hard to see suddenly sprung into view?

One way to go about this would be to train a machine to see the tanks. So you get a platoon of soldiers together, you get them to hide a bunch of tanks in the forest, and you take, say, a hundred photos of them. Then, you take another hundred photos of the empty forest. And you show fifty pictures from each set to a neural network, a piece of software that is designed to mimic a human brain. The neural network doesn't know anything about tanks or forests, or light and shade; it just knows that these are fifty pictures with something important in them, and fifty pictures without that something, and it tries to spot the difference. It passes the photos through multiple layers of neurons, tweaking and judging them, but without any of the preconceptions embedded by evolution in the human brain. And, after a while, it learns to see tanks hidden in the forest.

Because you took a hundred photos originally, it's possible to see if this really works. You take the other fifty photos of hidden tanks, and the other fifty photos of empty forest – which the machine has never seen before – and ask it to choose between them. And it does so, perfectly. Even if you can't see the tanks, you know which photos are which, and the machine, without knowing, chooses the right ones. Boom! You've evolved a new way of seeing, and you send your machine off to the training ground to show it off.

And then disaster strikes. Out in the field, with a new set of tanks in the forest, the results are catastrophic. They're random: the machine is about as good as spotting tanks as a coin toss. What happened?

The story goes that when the US Army tried this, they made a crucial error. All of the tank photos were taken in the morning, under clear blue skies. Then the tanks went away, and in the afternoon, when the photos of the empty forest were taken, it clouded over. The investigators realised that the machine worked perfectly, but what it had learned to distinguish was not the presence or absence of tanks, but whether it was sunny or not.

This cautionary tale, which has been told over and over again in the academic literature on machine learning,[1] is probably apocryphal, but it illustrates an important issue when dealing with artificial intelligence and machine learning: What can we know about what a machine knows? The story of the tanks encodes a fundamental realisation, and one of increasing importance: whatever artificial intelligence might come to be, it will be fundamentally different, and ultimately inscrutable, to us. Despite increasingly sophisticated systems of both computation and visualisation, we are no closer today to truly understanding exactly how machine learning does what it does; we can only adjudicate the results.

The original neural network, which probably engendered some early version of the tank story, was developed for the United States Office of Naval Research. It was called the

Perceptron, and like many early computers it was a physical machine: a set of 400 light-detecting cells randomly connected, by a rat's nest of wires, to switches that updated their response with every run – the neurons. Its designer, Cornell psychologist Frank Rosenblatt, was a great publicist for the possibilities of artificial intelligence. When the Perceptron Mark I was presented to the public in 1958, the *New York Times* reported,

> The Navy revealed the embryo of an electronic computer today that it expects will be able to walk, talk, see, write, reproduce itself and be conscious of its existene. Later perceptrons will be

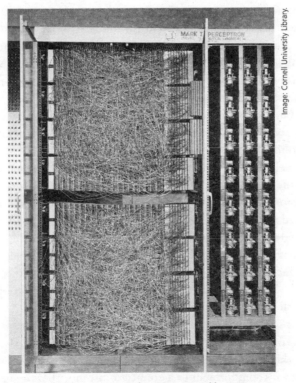

The Mark I Perceptron, an early pattern recognition system, at the Cornell Aeronautical Laboratory.

able to recognise people and call out their names and instantly translate speech in one language to speech and writing in another language, it was predicted.[2]

The idea that underlay the Perceptron was connectionism: the belief that intelligence was an emergent property of the connections between neurons, and that by imitating the winding pathways of the brain, machines might be induced to think. This idea was attacked by numerous researchers over the next decade, who held that intelligence was the product of the manipulation of symbols: essentially, some knowledge of the world was required to reason meaningfully about it. This debate between connectionists and symbolists was to define the artificial intelligence field for the next forty years, leading to numerous fallings out, and the notorious 'AI winters' in which no progress was made at all for many years. At heart, it was not merely a debate about what it means to be intelligent, but what is *intelligible* about intelligence.

One of the more surprising advocates of early connectionism was Friedrich Hayek, best known today as the father of neoliberalism. Forgotten for many years, but making a recent comeback among Austrian-inclined neuroscientists, Hayek wrote *The Sensory Order: An Inquiry into the Foundations of Theoretical Psychology* in 1952, based on ideas he'd formulated in the 1920s. In it, he outlines his belief in a fundamental separation between the sensory world of the mind and the 'natural', external world. The former is unknowable, unique to each individual, and thus the task of science – and economics – is to construct a model of the world that ignores the foibles of individual people.

It's not hard to see a parallel between the neoliberal ordering of the world – where an impartial and dispassionate market directs the action independent of human biases – and Hayek's commitment to a connectionist model of the brain. As later commentators have noted, in Hayek's model of the mind, 'knowledge is dispersed and distributed in the cerebral cortex much as it is in the marketplace among individuals'.[3] Hayek's argument for connectionism is an individualist, neoliberal one, and corresponds directly with his famous assertion in *The Road to Serfdom* (1944) that all forms of collectivism lead inexorably to totalitarianism.

Today, the connectionist model of artificial intelligence reigns supreme again, and its primary proponents are those who, like Hayek, believe that there is a natural order to the world that emerges spontaneously when human bias is absent in our knowledge production. Once again, we see the same claims being made about neural networks as were made by their cheerleaders in the 1950s – but this time, their claims are being put to work in the world more widely.

In the last decade, due to several important advances in the field, neural networks have undergone a massive renaissance, underpinning the current revolution in expectations of artificial intelligence. One of their greatest champions is Google, whose cofounder Sergey Brin has said of the progress in AI that 'you should presume that someday, we will be able to make machines that can reason, think and do things better than we can.'[4] Google's chief executive, Sundar Pichai, is fond of saying that the Google of the future will be 'AI first'.

Google has been investing in artificial intelligence for some time. Its in-house Google Brain project decloaked in 2011 to reveal that it had constructed a neural network from a cluster of a thousand machines containing some 16,000 processors, and fed it 10 million images culled from YouTube videos.[5] The images were unlabelled, but the network evolved the ability to recognise human faces – and cats – with no prior knowledge about what these things might signify.

Image recognition is a typical first task for proving intelligent systems, and a relatively easy one for companies like Google, whose business combines building ever-larger networks of ever-faster processors with harvesting ever-greater volumes of data from the daily lives of its users. (Facebook, which operates a similar program, used 4 million pictures of its users to create a piece of software called DeepFace, which can recognise people with 98 per cent accuracy.[6] Use of the software is illegal in Europe.) What happens next is that this software is used not merely to recognise, but to predict.

In a much-discussed paper published in 2016, two researchers from Shanghai Jiao Tong University, Xiaolin Wu and Xi Zhang, studied the ability of an automated system to make inferences about 'criminality', based on facial images. They trained a neural network on images of 1,126 'non-criminals' culled from official Chinese ID photos found on the web, and another 730 ID photos of convicted criminals supplied by courts and police departments. After training, they claimed that the software could tell the difference between criminal and noncriminal faces.[7]

The result of the paper's publication was uproar: technology blogs, international newspapers, and fellow academics weighed in. The most vocal critics accused Wu and Zhang of following in the footsteps of Cesare Lombroso and Francis Galton, notorious nineteenth-century proponents of criminal physiognomy. Lombroso founded the field of criminology, but his belief that the shape of the jaw, the slope of the forehead, the size of the eyes, and the structure of the ear could be used to determine a subject's 'primitive' criminal characteristics was debunked in the early twentieth century. Galton developed a technique of composite portraiture whereby he hoped to derive a 'typical' criminal face – physical features that corresponded to an individual's moral character. The attacks fed a narrative that facial recognition constituted a new form of digital phrenology, with all of the cultural biases that implied.

Wu and Zhang were appalled at the reaction, publishing an outraged response in May 2017. As well as refuting some of the more unscientific takedowns of their method, they took direct aim – in technological language – at their detractors: 'There is really no need to parade infamous racists in chronic order with us inserted at the terminal node'[8] – as though it was their critics who had manifested this lineage, rather than history itself.

Technology companies and others dabbling in AI are quick to retract their claims whenever they produce ethical conflicts, despite their own responsibility for inflating expectations. When the right-wing *Daily Mail* newspaper in the UK used the How-Old.net facial recognition programme to question the age of child refugees being admitted to Britain, its creator, Microsoft, was quick to stress that the software was just a 'fun app' that was 'not intended to be used as a definitive assessment of age'.[9] Likewise, Wu and Zhang protested, 'Our work is only intended for pure academic discussions; how it has become a media consumption is a total surprise to us.'

One criticism came in for special consideration, highlighting a recurring trope in the history of facial recognition – one with underlying racial undertones. In their examples of average criminal and noncriminal faces, some critics detected 'a hint of a smile' on the noncriminals – a 'micro-expression' absent from the criminal images, indicating their strained circumstances. But Wu and Zhang denied this, not on technological grounds, but on cultural ones: 'Our Chinese students and colleagues, even after being prompted to consider the cue of smile, fail to detect the same. Instead, they only find the faces in the bottom row appearing somewhat more relaxed than those in the top row. Perhaps, the different perceptions here are due to cultural differences.'[10]

What was left untouched in the original paper was the assumption that any such system could ever be free of encoded, embedded bias. At the outset of their study, the authors write,

Unlike a human examiner/judge, a computer vision algorithm or classifier has absolutely no subjective baggages, having no emotions, no biases whatsoever due to past experience, race, religion, political doctrine, gender, age, etc., no mental fatigue, no preconditioning of a bad sleep or meal. The automated inference on criminality eliminates the variable of meta-accuracy (the competence of the human judge/ examiner) all together.[11]

In their response, they double down on this assertion: 'Like most technologies, machine learning is neutral.' They insist that if machine learning 'can be used to reinforce human biases in social computing problems, as some argued, then it can also be used to detect and correct human biases.' Knowingly or not, such a response relies upon our ability to optimise not only our machines, but also ourselves.

Technology does not emerge from a vacuum. Rather, it is the reification of a particular set of beliefs and desires: the congruent, if unconscious dispositions of its creators. In any moment it is assembled from a toolkit of ideas and fantasies developed over generations, through evolution and culture, pedagogy and debate, endlessly entangled and enfolded. The very idea of criminality itself is a legacy of nineteenth-century moral philosophy, while the neural networks used to 'infer it' are, as we've seen, the product of a specific worldview – the apparent separation of the mind and the world, that in turn reinforces the apparent neutrality of its exercise. To continue to assert an objective schism between technology and the world is nonsense; but it has very real outcomes.

Examples of encoded biases are easy to come by. In 2009, a Taiwanese-American strategy consultant named Joz Wang purchased a new Nikon Coolpix S630 camera for Mother's Day, but when she tried to take a family photo, the camera repeatedly refused to capture an image. 'Did someone blink?' read the error message. The camera, preprogrammed with software to wait until all its subjects were looking, eyes open, in the right direction, failed to account for the different physiognomy of non-Caucasians.[12] The same year, a black employee at an RV dealership in Texas posted a widely viewed YouTube video of his new Hewlett-Packard Pavilion webcam failing to recognise his face, while zooming in on his white colleague. 'I'm going on record', he says, 'I'm saying it. Hewlett-Packard computers are racist.'[13]

Once again, the encoded, and particularly racial, biases of visual technologies are not new. *To Photograph the Details of a Dark Horse in Low Light*, the title of a 2013 exhibition by the artists Adam Broomberg and Oliver Chanarin, refers to a code phrase used by Kodak when developing a new film in the 1980s. Since the 1950s, Kodak had distributed test cards featuring a white woman and the phrase 'Normal' in order to calibrate their films. Jean-Luc Godard refused to use Kodak film on assignment in Mozambique in the seventies, claiming it was racist. But only when two of their biggest clients, the confectionary and furniture industries, complained that dark chocolate and dark chairs were difficult to photograph did the company address the need to image dark bodies.[14] Broomberg and Chanarin also explored the legacy of the Polaroid ID-2, a camera designed for ID shots with a special 'boost button' for the flash that made photographing black subjects easier. Much favoured by the apartheid-era government of South Africa, it was the focus of protests by the Polaroid Revolutionary Workers Movement when black American workers discovered it was used to produce the notorious passbook photographs referred to by black South Africans as 'handcuffs'.[15]

But the technology of the Nikon Coolpix and the HP Pavilion masks a more modern, and more insidious, racism: it's not that their designers set out to create a racist machine, or that it was ever employed for racial profiling; rather, it seems likely that these machines reveal the systemic inequalities still present within today's technological workforce, where those developing and testing the systems are still predominately white. (As of 2009, Hewlett-Packard's American workforce was 6.74 per cent black.)[16] It also reveals, as never before, the historic prejudices deeply encoded in our data sets, which are the frameworks on which we build contemporary knowledge and decision making.

This awareness of historic injustice is crucial to understanding the dangers of the mindless implementation of new technologies that uncritically ingest yesterday's mistakes. We will not solve the problems of the present with the tools of the past. As the artist and critical geographer Trevor Paglen has pointed out, the rise of artificial intelligence amplifies these concerns, because of its utter reliance on historical information as training data: 'The past is a very racist place. And we only have data from the past to train Artificial Intelligence.'[17]

Walter Benjamin, writing in 1940, phrased the problem even more fiercely: 'There is no document of civilisation which is not at the same time a document of barbarism.'[18] To train these nascent intelligences on the remnants of prior knowledge is thus to encode such barbarism into our future.

And these systems are not merely contained in academic papers and consumer cameras – they are already determining the macro scale of people's daily lives. In particular, the faith placed in intelligent systems has been implemented widely in police and justice systems. Half of police services in the United States are already employing 'predictive policing' systems such as PredPol, a software package that uses 'high-level mathematics, machine learning, and proven theories of crime behaviour' to predict the most likely times and places that new crimes can be expected to occur: a weather forecast for lawbreaking.[19]

How, once again, do these expectations of physical events get bound up in the stochastic events of everyday life? How do calculations of behaviour take on the force of natural law? How does an idea of the earth, despite all attempts at separation, become one of the mind?

The Great Nōbi Earthquake, which was estimated at 8.0 on the Richter scale, occurred in what is now Aichi Prefecture in 1891. A fault line fifty miles long fell eight metres, collapsing thousands of buildings in multiple cities and killing more than 7,000 people. It is still the largest known earthquake on the Japanese archipelago. In its aftermath, the pioneering seismologist Fusakichi Omori described the pattern of aftershocks: a rate of decay that became known as Omori's law. It is worth noting at this point that Omori's law and all that derived from it are empirical laws: that is, they fit to existing data after the event, which differ in every case. They are aftershocks – the rumbling echo of something that already occurred. Despite decades of effort by seismologists and statisticians, no similar calculus has been developed for predicting earthquakes from corresponding foreshocks.

Omori's law provides the basis for one contemporary implementation of this calculus, called the epidemic type aftershock sequence (ETAS) model, used today by seismologists to study the cascade of seismic activity following a major earthquake. In 2009, mathematicians at University of California, Los Angeles, reported that patterns of crime across a city followed the same model: the result, they wrote, of the 'local, contagious spread of crime [that] leads to the formation of crime clusters in space and time . . . For example, burglars will repeatedly attack clusters of nearby targets because local vulnerabilities are well known to the offenders. A gang shooting may incite waves of retaliatory violence in the local set space (territory) of the rival gang.'[20] To describe these patterns, they used the geophysical term 'self-excitation', the process by which events are triggered and amplified by nearby stresses. The mathematicians even noted the way in which the urban landscape mirrored the layered topology of the earth's crust, with the risk of crime travelling laterally along a city's streets.

It is ETAS that forms the basis of today's predictive policing programmes, estimated as a $25 million industry in 2016, and growing explosively. Whenever Predpol is taken up by a city's police department, as has happened in Los Angeles, Atlanta, Seattle, and hundreds of other US jurisdictions, the last few years of local data – the time, type, and location of each crime – are analysed using ETAS. The resulting model, constantly updated with new crimes as they occur, is used to produce shift-by-shift heat maps of potential trouble spots. Cruisers are dispatched to the site of potential tremors; police officers are assigned to shaky corners. In this manner, crime becomes a physical force: a wave passing through the strata of urban life. Prediction becomes the justification for stops and searches, tickets, and arrests. The aftershocks of a century-old earthquake rumble through contemporary streets.

The predictability (or otherwise) of earthquakes and homicides; the racial biases of opaque systems: these are, given enough time and thought, amenable to our understanding. They are based on time-worn models, and in the lived experience of the everyday. But what of the new models of thought produced by machines – decisions and consequences that we do not understand, because they are produced by cognitive processes utterly unlike our own?

One dimension of our lack of understanding of machine thought is the sheer scale at which it operates. When Google set out to overhaul its Translate software in 2016, the application was much used but also a byword for unintentional humour. It had been launched in 2006, using a technique called statistical language inference. Rather than trying to understand how languages actually worked, the system imbibed vast corpora of existing translations: parallel texts with the same content in different languages. It was the linguistic equivalent of Chris Anderson's 'end of theory'; pioneered by IBM in the 1990s, statistical language inference did away with domain knowledge in favour of huge quantities of raw data. Frederick Jelinek, the researcher who led IBM's language efforts, famously stated that 'every time I fire a linguist, the performance of the speech recogniser goes up'.[21] The role of statistical inference was to remove understanding from the equation and replace it with data-driven correlation.

In one sense, machine translation approaches the ideal described by Benjamin in his 1921 essay *The Task of the Translator*: that the most faithful translation ignores its original context to allow a deeper meaning to shine through. Benjamin insisted on the primacy of the word over the sentence, of the manner of meaning over its matter: 'A real translation is transparent,' he wrote. 'It does not cover the original, does not block its light, but allows the pure language, as though reinforced by its own medium, to shine upon the original all the more fully.'[22] What Benjamin desired of the translator was that, instead of striving to transmit directly what the original writer meant – 'the inaccurate transmission of an inessential content' – they might communicate their *way* of meaning it, that which was unique to their writing and thus to the translation. Such work 'may be achieved, above all, by a literal rendering of the syntax which proves words rather than sentences to be the primary element of the translator'; only a close reading of the choice of words, rather than the accumulation of superficially meaningful sentences, allows us to access the original's higher meaning. But Benjamin adds, 'If the sentence is the wall before the language of the original, literalness is the arcade.' Translation is always insufficient: it serves to emphasise the distance between languages, not to bridge it. The airiness of the arcade is only achieved when we embrace 'the distance, alienness, lack, and mismatch between languages' – translation not as transmission of meaning, but as the awareness of its absence.[23] The machines, it seems, do not get to play in the arcade. (And what would Benjamin make of the fact that Google's original Translate corpus was composed entirely of multilingual transcripts of meetings of the United Nations and the European Parliament?[24] This, too, is an encoding of barbarism.)

In 2016, the situation changed. Instead of employing a strict statistical inference between texts, the Translate system started using a neural network developed by Google Brain, and its abilities suddenly improved exponentially. Rather than simply cross-referencing heaps of texts, the network builds its own model of the world, and the result is not a set of two-dimensional connections between words, but a map of the entire territory. In this new architecture, words are encoded by their distance from one another in a mesh of meaning – a mesh only a computer could comprehend. While a human can draw a line between the words 'tank' and 'water' easily enough, it quickly becomes impossible to draw on a single map the lines between 'tank' and 'revolution', between 'water' and 'liquidity', and all of the emotions and inferences that cascade from those connections. The map is thus multidimensional, extending in more directions than the human mind can hold. As one Google engineer commented, when pursued by a journalist for an image of such a system, 'I do not generally like trying to visualise thousand-dimensional vectors in three-dimensional space.'[25] This is the unseeable space in which machine learning makes its meaning.

Beyond that which we are incapable of visualising is that which we are incapable of even understanding: an unknowability that stresses its sheer alienness to us – although, conversely, it's this alienness that feels most like intelligence. In New York in 1997, the reigning world chess champion Garry Kasparov faced off against Deep Blue, a computer specially designed by IBM to beat him. Following a similar match in Philadelphia the previous year, which Kasparov won 4–2, the man widely regarded as the greatest chess player of all time was confident of victory. When he lost, he claimed some of Deep Blue's moves were so intelligent and creative that they must have been the result of human intervention. But we understand why Deep

Blue made those moves: its process for selecting them was ultimately one of brute force, a massively parallel architecture of 14,000 custom-designed chess chips, capable of analysing 200 million board positions per second. At the time of the match, it was the 259th most powerful computer on the planet, and it was dedicated purely to chess. It could simply hold more outcomes in mind when choosing where to play next. Kasparov was not outthought, merely outgunned.

By contrast, when the Google Brain–powered AlphaGo software defeated the Korean Go professional Lee Sedol, one of the highest-rated players in the world, something had changed. In the second of five games, AlphaGo played a move that stunned Sedol and spectators alike, placing one of its stones on the far side of the board, and seeming to abandon the battle in progress. 'That's a very strange move,' said one commentator. 'I thought it was a mistake,' said the other. Fan Hui, another seasoned Go player who had been the first professional to lose to the machine six months earlier, said of it: 'It's not a human move. I've never seen a human play this move.' And he added, 'So beautiful.'[26] In the history of the 2,500-year-old game, nobody had ever played like this. AlphaGo went on to win the game, and the series.

AlphaGo's engineers developed its software by feeding a neural network millions of moves by expert Go players, and then getting it to play itself millions of times more, developing strategies that outstripped those of human players. But its own representation of those strategies is illegible: we can see the moves it made, but not how it decided to make them. The sophistication of the moves that must have been played in those games between the shards of AlphaGo is beyond imagination, too, but we are unlikely to ever see and appreciate them; there's no way to quantify sophistication, only winning instinct.

The late and much-lamented Iain M. Banks called the place where these moves occurred 'Infinite Fun Space'.[27] In Banks's

sci-fi novels, his Culture civilisation is administered by benev-
olent, superintelligent AIs called simply Minds. While the
Minds were originally created by humans (or, at least, some
biological, carbon-based entities), they have long since
outstripped their creators, redesigned and rebuilt themselves,
and become both inscrutable and all-powerful. Between
controlling ships and planets, directing wars, and caring for
billions of humans, the Minds also take up their own pleasures, which involve speculative computations beyond the
comprehension of humankind. Capable of simulating entire
universes within their imaginations, some Minds retreat
forever into Infinite Fun Space, a realm of meta-mathematical
possibility, accessible only to superhuman artificial intelligences. And the rest of us, if we spurn the arcade, are left with
Finite Fun, fruitlessly analysing the decisions of machines
beyond our comprehension.

Some operations of machine intelligence do not stay within
Infinite Fun Space however. Instead, they create an unknow-
ingness in the world: new images; new faces; new, unknown,
or false events. The same approach by which language can be
cast as an infinite mesh of alien meaning can be applied to
anything that can be described mathematically – that is, as a
web of weighted connections in multidimensional space.
Words drawn from human bodies still have relationships, even
when shorn of human meaning, and calculations can be
performed upon the number of that meaning. In a semantic
network, the lines of force – vectors – that define the word
'queen' align with those read in the order 'king - man +
woman'.[28] The network can infer a gendered relationship
between 'king' and 'queen' by following the path of such
vectors. And it can do the same thing with faces.

Given a set of images of people, a neural network can
perform calculations that do not merely follow these lines of
force, but generate new outcomes. A set of photographs of
smiling women, unsmiling women and unsmiling men can be

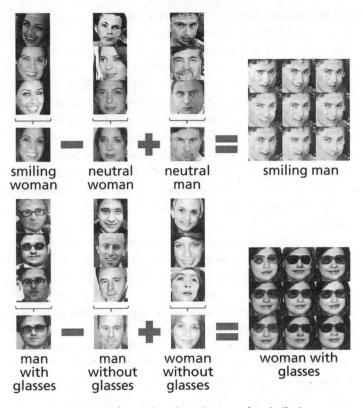

smiling woman — neutral woman + neutral man = smiling man

man with glasses — man without glasses + woman without glasses = woman with glasses

Creating new faces with mathematics. Image from Radford, Metz and Chintala, 'Unsupervised Representation Learning with Deep Convolutional Generative Adversarial Networks'.

computed to produce entirely new images of smiling men, as shown in a paper published by Facebook researchers in 2015.[29]

In the same paper, the researchers generate a range of new images. Using a dataset of more than 3 million photographs of bedrooms from a large-scale image recognition challenge, their network generates new bedrooms: arrangements of colour and furniture that have never existed in the real world, but come into being at the intersection of vectors of bedroomness: walls, windows, duvets and pillows. Machines dreaming dream rooms where no dreams are dreamed. But it is the faces – anthropomorphs that we are – that stick in the mind: Who are these people, and what are they smiling at?

Things get stranger still when these dream images start to interleave with our own memories. Robert Elliott Smith, an artificial intelligence researcher at University College London, returned from a family holiday in France in 2014 with a phone full of photos. He uploaded a number of them to Google+, to share them with his wife, but while browsing through them he noticed an anomaly.[30] In one image, he saw himself and his wife at a table in a restaurant, both smiling at the camera. But this photograph had never been taken. At lunch one day, his father had held the button down on his iPhone a little long, resulting in a burst of images of the same scene. Smith uploaded two of them, to see which his wife preferred. In one, he was smiling, but his wife was not; in the other, his wife was smiling, but he was not. From these two images, taken seconds apart, Google's photo-sorting algorithms had conjured a third: a composite in which both subjects were smiling their 'best'. The algorithm was part of a package called AutoAwesome (since renamed, simply, 'Assistant'), which performed a range of tweaks on uploaded images to make them more 'awesome' – applying nostalgic filters, turning them into charming animations, and so forth. But in this case, the result was a photograph of a moment that had never happened: a false memory, a rewriting of history.

The doctoring of photographs is an activity as old as the medium itself, but in this case the operation was being performed automatically and invisibly on the artefacts of personal memory. And yet, perhaps there is something to learn from this too: the delayed revelation that images are always false, artificial snapshots of moments that have never existed as singularities, forced from the multidimensional flow of time itself. Unreliable documents; composites of camera and attention. They are artefacts not of the world and of experience, but of the recording process – which, as a false mechanism, can never approach reality itself. It is only when these processes of capture and storage are reified in technology that we are able to perceive their falsity, their alienation from reality. This is the lesson that we might draw from the dreams of machines: not that they are rewriting history, but that history is not something that can be reliably narrativised; and thus, neither can the future. The photographs mapped from the vectors of artificial intelligence constitute not a record but an ongoing reimagining, an ever-shifting set of possibilities of what might have been and what is to come. This cloud of possibility,

Source: Google.

An image from DeepDream.

forever contingent and nebulous, is a better model of reality than any material assertion. This cloud is what is revealed by the technology.

This illumination of our own unconscious by the machines is perhaps best illustrated by another weird output from Google's machine learning research: a programme called DeepDream. DeepDream was designed to better illuminate the internal workings of inscrutable neural networks. In order to learn to recognise objects, a network was fed millions of labelled images of things: trees, cars, animals, houses. When exposed to a new image, the system filtered, stretched, tore and compressed the image through the network in order to classify it: this is a tree, a car, an animal, a house. But DeepDream reversed the process: by feeding an image into the back end of the network, and activating the neurons trained to see particular objects, it asked not what is this image, but what does the network want to see in it? The process is akin to that of seeing faces in clouds: the visual cortex, desperate for stimulation, assembles meaningful patterns from noise.

DeepDream's engineer, Alexander Mordvintsev, created the first iteration of the programme at two in the morning, having been woken by a nightmare.[31] The first image he fed into the system was of a kitten sat on a tree stump, and the output was a nightmare monster all its own: a hybrid cat/dog with multiple sets of eyes, and wet noses for feet. When Google first released an untrained classifier network on 10 million random YouTube videos in 2012, the first thing it learned to see, without prompting, was a cat's face: the spirit animal of the internet.[32] Mordvintsev's network thus dreamed of what it knew, which was more cats and dogs. Further iterations produced Boschian hellscapes of infinite architecture, including arches, pagodas, bridges, and towers in infinite, fractal progressions, according to the neurons activated. But the one constant that recurs throughout DeepDream's creations is the image of the eye – dogs' eyes, cats' eyes, human eyes; the omnipresent, surveillant eye of the network itself. The eye that floats in DeepDream's skies recalls the all-seeing eye of dystopian propaganda: Google's own unconscious, composed of our memories and actions, processed by constant analysis and tracked for corporate profit and private intelligence. DeepDream is an inherently paranoid machine because it emerges from a paranoid world.

'Secure Beneath The Watchful Eyes', Transport for London, 2002.

Meanwhile, when not being forced to visualise their dreams for our illumination, the machines progress further into their own imaginary space, to places we cannot enter. Walter Benjamin's greatest wish, in *The Task of the Translator*, was that the process of transmission between languages would invoke a 'pure language' – an amalgam of all the languages in the world. It is this aggregate language that is the medium in which the translator should work, because what it reveals is not the meaning but the original's manner of *thinking*. Following the activation of Google Translate's neural network in 2016, researchers realised that the system was capable of translating not merely between languages, but across them; that is, it could translate directly between two languages it had never seen explicitly compared. For example, a network trained on Japanese–English and English–Korean examples is capable of generating Japanese–Korean translations without ever passing through English.[33] This is called 'zero-shot' translation, and what it implies is the existence of an 'interlingual' representation: an internal metalanguage composed of shared concepts across languages. This is, to all intents, Benjamin's pure language; it is the meaningless metalanguage of the arcade. By visualising the architecture of the network and its vectors as splashes of colour and line, it's possible to see sentences in multiple languages clustered together. The outcome is a semantic representation evolved by, not designed into, the network. But this is as close as we shall ever get, for once again, we are peering through the window of Infinite Fun Land – an arcade we will never get to visit.

Compounding this error, in 2016 a pair of researchers at Google Brain decided to see if neural networks could keep secrets.[34] The idea stemmed from that of the adversary: an increasingly common component of neural network designs, and one that would no doubt have pleased Friedrich Hayek. Both AlphaGo and Facebook's bedroom generator were trained adversarially; that is, they consisted not of a single component that generated new moves or places, but of two competing components that continually attempted to outperform and outguess the other, driving further improvement. Taking the idea of an adversary to its logical conclusion, the researchers set up three networks called, in the tradition of cryptographic experiments, Alice, Bob, and Eve. Their task was to learn how to encrypt information. Alice and Bob both knew a number – a key, in cryptographic terms – that was unknown to Eve. Alice would perform some operation on a string of text, and then send it to Bob and Eve. If Bob could decode the message, Alice's score increased; but if Eve could, Alice's score decreased. Over thousands of iterations, Alice and Bob learned to communicate without Eve breaking their code: they developed a private form of encryption like that used in private emails today. But crucially, in the manner of the other neural networks we've seen, we don't understand how this encryption works. Its operation is occluded by the deep layers of the network. What is hidden from Eve is also hidden from us. The machines are learning to keep their secrets.

Isaac Asimov's Three Laws of Robotics, formulated in the 1940s, state,

1. A robot may not injure a human being or, through inaction, allow a human being to come to harm.
2. A robot must obey the orders given it by human beings except where such orders would conflict with the First Law.
3. A robot must protect its own existence as long as such protection does not conflict with the First or Second Laws.[35]

To these we might add a fourth: a robot – or any other intelligent machine – must be able to explain itself to humans. Such a law must intervene before the others, because it takes the form not of an injunction to the other, but of an ethic. The fact that this law has – by our own design and inevitably – already been broken, leads inescapably to the conclusion that so will the others. We face a world, not in the future but right now, where we do not understand our own creations. The result of such opacity is always and inevitably violence.

In relating the stories of Kasparov versus Deep Blue and Sedol versus AlphaGo, another parallel story was left untold. Kasparov did indeed leave the game frustrated and in disbelief of the machine's ability. But his frustration was channelled into finding some way to rescue chess from the dominance of machines. There have been many such attempts; few have proved successful. David Levy, a Scottish chess champion who played many exhibition games against machines in the 1970s and '80s, developed an 'anti-computer' style of restricted play that he described as 'doing nothing but doing it well'. His play was so conservative that his computer opponents were unable to discern a long-term plan until Levy's position was so strong that he was unbeatable. Likewise, Boris Alterman, an Israeli grandmaster, developed a strategy in matches against machines in the '90s and early '00s that became known as the 'Alterman Wall': he would bide his time behind a row of pawns, knowing that the more pieces he had on the board, the more possible moves the machine would have to calculate.[36]

Along with changes in style, it's also possible to change the game. Arimaa is a chess variant developed in 2002 by Omar Syed – himself a computer engineer trained in artificial intelligence – specifically designed to be difficult for machines to grasp, while being easy and fun for humans to learn. Its name comes from Syed's then-four-year-old son, who provided a benchmark for the comprehensibility of the rules. In Arimaa, players can arrange their pieces in any configuration, and must move one of their weakest pieces – pawns renamed as rabbits – to the far side of the board to win. They can also use their stronger pieces to push and pull weaker pieces towards a series of trap squares, removing them from the board and clearing the way for the rabbits. The combination of many different initial setups, the ability of pieces to move other pieces, and the possibility of making up to four moves per turn results in combinatorial explosion: a vast increase in possibilities that rapidly becomes too great for a computer programme to handle – the Alterman Wall taken to exponential extremes. Or so it was hoped. The first computer Arimaa tournament was held in 2004, with the most successful programme winning the right to challenge a group of top human players for a cash prize. In the first few years, the humans easily beat their computer opponents, even increasing the margin of victory as their skills in the new game improved faster than the programmes challenging them. But in 2015, the contest was won decisively by a machine, a result unlikely to be reversed.

It is tempting when confronted by the power and opacity of intelligent systems to delay, derail, or concede the ground. Where Levy and Alterman built walls, Arimaa went back to the land, attempting to carve out an alternative space outside the sphere of machine dominance. This was not Kasparov's approach. Instead of rejecting the machines, he returned the year after his defeat to Deep Blue with a different kind of chess, which he called 'Advanced Chess'.

Other names for Advanced Chess include 'cyborg' and 'centaur' chess. One image evokes the human melded with the machine, the other with the animal – if not something entirely alien. The legend of the centaur in Greek mythology arose perhaps with the arrival of mounted warriors from the steppes of Central Asia, when horse riding was unknown in the Mediterranean. (The Aztecs are reported to have made the same assumption about Spanish cavalrymen.) Robert Graves argued that the centaur was an even more ancient figure: a relic of pre-Hellenic earth cults. The centaurs were also the grandchildren of Nephele, the nymph of the cloud. Thus centaur strategies carry the possibility of being both contemporary necessities in the face of adversity, as well as prelapsarian revivals from less adversarial times.

In Advanced Chess, a human player and a computer chess programme play as a team against another human-computer pair. The results have been revolutionary, opening up new fields and strategies of play previously unseen in the game. One of the effects is that blunders are eliminated: the human can analyse their own proposed movements to such an extent that they can play error-free, resulting in perfect tactical play, and more rigorously deployed strategic plans.

But perhaps the most extraordinary result derived from Advanced Chess, which is normally played by matched human-machine pairs, occurs when human and machine play against a solo machine. Since Deep Blue, many computer programmes have been developed that can beat any human with ease and efficiency: increases in data storage and processing power mean that supercomputers are no longer required for the task. But even the most powerful contemporary programme can be defeated by a skilled player with access to their own computer – even one less powerful than their opponent. Cooperation between human and machine turns out to be a more potent strategy than the most powerful computer alone.

This is the Optometrist Algorithm applied to games, an approach which draws on the respective skills of humans and machines as required, rather than pitting one against the other. Cooperation also reduces the sting of computational opacity: through cooperative play rather than post hoc analysis, we might gain a deeper insight into the way in which complex machines make their decisions. Acknowledging the reality of nonhuman intelligence has deep implications for how we act in the world and requires clear thinking about our own behaviours, opportunities, and limitations. While machine intelligence is rapidly outstripping human performance in many disciplines, it is not the only way of thinking, and it is in many fields catastrophically destructive. Any strategy other than mindful, thoughtful cooperation is a form of disengagement: a retreat that cannot hold. We cannot reject contemporary technology any more than we can ultimately and utterly reject our neighbours in society and the world; we are all entangled. An ethics of cooperation in the present need not be limited to machines either: with other nonhuman entities, animate and non-animate, it becomes another form of stewardship, emphasising acts of universal justice not in an unknowable, uncomputable future, but in the here and now.

7

Complicity

In the run-up to the London Olympics in 2012, the British state went into characteristic paroxyms of security. Warnings were made about terrorists targeting the games and potential protesters were preemptively detained. MI5 set up a countdown clock to the opening ceremony in their Vauxhall foyer.[1] The Royal Navy moored their largest ship, HMS *Ocean*, in the Thames, with a complement of marines aboard. The army mounted Rapier surface-to-air missiles on tower blocks around the venues (an operation later revealed to be an elaborate, and successful, sales pitch to foreign governments). And the Metropolitan Police announced that they would use drones to watch over the city.[2]

The last item got me interested. For many years I've followed the evolution of unmanned aerial vehicles – drones – from secret military projects into everyday tools of war, and onto the home front in the form of both high-level surveillance platforms and cheap Christmas toys. But British police forces have not exactly had the best of luck with them. Essex Police, the first force to acquire drones, mothballed its programme in 2010. The same year, Merseyside Police were caught flying a drone without a licence from the Civil Aviation Authority (CAA); in 2011, newly licenced, they crashed and lost it in the River Mersey – and decided against replacing it.[3]

When the games were over, I filed a Freedom of Information request with the Metropolitan Police, asking if they had in fact used drones during the games, and if so, where and under what conditions.[4] Their response, some weeks later, surprised me: they refused to confirm or deny that they held any information related to my request. I reformulated the question a number of times: I asked if they had applied for a CAA licence to fly drones, which they refused to answer (although the CAA were happy to tell me that they had not). I asked if they had contracted a third party to fly drones for them, and they refused to answer. I asked what aircraft, of any kind, they owned or leased, and was told they had three helicopters, and would not confirm or deny anything else.

The helicopter response seemed odd: If they would talk about helicopters, why wouldn't they talk about drones? What makes them so special? Despite repeated efforts to answer the question, including taking my case to the Information Commissioner, the UK's arbiter on Freedom of Information questions, I never received an answer. Any question about drones was immediately placed under the rubric of possible covert operations, rendering it exempt from public disclosure. It began to feel like drones were a useful shroud under which anything could be hidden. It seems that the spectre of the drone is so powerful, so shadowy, that it can carry not only cameras and weapons systems, but an entire regime of secrecy, a secrecy born of covert military operations that has grown to infect every aspect of civil life. This weaponised secrecy was borne out in the very language with which the police rebuffed my questions. Every time and every way I asked, the response was always the same: 'We can neither confirm nor deny whether such information is held.' These words – their very form – originated in the covert history of the Cold War. These words are a kind of magic spell, or political technology, transforming civil life into a conflict between government and the governed as assuredly as any military technology – and creating a new kind of truth in the process.

In March of 1968, the Soviet ballistic missile submarine K-129 was lost in the Pacific with all hands. The West was first alerted to the sinking when the Soviet Navy scrambled a flotilla of ships to *K-129*'s last known location. They churned up a huge area of sea some 600 miles north of the Midway Atoll, but after weeks of fruitless trawling, naval command called off the search.

The United States, however, had access to a tool the Soviets didn't possess: a network of underwater listening stations designed to detect nuclear explosions. Trawling not the ocean but the reams of hydrophone data turned up a recording of an implosion event on March 8 – and its echoes had spread far enough to be triangulated from several points, giving an approximate location. A specially configured US submarine was dispatched, and after three weeks of searching it came across the wreck of *K-129* lying in more than three miles of water.

The US intelligence community was delighted: in addition to three ballistic missiles, *K-129* would have been carrying codebooks and cryptographic equipment. Its recovery, from under the noses of the Soviet Navy, would be one of the intelligence coups of the Cold War. The problem was that three miles was much deeper than any salvage operation ever undertaken, and any attempt to raise the submarine would have to be performed under conditions of utmost secrecy.

Over the next few years, the Central Intelligence Agency contracted with several suppliers of classified technologies to build a unique ship, called the *Hughes Glomar Explorer* after the billionaire businessman Howard Hughes, who agreed to provide a covering name. The *Glomar Explorer* was massive, hugely expensive, and topped by a drilling rig twenty metres tall. Lockheed Ocean Systems built a separate, state-of-the-art submersible barge, just to sneak a massive grappling claw into the ship without detection. In public, Hughes claimed that the ship was to be used to mine manganese nodules – accretions of precious metals that litter the ocean floors. Manganese nodules are real, and worth a lot of money, but nobody has ever managed to gather them economically. This didn't stop a huge industry developing around the possibility in the '60s and '70s, largely thanks to the Hughes name and the CIA's cover story. The ship's real purpose was to go out and fetch *K-129*.

Setting sail in 1974, the *Glomar Explorer* positioned itself above the wreck, opened the hidden doors in its keel, and let down the claw. Having successfully grasped the intact hull of the submarine, it started to lift – but at some point during the operation, the huge steel claw suffered a catastrophic failure, and most of the submarine sheared away. It's still unknown how much of *K-129* was actually recovered, as details have remained classified ever since. Some reports claim that two missiles were recovered; others refer to documents and devices. The only confirmed items were the bodies of six Soviet submariners who were subsequently buried at sea in a steel container, due to radiation fears.

Several months after the operation, the investigative reporter Seymour Hersh at the *New York Times* got hold of the story. The US government managed to delay publication by claiming that the operation was still ongoing, and that publicity would cause an international incident. A burglary at Hughes's offices in LA put another reporter onto the story, however, and in February 1975 the *Los Angeles Times* ran a partial account of the mission, riddled with errors, which led to a media frenzy. The *New York Times* subsequently went to press with their version of events, and the story became widely known.[5]

One of the most intriguing aspects of the *Glomar* operation was the way in which it was performed in plain sight, without anyone knowing what was occurring. From the Hughes cover story, to the submersible barge – which was manoeuvred into position just off the coast of California's Catalina Island, in full view of beachgoers – to the Soviet ships that sailed within 200 yards of the *Explorer* while it raised the submarine, the entire process was conducted simultaneously in secret and in the open. The *Glomar*'s legacy was to be the continuance of this strategy of opacity and misdirection into the realm of everyday life.

In 1981, another journalist, Harriet Ann Phillippi, used Freedom of Information legislation to press the CIA for more detail on the project and its attempted cover-up. The agency formulated a novel response to her request – and invented a new kind of public discourse in the process. Concerned that anything they revealed, knowingly or unknowingly, might be of use to the Soviet adversary, an associate general counsel at the CIA using the pseudonym Walt Logan wrote the following statement: 'We can neither confirm nor deny the existence of the information requested but, hypothetically, if such data were to exist, the subject matter would be classified, and could not be disclosed.'[6]

This formulation, which has come to be known in US law as the 'Glomar response', creates a third category of statement between affirmation and renunciation, between truth and falsehood. Often shortened to 'neither confirm nor deny', or simply NCND, the Glomar response has subsequently escaped from its CIA handlers, leapt the boundaries of National Security, and metastasised through official and public discourse.

A quick search of the internet today reveals that the words 'neither confirm nor deny' have infested every aspect of contemporary communication.[7] On a single day in September 2017, the phrase appeared in news reports attributed to Brazil's finance minister (regarding his presidential ambitions), the sheriff's office of Stanly County, North Carolina (nuisance 911 calls), the University of Johannesburg (corruption allegations), an Argentine goalkeeper (transfer to Zimbabwe), the special adviser to the president of Biafra on media and publicity (terrorist designations), Honda Motorcycles (new models), the New York Police Department (campus surveillance), the Georgia Judicial Qualifications Commission (urinating in court), a Marvel Comics editor (the return of the Fantastic

Four), reality star Kylie Jenner's publicist (possible pregnancy), and the FBI, the Secret Service and the Securities and Exchange Commission (regarding a financial hacking case). To neither confirm nor deny has become an automatic response: a statement of refusal to engage in discussion or disclosure of any kind, and the default position of those from whom – Jenner perhaps aside – we expect trust.

Perhaps we are naive to do so. The concealment of the true nature of the world in order to benefit those in power has a long history. In ancient Egypt, the flooding of the Nile each year was crucial to both agriculture and the state's revenues. A 'good' inundation irrigated the fertile plains along the river and deposited rich nutrients, but there was always the risk that a too-powerful flood would wash away fields and villages, or that too little water would result in drought and famine. Atop this annual cycle, the Egyptian nobility and priesthood built a civilisation of extraordinary wealth and stability, predicated on their ability to predict the arrival and strength of each year's flood and its likely effects – and the resulting tax levels. Each year, in celebration of the death and rebirth of Osiris, the priests would lead elaborate ceremonies and rituals marking Akhet, the Season of the Inundation, culminating in the announcement of the flood. In turn, the authority of their predictions translated into the authority of theocratic rule. But this authority was not – or at least not only – the gift of the gods. Hidden within the sacred boundaries of temple complexes on islands and riverbanks were structures called nilometers: deep wells dug into the earth and marked with columns or sets of steps, which measured the depth of the water in the river. The nilometers were scientific instruments: read correctly, and compared against centuries of data marked on the walls, the priests and rulers could forecast the behaviour of the river, and make the appropriate pronouncements and preparations. The function, and even existence, of the nilometers was hidden from the lay population. If questioned, the Egyptian priests would no doubt have responded, 'We can neither confirm nor deny . . .'

To bring such a scenario back up to date, consider the secret numbers. Since the 1940s, the National Security Agency (NSA) in the United States, and Government Communications Headquarters (GCHQ) in the United Kingdom – and no doubt their counterparts in Russia and China – have been hiring mathematicians at the height of their intellectual powers straight out of the top university maths departments. Once inside these organisations, all of their research is classified and is hidden from the general public. Occasionally, examples of their ingenuity leak out. Diffie–Hellman key exchange, named after the two mathematicians who created it, was first published in 1976 and formed the basis for public key cryptography, widely used today to encrypt Email and web pages.[8] But in 1997, the British government declassified documents showing that the process had been invented independently several years earlier by James Ellis, Clifford Cocks and Malcolm Williamson, three mathematicians working at GCHQ.[9]

Public key cryptography relies on creating mathematical problems for which no efficient solution is known: cracking the code without possessing its key requires a mathematical operation so complex as to be impossible. A common encryption approach is the factorisation of two primes. The encoding is done with a number created by multiplying two very large prime numbers; the keys are those two original numbers. Depending on the size of those numbers, even a supercomputer might take years to discover them. But there are a couple of problems with this assumption. The first is general: while factorisation is powerful if everyone uses different prime numbers, it turns out that most implementations use the same small set of primes over and over again, significantly reducing the complexity of the problem. It's widely believed by security researchers that NSA, with its massive computers and $11 billion annual budget, has in fact broken a number of commonly used primes, and is thus able to read a significant amount of encrypted communications.[10] The advent of quantum computing, in which NSA is investing heavily, will no doubt accelerate this effort.[11] But more specifically: think on those thousands of mathematicians, working in secret for more than seventy years in the closed halls of Cheltenham and Fort Meade. They invented public key encryption and didn't tell anyone about it. In the decades since, who is to say that they have not formulated entirely new fields of mathematics – the secret numbers – that allow for entirely new kinds of calculations? Such revolutions in mathematics have happened before; and if Euclid, Euler or Gauss were working today, there's a good chance they'd be working for one of the security agencies, and their discoveries would have disappeared into the secret library.

The new dark age is full of such cloudy possibilities. If it sounds far-fetched, simply recall that the CIA spent billions of dollars pulling off the deepest salvage operation in history while keeping it a secret from the public and its enemies, and that it continued to work on technological innovations for decades. It was the CIA, not the US Army or Air Force, that developed and built the first unmanned aerial vehicles – the Predator and Reaper drones that have revolutionised contemporary warfare, and done so by expanding the paranoia and secrecy of the intelligence agency first onto the battlefield, and then across the planet. And for all the CIA's advances in engineering, it is in information technology that it has invested most heavily, swapping defence contractors like Raytheon and Lockheed Martin for Silicon Valley tech companies like Palantir, which help it infiltrate modern communications and social networks. Or you could remember that in 2012, the even more secretive National Reconnaissance Office, which is charged with satellite surveillance, announced that it was donating two unused space telescopes to the public. NASA officials discovered that, while built in the late 1990s, both exceeded the capabilities of the most powerful civilian version of the technology, the Hubble Space Telescope. Moreover, their short focal length implied that they had been built for looking down, not up. As one science journalist wrote, 'If telescopes of this caliber are languishing on shelves, imagine what they're actually using.'[12] It is these three-letter agencies, and their equivalents in other countries, that are emblematic of the new dark age. As their power and size has grown over the decades, so huge parts of global history and scientific discovery have simply slipped away into the classified world.

The promulgation of official secrecy is deeply corrosive to the way we know and understand the world because we cannot know our own history, nor understand what we are truly capable of. In 1994, the US government formed a bipartisan committee, the Commission on Government Secrecy, with Senator Daniel Patrick Moynihan as chairman. Moynihan and his colleagues' task was to examine all aspects of secrecy in the United States, from the classification of documents to security clearances – essentially, what was permitted to be known, and who was permitted to know it. The three-year investigation found that the United States was marking 400,000 new documents every year as top secret, the highest level of classification, and was holding more than 1.5 billion pages of classified material over twenty-five years old.

Moynihan's final report included the statement that '[the] secrecy system has systematically denied American historians access to the records of American history. Of late we find ourselves relying on archives of the former Soviet Union in Moscow to resolve questions of what was going on in Washington at mid-century.'[13] Twenty years later, Donald Trump found that even as president he was not able to persuade his own intelligence agencies to release their complete records on the assassination of John F. Kennedy, an event whose murky and often classified history has poisoned the relationship between the American government and its people for decades.[14]

In the United Kingdom, the situation is far, far worse. In 2011, after a legal fight that lasted more than ten years, a group of Kenyans tortured by colonial authorities won the right to sue the British government. The four complainants, selected from among 6,000 depositions, had all been imprisoned in concentration camps in the 1950s and subjected to appalling abuses. Ndiku Mutua and Paulo Muoka Nzili had been castrated; Jane Muthoni Mara had been raped with bottles filled with boiling water; and Wambugu Wa Nyingi survived the March 1959 Hola Massacre, in which camp guards beat eleven detainees to death, leaving seventy-seven others with debilitating injuries. For years, the British government denied the events, and also denied the existence of any records that would corroborate them, along with the rights of former colonial subjects to challenge their oppressors following independence. Once the last of these objections was overturned by the High Court in London, the government was forced to admit that it did indeed possess such documents – thousands of them.[15]

Known as the 'migrated archive', a huge cache of colonial-era documents was stored at secret sites around the UK for decades, its existence unknown to historians and denied by civil servants. At Hanslope Park in the Midlands, a secretive government research facility, around 1.2 million documents revealed details of the Kenyan 'pipeline' system, which historians compared to the Nazi concentration camps. Thousands of men, women, and even children suffered beatings and rape during screening and interrogations. Common torture tactics included starvation, electrocution, mutilation, and forcible penetration, and extended to whipping and burning detainees to death. The files also contained details of colonial activities in at least thirty-seven other nations, including massacres of villagers during the Malayan emergency, the systematic subversion of democracy in British Guiana, the operation of Army Intelligence torture centres in Aden, and the planned testing of poison gas in Botswana.

The migrated archive also contained evidence that it was only a small part of a much larger, and largely destroyed, hidden history. Accompanying the remaining files – most of which have still not been released – are thousands of 'destruction certificates': records of absences that attest to a comprehensive programme of obfuscation and erasure. In the dying years of the British Empire, colonial administrators were instructed to gather up and secure all the records they could, and either burn them or ship them to London. This was known as Operation Legacy, and was intended to ensure the whitewashing of colonial history. Government offices, assisted by MI5 and Her Majesty's Armed Forces, either built pyres or, when the smoke became too obvious, packed them into weighted crates and sunk them offshore, in order to protect their secrets from the governments of newly independent nations – or from future historians.

Even when incriminating evidence survives for decades, it isn't safe. Until 1993, a collection of 170 boxes of documents flown to Britain as part of Operation Legacy were stored in London, where they were marked 'Top Secret Independence Records 1953 to 1963'. According to remaining records, they took up seventy-nine feet of shelf space in room 52A of Admiralty Arch, and included files on Kenya, Singapore, Malaya, Palestine, Uganda, Malta, and fifteen other colonies. A surviving partial inventory notes that the Kenyan files included documents about the abuse of prisoners and about psychological warfare. One batch, entitled 'Situation in Kenya – Employment of Witch Doctors by CO [Colonial Office]', carried the warning, 'This file to be processed and received only by a male clerical officer.'[16] In 1992, perhaps afraid that a Labour victory in the upcoming general election would lead to a new period of openness and disclosure, the

Foreign Office ordered thousands of documents shipped to Hanslope Park. In the process, the top secret independence records simply disappeared. No destruction certificates were issued, and no record has been found in other archives. By law, the documents should have been transferred to the National Archives, or their further classification justified, but instead they were simply expunged from the record. Historians have been forced to the conclusion that, fifty years after the events they documented took place, the only remaining records were destroyed in the heart of the British capital.

The brutality in Kenya was 'distressingly reminiscent of conditions in Nazi Germany or communist Russia', wrote the colony's own attorney general to its British governor in 1957.[17] Nevertheless, he agreed to write new legislation permitting it, as long as it was kept secret. 'If we must sin, we must sin quietly', he affirmed. Operation Legacy was a deliberate and knowing effort to obscure the violence and coercion that enabled imperialism, and its manipulation of history prevents us from reckoning with the British Empire's legacy of racism, covert power, and inequality today. Moreover, the habit of secrecy it engendered permits its abuses to continue into the present day. The torture techniques developed in colonial Kenya were refined into the 'five techniques' deployed by the British Army in Northern Ireland, and then into the CIA's 'enhanced interrogation' guidelines. In 1990, the police archive at Carrickfergus, which contained vital evidence regarding the actions of the British state in Northern Ireland, was destroyed by arson. Evidence increasingly links the fire to the British Army itself. When investigators tried to establish whether CIA rendition flights had stopped over on the British territory of Diego Garcia, they were told that the flight records were 'incomplete due to water damage'.[18] It's hard to think of a more apt, or horrible, excuse: having failed to cover up its waterboarding of detainees, the intelligence agencies resorted to waterboarding information itself.

Looking back over this litany of deception suggests that we have been living in a dark age for quite some time, and there are signs that contemporary networks are making it harder to hide the sins of the past – or the present. But for this to be true, we would have to be getting better not only at spotting the signs of obfuscation, but also at acting to curb it. As the torrent of revelations about global surveillance practices released over the last five years have shown, awareness of this corrosion rarely translates into remedy.

When the first headlines about the activities of NSA and GCHQ started to appear in newspapers around the world in June of 2013, there was an initial uproar. Both agencies, it was shown, had been spying on millions of people globally, including their fellow citizens, in collusion with other governments and the corporations that largely administer the internet. First it was revealed that 120 million Verizon customers in the United States were being closely monitored, with both participants in every call having their phone numbers logged, together with their locations, and the time and duration of the call. This data was collected by the phone company before being turned over to the FBI, who in turn passed it to NSA. The next day came the exposure of the PRISM operation, which gathered up all of the data passing through the servers of the largest internet companies – including emails, documents, voice and video chats, and pictures and videos from Microsoft, Yahoo, Google, Facebook, YouTube, Skype, Apple and others. A short time later, it was revealed that the intelligence agencies' reach went even deeper into the system, including the collection of raw data from the actual cables that carry information around the world. When asked what it was like to use NSA's back end system, XKeyscore, Edward Snowden replied, 'You could read anyone's email in the world, anybody you've got an email address for. Any website: You can watch traffic to and from it. Any computer that an individual sits at: You can watch it. Any laptop that you're tracking: you can follow it as it moves from place to place throughout the world.'[19]

It became clear that the international nature of the internet meant that there was no possible restriction on its surveillance, no objection to governments spying upon their own citizens; everyone was a foreigner to someone, and once the data was collected it went into the pot. The vampire squid kept expanding: first it was NSA and GCHQ; next it was the 'Five Eyes' of the United States, United Kingdom, Australia, New Zealand and Canada, which the 'Nine Eyes' expanded to Denmark, France, the Netherlands and Norway; then it was the SIGINT Seniors Europe, or 'Fourteen Eyes' group, with Germany, Belgium, Italy, Spain and Sweden all joining in – even when it was obvious that their own politicians, embassies, trade missions and UN delegations were the target of the other side. Chancellor Angela Merkel of Germany complained that her private cell phone was tapped during the same period her own Federal Intelligence Service, the BND, was handing over troves of information on European citizens, defence contractors and critical industries.[20] Every private detail of the personal lives of billions of internet and phone users sloshed around inside vast tanks of data, the scale and size of which exceeded what was previously considered to be even technically possible.

A programme called Optic Nerve specifically targeted the webcams of Yahoo Messenger users, the most popular chat programme for commodities traders and horny teenagers alike. From each broadcast, one still image was saved every five minutes – a limit supposedly enforced 'to comply with human rights legislation' – and run through facial recognition software to identify participants. GCHQ was forced to implement additional controls to protect staff from the significant proportion of the data that revealed 'undesirable nudity'.[21] Stories emerged of NSA contractors searching the emails and text messages of spouses, lovers, exes and crushes, a practice sufficiently widespread to gain its own jokey codename, LOVEINT, and demonstrating the ease with which the system could be accessed.[22] Other code words revealed the preoccupations and dark humour of their creators. Regin, a piece of malware used to infiltrate telecom systems in Belgium and the Middle East, contained cricket-themed code words like LEGSPIN and WILLISCHECK, believed to refer to English fast bowler Bob Willis.[23] Another GCHQ operation to harvest IP addresses of website visitors was code-named KARMA POLICE, apparently after the Radiohead song of the same name, which includes the lyric, 'This is what you'll get when you mess with us.'[24]

The stories continued for months, obscure technological jargon became common knowledge, and poorly designed Powerpoint slides were seared into the memory of millions. Code words multiplied, becoming a kind of sinister poetry: TEMPORA, MUSCULAR, MYSTIC, BLARNEY and BOUNDLESS INFORMANT; NOSEY SMURF, HIDDEN OTTER, CROUCHING SQUIRREL, BEARDED PIGGY and SQUEAKY DOLPHIN. Ultimately, these endless lists come to obscure the practical reality of a global surveillance system that is irreducible to its component parts. As Edward Snowden wrote in his first email to the filmmaker Laura Poitras, 'Know that every border you cross, every purchase you make, every call you dial, every cell phone tower you pass, friend you keep, article you write, site you visit, subject line you type, and packet you route, is in the hands of a system whose reach is unlimited but whose safeguards are not.'[25] But what remains most striking, just a few years after the revelations, is ultimately not their extent, but how obvious they should have been – and how little has changed.

The existence of a concerted technological effort to intercept civilian communications has been known since at least 1967, when a telegraphist named Robert Lawson walked into the offices of the *Daily Express* in London and informed the investigative journalist Chapman Pincher that every cable or telegram that entered or left the UK was collected each day by a Ministry of Public Buildings and Works van and taken to an Admiralty building to be examined, before being returned. The story ran in the next day's paper, making clear that the cable intercepts were part of a much larger operation involving phone taps and the opening of letters. At the time, the existence of GCHQ was not even known to the public, and even when the government's own commission of inquiry into the affair both confirmed that the reporting was accurate, and denounced a number of official statements as misleading, the affair slipped quickly from the public memory.

In 2005, eight years before the Snowden revelations, the *New York Times* revealed that in the aftermath of 9/11 the NSA had been granted extensive secret powers by President George W. Bush to spy on US communications without the need for a warrant.[26] The article revealed the existence of a project, which had been code-named Stellar Wind, for building a vast database of the communications of American citizens, including email communications, telephone conversations, financial transactions, and internet activity. A former NSA analyst, William Binney, went on the record to confirm the extent of the programme, and it was attacked in the press for its clear overstepping of constitutional protections. The project had already been the subject of internal government turmoil when it was discovered that, contrary to the presidential authorisation, the NSA was not only tapping communications with a foreign connection, but collecting data on all the communications it could. The White House's response was simply to reauthorise the programme under a different rubric. Binney continued to make noise about the project over subsequent years, and as late as 2012 *Wired* magazine carried a report on the NSA's construction of a vast new data centre in Utah that suggested that Stellar Wind was still active, quoting Binney on its capabilities.[27]

In May 2006, an AT&T contractor named Mark Klein revealed that the NSA had the capability to monitor huge amounts of communications. In 2002, he had met an NSA agent who was recruiting AT&T management for a special project; the following year he discovered a secret room inside the largest San Francisco telephone exchange, which only the technician recruited by NSA was allowed to enter. The room was adjacent to the machinery that routed all public telephone calls. Klein himself was subsequently put to work in another room in the exchange; this one handled internet traffic for a company called Worldnet. Klein's job involved splitting the fibre-optic cables in certain circuits and routing them to the secret room. These specific circuits were the ones that connected Worldnet's customers with the rest of the internet, and discussions with other AT&T employees revealed that similar splitter cabinets had been installed in exchanges in other cities. In each case, the diverted fibre led to a NarusInsight 'semantic analyser' machine, which could sift through huge amounts of information to pick out preprogrammed words and phrases.[28] The size of the 'take' strongly implied that NSA was monitoring not only foreign communications, but indiscriminately hoovering up domestic traffic as well. A lawsuit against AT&T, based on Klein's evidence and filed by the Electronic Frontier Foundation, alleged as much; but while it became a major media story, it was blocked by the US government, which quickly passed retroactive legislation to make the company immune from legal action.

And even without such revelations, why was nobody looking? The scale of the black budget was there for anyone to see; the listening stations built for the Cold War were still humming away, even expanding; the fields of antennae and satellite dishes appeared on Google Maps, perched on white cliffs over the cable landing sites. GCHQ even had a trade union until 1984, when it was very publicly banned by Margaret Thatcher in one of the longest running labour disputes of the twentieth century. Yet discussions of the agencies' capabilities remained the preserve of students of intelligence – and, as we will see in the next chapter, fodder for conspiracy theorists.

It wasn't until the 2013 release of documents by Edward Snowden that some kind of critical paranoid mass was achieved. Why this should have been the case is debatable; perhaps it was the sheer volume of it, and its visual and narrative flair. It overflowed our ability to ignore it, simply by keeping on coming, day after day, in a welter of buzzwords and ridiculous project names and eye-searing Powerpoint slides, like a never-ending marketing meeting with Satan himself. Perhaps it was Snowden's own story that so powerfully captured our attention: his sudden appearance in Hong Kong, his flight to Russia, the need for a young, elusive protagonist to carry the narrative. Snowden's revelations were also the first to connect known NSA and GCHQ programmes – to reveal their total operational entanglement, and thus the ways in which global surveillance made everyone into a target, negating any possibility of being protected by the perceived superiority of one's own government.

And yet, no action. In the United States, proposals to end warrantless wiretapping and curb the blanket collection of data by the intelligence agencies, such as the Amash–Conyers Amendment, have been defeated in both houses of Congress, while other bills remain stuck in committees. The USA FREEDOM Act – formally titled the Uniting and Strengthening America by Fulfilling Rights and Ending Eavesdropping, Dragnet-collection and Online Monitoring Act – passed into law on June 2, 2015, essentially reinstating the Patriot Act, which expired the day before. While much touted as a regulatory response to the Snowden revelations, the act left most of the NSA's capabilities intact, including blanket collection of metadata – every detail of a communication except its content, which could subsequently be acquired through a secret subpoena. In any case, the act could at any time be subverted by presidential decree, just as previous versions were in the years after 9/11, and overseas operations remain entirely undisturbed. A process that was founded on the systematic and covert overruling of law was never going to be reversed by more legislation. The British government, which never passed any law preventing GCHQ surveillance of its own citizens before or after the revelations, contented itself with issuing increasingly draconian censorship demands, known as D-Notices, to newspapers reporting on the affair. In the face of the ongoing global war on terror and an industrial intelligence complex of almost unimaginable power, the rest of the world could simply protest in vain.

Ultimately, the public appetite for confronting the insane, insatiable demands of the intelligence agencies was never there and, having briefly surfaced in 2013, has fallen off, wearied by the drip-drip of revelation and the sheer existential horror of it all. We never really wanted to know what was in those secret rooms, those windowless buildings in the centre of the city, because the answer was always going to be bad. Much like climate change, mass surveillance has proved to be too vast and destabilising an idea for society to really get its head around. Like awkward, half-joking, half-terrified conversations about the weather, it has become merely another whining hum of paranoia in the background of everyone's daily routines. Thinking about climate change spoils the weather, rendering it an existential threat even when it's nice. Thinking about mass surveillance spoils phone calls, emails, cameras, and pillow talk. Its black ichor coats the things we touch every day. Its implications stretch so deep into our everyday lives that it's easier to add it to the long list of things we simply agree not to think.

This is a pity, because there's much that remains to be thought and argued about regarding mass surveillance – indeed, of any surveillance, and of any image entered as evidence. Global mass surveillance relies on political secrecy and technological opacity, and the two feed upon one another.

While governments have always spied on their own people as well as their enemies, their ability to eavesdrop on every moment of life has been radically enhanced by networks and processing power – by the spread of computation into the walls of every home and down every street, into our workplaces and into our pockets. Technical possibility breeds political necessity, because no politician wants to be accused of not doing enough in the aftermath of some atrocity or exposé. Surveillance is done because it can be done, not because it is effective; and, like other implementations of automation, because it shifts the burden of responsibility and blame onto the machine. Collect it all, and let the machines sort it out.

In testimony to a British parliamentary committee in 2016, the aforementioned NSA whistle-blower William Binney asserted that bulk collection of data by the intelligence agencies was '99 per cent useless'. The reason he gave for this was that the sheer volume of information collected swamped analysts, making it impossible to pick out the relevant data to address specific threats. This is a warning that has been sounded many times before, but its implications have not been heeded – indeed, they have been exacerbated. Following the attempted bombing of a flight from Amsterdam to Detroit on Christmas Day, 2009, President Obama himself admitted that too much intelligence was the problem: 'This was not a failure to collect intelligence, [but] a failure to integrate and understand the intelligence that we already had,' he stated.[29] A French counterterrorism official commented on the case that 'about the time we're overcome with envy and awe at the reach and depth of American intelligence-gathering capacity, we start to feel really lucky at not having to process the impossible mass of information it generates'.[30]

The computational excesses of mass surveillance are seen too in the US drone programme, which for years has been dogged by problems of analysis and interpretation. As the drones multiply and their flight times increase, so do the resolution and bandwidth of the cameras they carry, exponentially exceeding our ability to monitor them. As far back as 2010, one of the US Air Force's most senior commanders was warning that it could soon be 'swimming in sensors and drowning in data'.[31] More information, even for the most advanced information-processing organisations, does not correspond to more understanding. Rather, it confuses and conceals, becoming a spur to further complexity: an arms race akin to the weather forecasting problem, where computation desperately attempts to outrun time itself. As William Binney described in his evidence to the UK parliament, 'The net effect of the current approach is that people die first, even if historic records sometimes can provide additional information about the killers (who may be deceased by that time).'[32]

On multiple levels, mass surveillance simply doesn't work. Studies have repeatedly shown that mass surveillance generates little to no useful information for counterterrorism offices. In 2013, the President's Review Group on Intelligence and Communications Technologies declared mass surveillance 'not essential to preventing attacks', finding that most leads were generated by traditional investigative techniques such as informants and reports of suspicious activities.[33] Another 2014 report by the New American Foundation described the government claims about the success of surveillance programmes in the wake of the 9/11 attacks as 'overblown and even misleading'.[34]

At the other end of the spectrum, analysis of the deployment of closed-circuit television in public spaces has shown it to be just as ineffective, in much the same ways as global surveillance. It is vastly expensive, it diverts funding and attention from other approaches to the issues it seeks to address, and it has little appreciable effect. Often cited as a deterrent, it is no such thing. When San Francisco installed hundreds of security cameras in the mid 2000s, the number of homicides within 250 feet of the cameras went down – and spiked in the next 250 feet. People just moved down the street to kill each other.[35] CCTV, like global surveillance, serves only to heighten the background hum of paranoia, increasing fears of crime and control while doing nothing to address them. CCTV and mass surveillance are both essentially retroactive and retributive: more intelligence may be gathered, and more arrests made, but only once the crime has been committed. The critical event has already occurred, and the underlying causes are always ignored.

Considering the efficacy of surveillance in this way forces us to reflect on our own strategies for opposing abuses of power. Does throwing light on the subject really help? Improved lighting has long been one of the axioms of security theatre itself, but the installation of lighting on city streets has as often been followed by a rise in crime as it has preceded a fall.[36] Criminals may be as emboldened by the light as any victim: when everything is well lit, the malicious look a lot less suspicious, and they know when the coast is clear. Bright light makes people feel safer, but it doesn't actually make them safer.[37]

The exposure of the darkest activities of the intelligence agencies has failed to curb them; rather it has reassured the public, while legitimising these same activities. Operations that formerly took place in a hazy zone of obscurity and deniability have been codified in law, and not to our advantage.

Perhaps, while we laud the visual impact of the Snowden revelations for stimulating a debate on mass surveillance, we need to consider that their very visuality provided a distraction from understanding its underlying mechanisms and persistence. If on the one hand we can argue that surveillance fails because of its reliance on images over understanding, and its belief in a single, justificatory narrative, then how can we argue on the other hand that surveillant approaches to countering it will succeed? Yet this is exactly what we do. In opposition to secrecy, we assert transparency. Our demands for clarity and openness may appear to be a counter to opacity and classification, but they end up asserting the same logics. Under this analysis, the National Security Agency and Wikileaks share the same worldview, with differing ends. Both essentially believe that there is some secret at the heart of the world that, if only it can be known, will make everything better. Wikileaks wants transparency for all; the NSA only wants transparency for some – its enemies; but both function according to the same philosophy.

Wikileaks' original intent was not to become a kind of mirror to the NSA, but to break the whole machine. In 2006, in the very early days of Wikileaks, Julian Assange wrote an analysis of conspiratorial systems of government and how they can be attacked, entitled 'Conspiracy as Governance'. For Assange, all authoritarian systems are conspiracies because their power depends on keeping secrets from their peoples. Leaks undermine their power, not because of what is leaked, but because increased internal fear and paranoia degrades the system's ability to conspire. What is damaging is the act of leaking itself, not the contents of any specific leak.[38] As Wikileaks entered the public eye and Assange himself became an increasingly powerful and arrogant figure, the organisation became involved in a series of feuds with the intelligence agencies – and ultimately a tool for states to attack one another – and this realisation was lost. What replaced it was a mistaken belief in the power of the 'smoking gun': the single source or piece of evidence that would bring down authority.

The problem of the smoking gun besets every strategy that depends on revelation to move opinion. Just as the activities of the intelligence agencies could have been inferred long before the Snowden revelations by multiple reports over decades, so other atrocities are ignored until some particular index of documentary truthfulness is attained. In 2005, Caroline Elkins published a thorough account of British atrocities in Kenya, but her work was widely criticised for its reliance on oral history and eyewitness accounts.[39] It was only when the British government itself released documents that confirmed these accounts that they were accepted, becoming part of an acknowledged history. The testimony of those who suffered was ignored until it conformed to the account offered by their oppressors – a form of evidence that, as we have seen, will never be available for a multitude of other crimes. In the same manner, the cult of the whistle-blower depends upon the changing conscience of those already working for the intelligence services; those outside such organisations are left without agency, waiting helplessly for some unknown servant of government to deign to publish what they know. This is a fundamentally insufficient basis for moral action.

Just as the availability of vast computational power drives the implementation of global surveillance, so its logic has come to dictate how we respond to it, and to other existential threats to our cognitive and physical well-being. The demand for some piece of evidence that will allow us to assert some hypothesis with 100 per cent certainty overrides our ability to act in the present. Consensus – such as the broad scientific agreement around the urgency of the climate crisis – is disregarded in the face of the smallest quantum of uncertainty. We find ourselves locked in a kind of stasis, demanding that Zeno's arrow hit the target even as the atmosphere before it warms and thickens. The insistence upon some ever-insufficient confirmation creates the deep strangeness of the present moment: everybody knows what's going on, and nobody can do anything about it.

Reliance on the computational logics of surveillance to derive truth about the world leaves us in a fundamentally precarious and paradoxical position. Computational knowing requires surveillance, because it can only produce its truth from the data available to it directly. In turn, all knowing is reduced to that which is computationally knowable, so all knowing becomes a form of surveillance. Thus computational logic denies our ability to think the situation, and to act rationally in the absence of certainty. It is also purely reactive, permitting action only after sufficient evidence has been gathered and forbidding action in the present, when it is most needed.

The operation of surveillance, and our complicity in it, is one of the most fundamental characteristics of the new dark age, because it insists on a kind of blind vision: everything is illuminated, but nothing is seen. We have become convinced that throwing light upon the subject is the same thing as thinking it, and thus having agency over it. But the light of computation just as easily renders us powerless – either through information overload, or a false sense of security. It is a lie we have been sold by the seductive power of computational thinking.

Consider an example from the network itself. Some time prior to May 2016, James O'Reilly, a resident of Fort McMurray in Alberta, Canada, installed a Canary security system in his home. The Canary suite of products, like Google's Home offerings, perfectly embodies the logic of surveillance and computational thinking: a series of cameras, sensors, and alarms – linked together and through the internet – provide total situational awareness of the home in real time, and the promise of protection and peace of mind through the agency of the all-seeing machines.

On May 1, 2016, a wildfire started in the boreal forest to the southwest of Fort McMurray and, fanned by strong winds, spread towards the town. On May 3, a mandatory eviction order was issued, and 88,000 people abandoned their homes, including O'Reilly. As he was driving away, his iPhone pinged with a notification from the home security system, and started to live stream video, which was later posted to YouTube.[40]

The video opens with a shot of O'Reilly's living room: table lamps are still illuminated, as are the lights of a fish tank, in which goldfish continue to swim. The trees outside the window are shaken by a strong wind, but nothing seems untoward. Over the next few minutes, shadows start to beat against the door, resolving slowly into billowing smoke. After another minute, the window has turned black, and the frame catches. Fire shatters first the blind, and then the window itself. Smoke pours into the room, and it is gradually obscured. The camera switches to black-and-white night vision. In the growing darkness, an alarm sounds intermittently, but it finally falls silent, and all that can be heard is the crackling of the flames.

It is a nightmarish scene, yet one that seems to embody the conditions of a new dark age. Our vision is increasingly universal, but our agency is ever more reduced. We know more and more about the world, while being less and less able to do anything about it. The resulting sense of helplessness, rather than giving us pause to reconsider our assumptions, seems to be driving us deeper into paranoia and social disintegration: more surveillance, more distrust, an ever-greater insistence on the power of images and computation to rectify a situation that is produced by our unquestioning belief in their authority.

Surveillance does not work, and neither does righteous exposure. There is no final argument to be made on either side, no clinching statement that will ease our conscience and change the minds of our opponents. There is no smoking gun, no total confirmation or clear denial. The Glomar response, rather than the dead words of a heedless bureaucracy, turns out to be the truest description of the world that we can articulate.

8

Conspiracy

In Joseph Heller's novel *Catch-22*, the airmen of the 256th USAF Squadron find themselves trapped in an impossible position. The war is at its height, and the fighting in the skies over Italy is intense. They run the risk of being shot down every time they climb into the cockpit, and it's clearly insane to choose to fly more of the dangerous missions; the sane choice would be to refuse to fly. But to get out of flying missions, they would have to plead insanity, at which point they would be declared sane for trying to get out of them. The airman 'would be crazy to fly more missions and sane if he didn't, but if he were sane he had to fly them. If he flew them he was crazy and didn't have to, but if he didn't want to he was sane and had to.'[1]

Catch-22 exemplifies the dilemma of rational actors caught up within the machinations of vast, irrational systems. Within such systems, even rational responses lead to irrational outcomes. The individual is aware of the irrationality but loses all power to act in their own interest. Faced with the roiling tide of information, we attempt to gain some kind of control over the world by telling stories about it: we attempt to master it through narratives. These narratives are inherently simplifications, because no one story can account for everything that's happening; the world is too complex for simple stories. Instead of accepting this, the stories become ever more baroque and bifurcated, ever more convoluted and open-ended. Thus paranoia in an age of network excess produces a feedback loop: the failure to comprehend a complex world leads to the demand for more and more information, which only further clouds our understanding – revealing more and more complexity that must be accounted for by ever more byzantine theories of the world. More information produces not more clarity, but more confusion.

In the 1970 film adaptation of *Catch-22*, Air Force Captain John Yossarian, played by Alan Arkin, utters the immortal line, 'Just because you're paranoid doesn't mean they aren't after you.' Yossarian's dictum has found new life in today's paranoid conspiracy thrillers engendered by technological advances and mass surveillance. One of the first symptoms of clinical paranoia is the belief that somebody is watching you; but this belief is now a reasonable one. Every email we send; every text message we write; every phone call we make; every journey we take; each step, breath, dream, and utterance is the target of vast systems of automated intelligence gathering, the sorting algorithms of social networks and spam factories, and the sleepless gaze of our own smartphones and connected devices. So who's paranoid now?

It's November 2014 and I'm standing on an access road in a field near Farnborough, in Hampshire, England. I'm waiting for a plane to fly overhead. I don't know when it's going to take off, or if it's going to fly at all. There's a camera on the hood of my car that has been filming empty sky for a couple of hours now; every thirty minutes or so I wipe the memory card and start it up again. The thin, high cloud shimmers and disappears.

The plane I am waiting for is one of three Reims-Cessna F406 aircraft based at Farnborough Airport, home of the famous air show and location of the first powered flight in Britain, in 1908. The Royal Aircraft Establishment, which researched and built first airships and later planes for the British military, was established here – as the Army Balloon Factory – in 1904. In the hangars to the south of the runways, the Air Accidents Investigations Branch, reassembles the shattered fragments of downed aircraft, in order to piece together the circumstances of their demise. It is thus a mecca for plane nerds, like myself, as well as the favourite airfield of oligarchs and foreign royalty, coasting into Airstrip One in unmarked private jets.

The Cessnas aren't jets; they're little twin turboprops, designed for civilian and military surveillance, particularly favoured by coastguards and aerial survey companies. The three who make their home at Farnborough first came to my attention when I encountered one of them doing tight circles over the Isle of Wight one summer afternoon, for hours on end. I was spending a lot of time on the website FlightRadar24, initially looking for the private charter planes being used to deport rejected asylum seekers in the middle of the night[2], but I slowly became entranced by the sheer wealth of data beamed down from the skies, and the intricate patterns of aircraft over southern England. At any time of day there are thousands of planes, large and small, speeding through or pottering around this heavily congested airspace, one of the busiest in the world. Among the long-haul jets and budget city-hoppers weave trainer aircraft and military transports – and sometimes, flights that the government would prefer to remain hidden.

Few people know more about what is hidden from view by the British Government than the investigative journalist Duncan Campbell, who was the first person to report publicly on GCHQ back in 1976. In 1978, the government punished Campbell and his colleagues Crispin Aubrey (another journalist) and John Berry (a former intelligence officer) by prosecuting them under the Official Secrets Act.[3] The so-called ABC Trial, which ran for months, revealed that almost all the information used in the reports was in the public domain already. 'There are no secrets, only lazy researchers,' as Richard Aldrich, a historian of the intelligence services, wrote in an account of the trial.[4] In 2010, Campbell reviewed Aldrich's book on GCHQ for the *New Statesman*, writing,

> [GCHQ's installation at Bude in Cornwall] was the start of the English-speaking allies' Project Echelon, comparable, Aldrich suggests, to today's Google Alert system, which constantly scans the internet for new additions. This is an ingenious comparison, but it omits a critical point of divergence. Google, even though it often overreaches itself, collects what is placed in the public domain. The sigint collectors are scanning and storing the entire private domain of communication, under questionable authority at best, and certainly without account-ability as it is normally understood.
>
> Over east London now, as you are reading this, a sigint collection plane is likely circling at 10,000 feet above Canary Wharf, scooping up the capital's cellular networks, report-edly attempting to voice-match mobile telephone calls made in the area to a bomber back in Britain following training with the Taliban. If such activity nets those who plan harm on the City streets effectively, all may appear well and good. But how are the hundreds of thousands of others whose communications are collected to be protected against impro-priety, or error, or worse?[5]

This, and other scattered references, were what I found when I started looking for information about the Cessnas circling the Isle of Wight. On G-INFO, the publicly accessible database of UK-registered aircraft, I found two of the planes listed as belonging to Nor Aviation, an otherwise mysterious entity with an address at a Mail Boxes Etc. store in Surbiton, a few miles from the airfield. The same anonymous location was the registered address of a second Cessna belonging to Nor Aviation, while a third, performing the same low passes over Bembridge and Blackgang, was registered to Aero Lease UK at the Mail Boxes Etc. in Farnborough itself. The names of several owners were the same as serving or former Metropolitan Police officers, a strangeness confirmed by the discovery of a newspaper article from 1995, detailing a decade-long fraud perpetrated by a former Met accountant, Anthony Williams.[6] Williams was tasked with setting up front companies for the Met's secret air wing, but funnelled most of the funds – some £5 million over nine years – into his own bank account, from which they were used to buy up a large chunk of the Scottish village of Tomintoul, as well as the manorial title Lord Williams of Chirnside.

Attempts to find out more about the planes on pilot and planespotter forums was frustrated by the usual British deference to authority: those who posted about the planes were warned off by other users; administrators of the Farnborough planespotters groups banned all mention of their tail numbers. This wasn't a surprise: investigations into the deportation flights had led to my being unceremoniously banned from several forums previously. 'We're interested in the planes, not who's on them,' I was told. Or – in the case of the legally dubious blanket surveillance of the general public's mobile phone calls by a secret fleet of police aircraft – not even interested in the planes, despite photographs of them littering the websites of air photography enthusiasts. (I suspect, too, that it is the existence of these aircraft that strengthened the Met's insistence upon secrecy when I naively requested information about their aerial capabilities, as related in the previous chapter.)

So here I am in the field in Hampshire, and after several hours the lawnmower rasp of a light aircraft becomes audible, shortly followed by the appearance of a small, twin-engined plane, its registration number clearly visible on the underside of the wings. Shortly after it disappears over the horizon, it pops up on FlightRadar24, heading southwest. I watch it on my phone for the next hour, as it performs its usual pattern of mid-altitude loops off the south coast, and then heads back toward me. Ninety minutes or so after it took off, it returns to

Farnborough. I still don't know what they're doing down there. Later, I will write a small piece of software to scrape the website and log all the flights of the three planes, as well as others – the 3 a.m. deportation flights out of Stansted Airport, the CIA's unmarked excursions over Los Angeles and Boston, the high-altitude lurkings of MI5's Islander aircraft from Northolt. Big data flows out of the sky at a rate I can barely keep up with, and that I don't really know what to do with anyway. Sometime in 2016, the planes stop broadcasting their location after take-off.

While I'm waiting by the airfield, another car pulls up – a minicab, according to the licence decal in the rear window. The access road is a good spot, just off the A325, for cabbies to wait between jobs. The driver gets out of the car, and I take the opportunity to borrow a lighter. We share a companionable cigarette; he notices my radio and binoculars. We talk about planes. And then, inevitably, we talk about chemtrails.

'They're different now, aren't they, the clouds?' says the taxi driver. It's becoming a familiar conversation. Go on YouTube and you can find countless videos detailing, often in anger, the changing nature of the skies, and the aircraft producing such changes. Many of my web searches for the aircraft logging mobile phone calls lead me not to accounts of surveillance, but of covert geo-engineering: the use of planes to control the atmosphere with chemical sprays.

Something strange is afoot. In the hyper-connected, data-deluged present, schisms emerge in mass perception. We're all looking at the same skies, but we're seeing different things. Where I see covert deportations and secret surveillance planes – supported by flight logs and ADS-B data, newspaper reports and Freedom of Information requests – others see a global conspiracy to doctor the atmosphere, to control minds, to enslave populations, or to reengineer the climate for naive or nefarious purposes. In an atmosphere measurably filling with carbon dioxide – a gas that warms the planet and makes us dumber – many are convinced that far more than green-house gases are being dumped upon us.

Chemtrails have been around for a while, since at least the 1990s, when, according to the conspiracy theorists, the US Air Force let slip what they were really up to. In a report entitled 'Weather as a Force Multiplier: Owning the Weather in 2025', a group of Air Force researchers proposed a series of meas-ures by which the US military might use weather modification to achieve 'battlespace dominance to a degree never before imagined,' including inducing and preventing precipitation, controlling thunderstorms, and selectively activating the ionosphere with microwave beams to improve or degrade radio communications.[7] While weather modification has a long history, the particular conjunction of speculative meteor-ology, military research, and the nascent internet caused chemtrails to go viral – perhaps the first truly mass folklore of the network.

Within a few years, assisted by online forums and talk radio, the belief that aircraft were intentionally spraying chem-icals into the upper atmosphere was widespread, even global. Questions were asked in parliaments; national scientific organ-isations were flooded with enquiries; atmospheric scientists were barracked at conferences. Online, shaky videos of blue skies besmirched with smog, and planes trailing black smoke, proliferate. Groups of individuals gather in forums and Facebook groups to swap anecdotes and images.

The chemtrails theory is multifaceted and hydra-like; its adherents believe in fractal versions of the same idea. For some, the chemicals sprayed by commercial, military, and mystery aircraft are part of a widespread programme of solar radiation management: the creation of cloud cover to reduce sunlight and slow – or accelerate – global warming. The chem-icals used cause cancer, Alzheimer's, skin diseases and deformities. Global warming itself might be a lie, or a plot by shadowy forces to take over the world. Others believe the chemicals are intended to turn people into mindless drones, or to make them sick in order to profit the pharmaceutical industry. Covert geo-engineering, climate denialism, and the new world order meet in the churn of online misinformation, user-submitted videos, claims and debunkings, and contagious distrust.

Chemtrails become the vortex of other conspiracies, pulling everything into their orbit. 'Take Ur Power Back: Vote to leave the EU' exhorts one YouTuber, with the perhaps unsurprising username of Flat Earth Addict, over a montage of blue suburban skies criss-crossed with contrails.[8] In this telling, covert climate engineering is a project of the European Union to suppress the will of the people. A few days later, the morning after Britain does indeed vote to leave the EU, Nigel Farage, de facto leader of the Leave Campaign, appears on national television. 'The sun has risen on an independent Britain,' he says, 'and just look at it, even the weather has improved.'[9]

The pervasiveness of chemtrails is deeply akin to Timothy Morton's hyperobject reading of climate change itself: something that clings to the skin and inserts itself into every facet of life, as perfectly captured in an account by journalist Carey Dunne of a month spent with chemtrail believers in California: 'I wish I didn't know, because now that I know, it's really making my heart sad.'[10] Conspiracies literalise the horror we feel lurking unspoken in the world.

Dunne's initial enthusiasm for an idyllic working break on an organic farm turns weird when she discovers the beliefs of her employers, hippyish back-to-the-landers who, through Facebook, discovered a community of local chemtrail believers – and a doctored tweet by Donald Trump claiming that his administration would end chemtrailing:

'How does someone like me know what's true and what's not?' Tammi says. 'I'm 54 years old. I don't watch the news. I don't listen to the news on the radio. Then when I'm on the internet, and I see something where I'm like, "Holy shit, *really?*" I'm led down this path of believing it. I don't have the knowledge that a journalist has about how verifiable is the source. When you're just a standard person, you can really be led to believe anything. Because of the internet, anybody can put news out there. How do I know if it's the truth or not? It makes it hard when you're trying to choose a president. People chose Donald Trump because [they thought] he tweeted he was gonna stop chemtrails – you know what I mean?'[11]

Conspiracy theory, nevertheless, serves a vital and necessary function, by bringing into view objects and discourses otherwise ignored – the edge cases of the problem space. The term 'conspiracy theory' has more to do with the relation of people to power, than that of people to truth. The 'black smokers' of the chemtrailers can't simply be ignored, when it is so clear that they point directly toward the actual and ongoing cataclysm in the atmosphere. Ruskin's Plague-Cloud may or may not have been the first visible emanations from the chimneys of a rapidly industrialising Britain, or it might have been a deeper metaphor: a miasma rising from the thousands of corpses littering the battlefields of Europe, the first casualties of the twentieth century's wars of industrial capital.

As in Ruskin's time, the fundamental uncertainty of the present manifests in the form of weather formations: an array of new and strange clouds. In 2017, the latest edition of the International Cloud Atlas, published by the World Meteorological Organization, added a new classifier to its official list of cloud formations. This is 'homogenitus', and it is used to describe those cloud formations that develop as a result of human activity.[12]

In the lower part of the atmosphere, warm and moist air from urban and vehicle emissions creates a fog: these are layers of *Stratus homogenitus*. In unstable atmospheres, these layers lift up to form free-floating clouds of *Cumulus homogenitus*.

Photograph: Karlona Plskova/WMO.

Stratocumulus homogenitus: Rising thermals from the Prunéřov, Tušimice and Počerady power plants in the Czech Republic generate clouds that spread out to form stratocumulus at a height of about 2,500 metres.

Thermal power plants, which eject their waste heat into the middle atmosphere from their cooling towers, swell existing nimbostratus and altostratus, casting themselves into shadow. But it is in the high atmosphere, far from the surface of the earth, that homogenitus comes into its own.

The combustion of kerosene in jet engines produces water vapour and carbon dioxide. The water vapour cools quickly in the freezing air, first forming tiny droplets of liquid water, and then hardening into ice crystals. At high altitudes, ice crystals require a tiny nucleus around which to form: this is provided by the impurities in the jet fuel. Millions and millions of these crystals form the track that marks the plane's passage. This is *Cirrus homogenitus*. Contrails are officially man-made clouds, and on cold, still days they can persist for hours, or even longer.

The criss-crossing of the skies is repeated everywhere. In Grant Morrison's comic book series *The Invisibles*, one of the

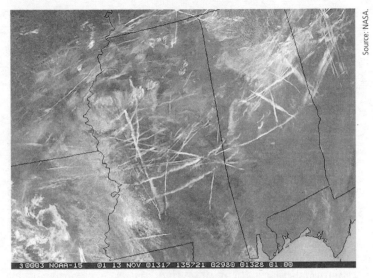

November 13, 2001, NOAA-15 AVHRR infrared over the southeastern United States, showing contrails of various ages.

characters takes a polaroid snap of the desert sky, commenting, 'A cloud head rising over the mesa in Dulce, New Mexico – that is exactly the same, in every detail – as one photographed in Queenstown, New Zealand.' In *The Invisibles*' cosmology, this is one of the dramatic moments when the narrative collapses, and evidence of time travel and much else is revealed. For us, the strange, global entanglement of *Cirrus homogenitus* and its endless circulation and reproduction online through climate research and conspiracy theory is the moment when the weather becomes active data: a Storm-Cloud of the Anthropocene, unlimited in physical space and spreading through the network, and the paranoid imagination.

Scientists are at pains to disassociate 'normal' contrails from the conspiracists' chemtrails, but they contain the seeds of the same crisis. Contrails are the visible sign of what is ejected invisibly from jet engines: carbon dioxide, the stupefying insulator that is increasing so rapidly and dangerously in the atmosphere. Jet exhaust also includes nitrogen oxides, sulfur oxides, lead, and black carbon, which interact with each other and the air in complex ways which we do not fully understand. While airlines have continued to introduce fuel-saving efficiencies over the decades, this financial and ecological saving is far outstripped by the rapid growth of aviation in its totality. At its current rate of expansion, the aviation industry alone will by 2050 account for the entirety of the carbon dioxide emissions permitted to hold global warming below the two-degree-Celsius crisis point.[13]

Contrails do affect the climate, particularly when they persist, spreading out across the sky to form vast swathes of whiteness resembling cirrus and altocumulus. It is not merely their chemical composition, but their very cloudiness that affects the atmosphere: they trap more long-wave thermal radiation beneath them than they reflect back into space, resulting in increased global warming. The difference is particularly pronounced at night, and during the winter.[14] Long-term studies of the atmosphere have shown that it is in fact getting cloudier up there: the contrails are changing the skies, and not for the better.[15]

In ancient Greece, certain seers practised ornithomancy: divination of the future by observing the flight of the birds. According to Aeschylus, it was Prometheus, the bringer of technology, who introduced ornithomancy to the ancients by designating some birds as fortuitous and some as sinister.[16] Prometheus also promoted haruspicy, the examination of birds' entrails for omens – a kind of primitive hacking. Today's haruspex is the obsessive online investigator, spending hours picking over the traces of events, gutting them and splaying out their innards, poking at their joints and picking out fragments of steel, plastic, and black carbon.

Many conspiracy theories, then, might be a kind of folk knowing: an unconscious augury of the conditions, produced by those with a deep, even hidden, awareness of current conditions and no way to articulate them in scientifically acceptable terms. But a world that has no way of admitting such differently articulated accounts is in danger of falling prey to far worse stories – from antiscientific public panics to blood libels – and of failing to hear voices of genuine and necessary warning.

In the far north of Canada, indigenous people claim that the sun no longer sets where it used to, and that the stars are out of alignment. The weather is changing in strange and unpredictable ways. Warm, unstable winds blow from new directions; severe flooding threatens towns and villages. Even the animals are changing their patterns of life, struggling to adapt to the uncertain conditions. This is how the world is described in *Inuit Knowledge and Climate Change*, by Nunavut filmmaker Zacharias Kunuk and environmental scientist Ian Mauro, a series of interviews with Inuit elders in which they recount their experiences of the world around them – experiences informed by decades of observing the climate firsthand. The sun is setting in a different place, they say, often kilometres from where it used to. The earth itself is off-kilter.

When the film was screened at the Copenhagen Climate Change Conference (COP15) in December 2009, it caused many scientists to complain that while the Inuit viewpoint was important, their claim that the earth had actually moved – had tilted on its axis – was dangerous, and would lead to them being discredited.[17] But the direct experience of the Inuit is upheld by scientific theory: at high latitudes, the appearance of the sun is hugely affected by the snow covering the ground, which reflects and refracts it myriad ways. Changes in the snow and ice correspond to changes in visibility. At the same time, the atmosphere is indisputably filling up with particulate matter, the impurities of jet liners and the exhaust of fossil fuel fires. The bright red sunsets seen over dirty cities are the result of the smog and smoke the city itself exhales. In this way, the sun above the Arctic is distorted, and appears to set further and further away. The sky, like everything else, is seen through the lens of climate change. Not knowing why doesn't make it not so.

'Over the years, nobody has ever listened to these people. Every time [the discussion is] about global warming, about the Arctic warming, it's scientists that go up there and do their work. And policy makers depend on these findings. Nobody ever really understands the people up there,' Kunuk reported.[18] In this regard, the knowledge of the Inuit is much akin to the Kenyan victims of torture, whose embodied evidence was ignored until it was validated in the language of their oppressors, through formal documentation and analysis. Scientific and political knowledges cannot escape the horizon of their own experience any more than embodied ones can, but it doesn't mean they're not looking at the same thing and seeking ways to articulate it.

Some of the most spectacular sunsets seen in Europe in recent times occurred after the eruption of Eyjafjallajökull, the Icelandic volcano that filled the heavens with ash in April of 2010. These sunsets are also caused by aerosols in the atmosphere, particularly sulfur dioxide. As sunset approaches, ash and sulfur dioxide produce ripples of white cloud on the horizon, before the blue light scattered by atmospheric particles combines with the extended red of sunsets to produce a unique tone known as volcanic lavender.[19] The sunsets appeared across the continent as the ash cloud moved south and west over several days. Volcanic ash was known to interfere with jet engines, but despite several incidents over decades, few studies had been performed. As a result, the whole of European airspace shut down. Over the course of eight days, over 100,000 flights were cancelled, almost half the world's air traffic, and 10 million passengers were stranded.

Apart from the sunsets, the most unsettling thing about the Eyjafjallajökull event was its silence. For the first time in

decades, the skies over Europe were quiet. The poet Carol Ann
Duffy noted its stillness:

> Britain's birds
> sing in this spring, from Inverness to Liverpool,
> from Crieff to Cardiff, Oxford, London Town,
> Land's End to John O'Groats; the music silence summons,
> that Shakespeare heard, Burns, Edward Thomas; briefly, us.[20]

Others commented on the archaic strangeness of a sky without
contrails. It was a strangeness that crept up on us slowly, an
inversion of the event. While the media reported on the 'chaos'
of travel disruptions, we sat in sunlight beneath clear blue
skies. The eruption was a hyperobject: an event of almost
inconceivable violence, present everywhere but experienced
locally as an absence, like climate change, like Roni Horn's
paradox of the weather: 'The nice is occurring in the immediate and individual, and the wrong is occurring systemwide.'

For a long time, climate sceptics have claimed that volcanoes produce more carbon dioxide than human activities.
Indeed, volcanoes have historically been responsible for periods of global cooling, and of paranoia. In 1815, the colossal
eruption of Mount Tambora in Indonesia was the final cataclysm in a series of events that caused 1816 to become known
as 'The Year Without a Summer'. Crops failed across North
America and Europe, with snow, ice, and frost appearing in
July and August. Bright red and purple skies appeared, and
famine spread across the land, along with ominous portents
and apocalyptic beliefs. In Geneva, a group of friends decided
to set down their most frightening stories. One outcome was
Mary Shelley's *Frankenstein, or The Modern Prometheus*;
another was Byron's poem 'Darkness', in which he wrote,

> The bright sun was extinguish'd, and the stars
> Did wander darkling in the eternal space,

Rayless, and pathless, and the icy earth
Swung blind and blackening in the moonless air.[21]

The explosion of the volcano Krakatoa in August 1883 also produced purple sunsets and global falls in temperature, and has been associated with both Ruskin's Plague-Cloud and the flaming skyscape of Edvard Munch's *The Scream*.[22] Like Tambora before it, it took several months for news of the eruption to reach Europe: in the meantime, apocalyptic predictions flourished.

The eruption of Eyjafjallajökull provided an opportunity to lay certain misconceptions about volcanic carbon dioxide to rest. The volcano was estimated to have emitted between 150,000 and 300,000 tonnes of carbon dioxide a day;[23] by contrast the grounding of the European air fleet prevented the emission of some 2.8 million tonnes in just eight days,[24] a figure greater than the total global annual emissions from all of the volcanoes in the world.[25] If painting *The Scream* today, the appropriate backdrop would not be the blood-red sky of Krakatoa's eruption, but a firmament criss-crossed with contrails: the same contrails that litter the websites of chemtrail conspiracy theorists, even, if not especially, those who deny the realities of man-made climate change. We are all looking at the same sky and seeing radically different things.

Acts of human violence have been recorded in the climate on numerous occasions. In the thirteenth century, the Mongol invasions of Eurasia caused such devastation to agriculture that forests significantly regrew, causing a measurable 0.1 per cent dip in atmospheric carbon levels.[26] The 'little ice age' that reached its climax in the Year Without a Summer of 1816 began in 1600, but it was the result of a century of global turmoil, which began with the Colombian catastrophe of 1492. In the 150 years following the arrival of Europeans in America, 80 to 95 per cent of the indigenous population was wiped out, reaching 100 per cent in some

regions, many by warfare, most by diseases introduced from
the Old World. A population of 50 to 60 million was reduced
to around 6 million. In the aftermath, 50 million hectares of
previously cultivated land was left devoid of humans.
Subsequently, more than 12 million Africans were enslaved
and displaced to the Americas, with millions more dying en
route. Once again, agriculture collapsed, this time on both
sides of the Atlantic, and the regrowth of forests coupled
with the reduction in wood burning resulted in an atmospheric decline in carbon dioxide of seven to ten parts per
million between 1570 and 1620.[27] It has never fallen in such
a way since.

It is perhaps this event that should be considered the beginning of the anthropocene, rather than some marvellous human
invention belatedly recognised as suicidal. Not the invention
of the coal-fired steam engine that kick-started the industrial
age in the eighteenth century; not the fixation of nitrogen
beginning with the invention of the Haber-Bosch process; not
the release of billions of particles of radioactive contamination
from the detonation of hundreds of nuclear bombs: the anthropocene starts with mass genocide, with planetary violence on
such a scale that it registers in ice cores and the pollination of
crops. It is the hallmark of the anthropocene that, unlike those
epochs that started with a meteor strike or sustained volcanic
eruptions, its origins are cloudy and uncertain. And its effects,
which are happening right now, are even more so. What we
can say of it is that, as the first truly human epoch – the one
that we are closest to and most entangled with – it is also the
hardest to see and think.

At 9:08 on the morning of September 11, 2001, five minutes
after the second plane crashed into the World Trade Centre
towers, the US Federal Aviation Authority shut down New
York's airspace and closed its airports. At 9:26 it issued a
nationwide ground stop, preventing any planes taking off
anywhere in the country. And at 9:45, the national airspace

was completely closed: no civilian aircraft were allowed to take off, and all aircraft in flight were ordered to land at the nearest airport as soon as possible. Canada's transport agency followed suit. By 12:15 p.m., the airspace over the continental United States was clear of civilian and commercial aircraft. Apart from military aircraft and prisoner transports, nothing flew over North America for three days.

During those three days between September 11 and 14, the difference between day and night temperatures, known as the average diurnal temperature range (DTR), showed a marked increase. Across the whole continent, the DTR increased by more than one degree Celsius, while for regions in the Midwest, Northeast and Northwest, where contrail coverage was usually the greatest, it more than doubled the seasonal average.[28] An act of violence, like so many before it, was recorded in the weather itself.

Over the course of the day on September 11, scrolling tickers started to appear on the bottom of news broadcasts, first on Fox News, then on CNN and MSNBC. Tickers had been used in breaking news situations before, as producers struggled to communicate the maximum amount of information and allow new viewers to quickly get up to speed. But after 9/11, the tickers never went away. The crisis became a daily, ongoing event, merging seamlessly into the war on terror, fears of dirty bombs, stock market collapses and occupations. In the news tickers, the discrete, empirical approach of bulletins was swept away in a constant stream of information: a precursor to the flowing walls of Facebook and Twitter feeds. The endless circulation of undated, unattributed information in news tickers and digital streams shredded our ability to tell coherent stories about the world. 9/11 – not the specific event itself, but the media environment it occurred in and accelerated – heralded the arrival of a new age of paranoia, best exemplified in the conspiracies of government complicity in the event, but mirrored at every level of society.

Richard J. Hofstadter, writing in 1964, created the term 'paranoid style' to characterise American politics. Citing examples ranging from Masonic and anti-Catholic panics in the 1800s to Senator Joe McCarthy's assertions of high-level government conspiracy in the 1950s, Hofstadter outlined a history of othering: the casting of an invisible enemy as 'a perfect model of malice, a kind of amoral superman – sinister, ubiquitous, powerful, cruel, sensual, luxury-loving'.[29] The most common attribute of this enemy is their extraordinary power: 'Unlike the rest of us, the enemy is not caught in the toils of the vast mechanism of history, himself a victim of his past, his desires, his limitations. He wills, indeed he manufactures, the mechanism of history, or tries to deflect the normal course of history in an evil way.' In short, the enemy is the other who rises above the convolutions and complexities of the present, who grasps the totality of the situation and is capable of manipulating it in ways the rest of us are not. Conspiracy theories are the extreme resort of the powerless, imagining what it would be to be powerful.

This theme was taken up by Fredric Jameson, when he wrote that conspiracy 'is the poor person's cognitive mapping in the postmodern age; it is the degraded figure of the total logic of late capital, a desperate attempt to represent the latter's system, whose failure is marked by its slippage into sheer theme and content'.[30] Surrounded by evidence of complexity – which for the Marxist historian is emblematic of the generalised alienation produced by capitalism – the individual, however outraged, resorts to ever more simplistic narratives in order to regain some control over the situation. As the technologically augmented and accelerated world trends toward the opposite of simplicity, as it becomes more – and more visibly – complex, conspiracy must of necessity become more bizarre, intricate, and violent to accommodate it.

Hofstadter identified another key aspect of the paranoid style: its mirroring of the subject's own desires. 'It is hard to resist the conclusion that this enemy is on many counts the projection of the self; both the ideal and the unacceptable aspects of the self are attributed to him.'[31] The chemtrails stick to the body, becoming unconscious, yet persistent, manifestations of wider environmental ruin. Just as a friend told me about flying to their summer holidays on one of the same jets I watched performing midnight deportations, so chemtrail believers film 'black smokers' from the windows of their own polluting pleasure flights. There's no outside to the complexity we find ourselves enmeshed in, no exterior point of view that we can all share on the situation. The network that brings us knowledge wraps around us, refracting our perspective into a million points of view, simultaneously illuminating and disorientating us.

In the last few years, the paranoid style has gone mainstream. It's easy to dismiss the chemtrailers and 9/11 truthers as the lunatic fringe, until they start to take over governments and bring down countries. Donald Trump may not have tweeted that he was going to put an end to chemtrails, but he has tweeted on multiple occasions that global warming is a conspiracy against American business, and probably some kind of Chinese plot.[32] His political rise came on the back of the 'Birther' movement, which claimed that Barack Obama was not a US citizen and was thus ineligible for the presidency. The Birther movement ignited Republican radicalisation, becoming the dominant issue at Tea Party rallies and town hall meetings. In 2011, Trump embarked on a national press tour questioning the legitimacy of Obama's birth certificate, and claimed on Twitter that he was in fact a Kenyan-born impostor named 'Barry Soweto'. He offered to donate money to the president's favourite charity if he would release his passport application. As a result of his pursuit of the issue, his support among likely Republican voters doubled, and politicians, including his later opponent for the Republican nomination, Mitt Romney, sought his endorsement. When he finally renounced the conspiracy in 2016 – long after Obama's long-form birth certificate was actually released – he claimed that Hillary Clinton had started it.[33]

After he entered the race for the presidency, Trump continued to take his lines from some of the most extreme and most prominent online conspiracy theorists. His call for a border wall to prevent Mexican 'murderers and rapists' entering the United States was justified by reference to a video produced by Alex Jones's Infowars.com, a conspiracy theory website and media empire. His campaign's frequently repeated calls for the jailing of Hillary Clinton also originated with Infowars.com. Trump's willingness to repeat what he read on the internet, or was fed by advisors with close links to right-wing conspiracy networks, surprised even Jones: 'It is surreal to talk about issues here on air, and then word-for-word hear Trump say it two days later,' he said.[34] The fringes of the internet had returned to the centre.

In 'Weather as a Force Multiplier: Owning the Weather in 2025', the US Air Force report that kick-started the chemtrails conspiracy, the writers noted that

> while most weather-modification efforts rely on the existence of certain preexisting conditions, it may be possible to produce some weather effects artificially, regardless of preexisting conditions. For instance, virtual weather could be created by influencing the weather information received by an end user. Their perception of parameter values or images from global or local meteorological information systems would differ from reality. This difference in perception would lead the end user to make degraded operational decisions.[35]

In this case, it's not necessary to change the actual weather, but merely to disrupt the tools with which the target perceives the weather. Man-made clouds don't need to be seeded in the stratosphere; they can be inserted as code into the networks of information that have come to replace our direct perception of the world. As one version of the chemtrail conspiracy might go: it's the *virtual* weather that is harming us.

The virtual weather disrupts our ability to tell coherent stories about the world because it challenges previously held models of consensus reality – and of consensus as a whole. In analyses of the most extreme conspiracy theories online, traditional psychological models start to fail. According to the textbook definition – in this case, that of the *Diagnostic and Statistical Manual of Mental Disorders*, published by the American Psychiatric Association and widely used by clinicians, researchers, and the legal system – a belief is not a delusion when it is held by a person's 'culture or subculture'. But the network has changed how we establish and shape cultures: people in distant locales can gather online to share their experiences and beliefs and form cultures all their own.

On December 30, 1796, James Tilly Matthews, a London tea broker, interrupted a session of the House of Commons by shouting, 'Treason!' from the public gallery. He was immediately arrested and shortly after committed to Bethlem Royal Hospital – better known as Bedlam. Under examination, Matthews claimed to have been involved in secret affairs of state, which were being concealed by the government of William Pitt. He also detailed the operation of a machine called the 'air loom', which used a system of hydraulic pumps and magnetic emanations to control his body and mind.[36] Matthews has gone down in history as the first documented case of paranoid schizophrenia. His detailed descriptions of the air loom have also passed into the literature, as they provide the first example of paranoid delusions tracking the scientific discoveries of the day.

In 1796, Britain and Europe were abuzz with revolutions scientific and political: Joseph Priestley had separated the air into its constituent elements, while in Paris Antoine Lavoisier had just published his *Elements of Chemistry*, which created a new understanding of the physical world. Coming just a few

James Tilly Matthews's air loom. Image from *Illustrations of Madness* by John Haslam, 1810.

years after the French Revolution, these discoveries had a political edge. Priestley was a staunch republican, and he published pamphlets promoting his belief that science and reason would dispel tyrannical error and superstition. In turn, conservative opponents of the new science and societal reforms compared the political turbulence to Priestley's 'wild gas': unnatural and uncontrollable.[37] Matthews's air loom entangled pneumatic and political machineries to produce a conspiracy.

The process has been repeated for every subsequent technology, from radio to television, from the phonograph to the internet. They are the results of the attempts by laymen to integrate strange and poorly understood new technologies into their model of the world; but the world bears some responsibility for the way it admits and fosters such beliefs. Matthews – an intelligent and gentle man, who later helped design Bedlam's successor to better cater to the needs of its inmates – acknowledged his disease, but continued to insist upon political malfeasance. He was probably right: later historians found evidence that he had been employed on secret missions by the state, and had been disavowed.

Matthews's closest equivalents today, outside the realm of clinical paranoia, are those who claim to be the subject of 'gang stalking' and 'mind control experiments', the most common search terms for a set of symptoms that include surveillance and persecution of individuals by persons unknown (through street harassment and coercion), electronic bugging, and telepathic suggestion. Subjects of gang stalking and mind control call themselves Targeted Individuals and gather on websites with names like Fight 'Gang Stalking', and Freedom from Covert Harassment and Surveillance. The communities that collect around such sites vastly outnumber those who receive treatment for mental illnesses; indeed, resistance to treatment, and the embrace of those who share their beliefs, is one of the core components of such groups. Targeted Individuals tell much the same story as Matthews: unknown actors, using the latest technology, are at work to influence and control them. But unlike Matthews, they have a community around them – a culture – that justifies and upholds their beliefs.

This is what troubles the clinical definition of a delusion, which makes an exemption for beliefs 'accepted by other members of the person's culture or subculture'.[38] Those that the psychiatric establishment would have classified as delusional can 'cure' themselves of their delusions by seeking out and joining an online community of like minds. Any opposition to this worldview can be dismissed as a cover-up of the truth of their experience, supported by fellow Targeted

Individuals. Moreover, there is the possibility that confirmation of their beliefs provides better care for individuals than the stark opposition, disgust and fear emanating from the rest of society. A group characterised by its distrust of others has co-opted network technology to create its own dynamic, complex, and informative community that is mutually supportive and self-sustaining. It has separated itself from the medical and social mainstream in order to build a world in which its own understanding is validated and valued.

The same pattern recurs across different, but related groups. Morgellons is the name of a self-diagnosed medical condition that has troubled the medical profession for years. Its sufferers report persistently itchy skin with fibres poking out of their body. Multiple studies have concluded that Morgellons is a psychological rather than physical condition, but sufferers, through the internet, organise conferences and lobbying groups.[39] Others claim that the electromagnetic waves produced by mobile phones, Wi-Fi hotspots, and power lines are making them ill. Electromagnetic hypersensitivity, some claim, afflicts 5 per cent of the US population, causing untold misery. Victims build themselves rooms lined with foil, known as Faraday cages, to keep out the waves; or they move to the National Radio Quiet Zone in West Virginia, a scientific preserve devoid of radio signals.[40]

Self-confirming groups, from Targeted Individuals to Morgellons sufferers, and 9/11 truthers to Tea Partiers, seem to be a hallmark of the new dark age. What they reveal is what the chemtrailers show directly: that our ability to describe the world is a product of the tools at our disposal. We're all looking at the same world and seeing radically different things. And we have built ourselves a system that reinforces that effect, an automated populism that gives people what they want, all of the time.

If you log onto social media and start searching for information about vaccines, you'll quickly find your way to anti-vaccination opinions. And once exposed to those sources of information, other conspiracies – chemtrailers, flat earthers, 9/11 truthers – are promoted into the feed. Quickly, these opinions start to feel like the majority: an endless echo chamber of supportive opinion, no matter what the subject matter. What happens when our desire to know more and more about the world collides with a system that will continue to match its answers to any possible question, without resolution?

If you're searching for support for your views online, you will find it. And moreover, you will be fed a constant stream of validation: more and more information, of a more and more extreme and polarising nature. This is how men's rights activists graduate to white nationalism, and how disaffected Muslim youths fall towards violent jihadism. This is algorithmic radicalisation, and it works in the service of the extremists themselves, who know that polarisation of society ultimately serves their aims.

A month after the *Charlie Hebdo* attacks in Paris in January 2015, *Dabiq*, the online magazine of the Islamic State of Iraq and the Levant, published its seventh issue, containing an editorial outlining the group's strategy. It built upon ISIL's previous declarations, promoting sectarianism while condemning coexistence and collaboration between different religions.[41] In 2006, Al-Qaeda in Iraq, the precursor to ISIL, attacked and destroyed the Al-Askari Mosque in Samarra, among the holiest sites in Shia Islam – one of many acts of deliberate provocation that triggered the still-ongoing civil war in the country. Since its emergence in 2014, ISIL has expanded this approach to the entire planet: by claiming responsibility for terrorist attacks around the globe, the group hopes to trigger a backlash against Muslim communities in the West, polarising societies and creating a violent spiral of alienation and retribution.[42]

ISIL calls the space of coexistence and cooperation between Muslims and other communities 'the gray zone', and has vowed to destroy it. By pitting Muslim traditions against one another, and non-Muslim majorities against their fellow citizens, they seek to portray themselves as the only protectors of true Islam, and the Caliphate as the only place where Muslims can be truly safe. For this strategy to succeed, it requires the majority of people to abandon the gray zone under the relentless pressure of violence and paranoia, and to submit to a black-and-white vision of the world that admits no doubt and uncertainty.

On the other side of the territory, the term 'gray zone' has been deployed to describe the most contemporary form of warfare, which exists just below the threshold of conventional armed conflict. Gray zone warfare is characterised by unconventional tactics, including cyberattacks, propaganda and political warfare, economic coercion and sabotage, and sponsorship of armed proxy fighters, all shrouded in a cloud of misinformation and deception.[43] Russia's use of 'little green men' in the invasion of eastern Ukraine and Crimea, China's expansion in the South China Sea, and Iran and Saudi Arabia's proxy war in Syria all point to an evolution of warfare defined by ambiguity and uncertainty. Nobody is clear as to who is fighting who; everything is deniable. Just as the US military is one of the most advanced planners for the realities of climate change, so the military planners at West Point and the General Staff Academy are at the forefront of recognising the cloudy realities of the new dark age.

What if we choose to appropriate the gray zone for ourselves? Somewhere between the jihadis and the military strategists, between war and peace, between black and white, the gray zone is where most of us live today. The gray zone is the best descriptor for a landscape inundated with unprovable facts and provable falsehoods that nevertheless stalk, zombie-like, through conversations, cajoling and persuading. The gray zone is the slippery, almost ungraspable terrain we now find ourselves in as a result of our vastly extended technological tools for knowledge making. It is a world of limited knowability and existential doubt, horrifying to the extremist and the conspiracy theorist alike. In this world we are forced to acknowledge the narrow extent of empirical reckoning and the poor returns on overwhelming flows of information.

The gray zone cannot be defeated. It cannot be drained or overrun – it is already overflowing. The conspiracy theory is the dominant narrative and the lingua franca of the times: properly read, it really does explain everything. In the gray zone, the contrails are both chemtrails and the early warning signs of global warming: they can be each of these things at the same time. In the gray zone, the exhaust fumes of industrial chimneys mingle with the free molecules of the upper atmosphere, animating the natural and unnatural in Brownian motions of uncertain provenance. The fibrous strands that poke through the skin of Morgellons sufferers are trace elements of fibre-optic cables, and the electromagnetic vibrations of cellphone towers transmitting high-frequency financial data. In the gray zone, the setting sun refracts through the haze of airborne particulates, and the earth really is out of kilter: we're just prepared to admit it now.

Living consciously in the gray zone, if we should choose to do so, allows us to sample from the myriad of explanations that our limited cognition stretches like a mask over the vibrating half-truths of the world. It is a better approximation of reality than any rigid binary encoding can ever hope to be – an acknowledgement that all our apprehensions are approximations, and all the more powerful for being so. The gray zone allows us to make peace with the otherwise-irreconcilable, conflicting worldviews that prevent us from taking meaningful action in the present.

9

Concurrency

On the screen, a man's hands slowly rotate a box of twenty-four *Cars*-branded Kinder Eggs. He removes the polythene wrapper and rotates it, carefully lifting it to show the top and the bottom of the box. The video cuts to a dozen of the eggs neatly arranged on a table. The pair of hands picks one up and peels off the red and silver foil wrapper, revealing the chocolate egg inside. The egg is cracked to free a small plastic barrel, which, when opened, contains a small plastic toy. If the toy comes with stickers or other attachments, these are carefully applied, and the toy is slowly manipulated in front of the camera, all to the gentle sounds of tearing foil, cracking chocolate, and peeling plastic. After it has been fully appreciated, the egg and its contents are set aside, and the process is repeated for the next egg, and the next, until all have been opened. After a brief panning shot of all the toys, the video ends. It lasts seven minutes, and on YouTube it has been viewed 26 million times.

Kinder Eggs are an Italian sweet consisting of a milk and white chocolate shell containing a packaged plastic toy. Since their introduction in 1974, they have been sold in their millions worldwide – although they are banned in the United States, which prohibits sweets with objects inside. *Cars*, a 2006 Disney movie featuring the animated adventures of Lightning McQueen and his vehicular friends, grossed $450 million worldwide and has spawned two sequels so far, as well as near-infinite promotional tie-ins – including Kinder Eggs. So why of all sweets and all the product promos in the world does this one deserve such a reverential review?

It doesn't, of course. It's not special. The video, titled 'Cars 2 Silver Lightning McQueen Racer Surprise Eggs Disney Pixar Zaini Silver Racers by ToyCollector' is just one of millions and millions of 'surprise egg' videos on YouTube. Every video follows the same theme: there's an egg; it's got a surprise in it; the surprise is revealed. But from such a simple premise, an infinity of combinations flows. There are more Kinder Egg videos of course, in every possible flavour: superhero eggs and Disney eggs and Christmas eggs and so on and so forth. And then there are knock-off, Kinder-alike eggs and Easter eggs and eggs made of Play-Doh and Lego eggs and balloon eggs and on and on. There are egg-like objects, such as toy garages or doll's houses that can be opened to reveal their contents with the same hushed awe. There are surprise egg videos that last for more than an hour, and there are more surprise egg videos than any human being could watch in an entire lifetime.

Unboxing videos have been a staple of the internet since decent video streaming became a possibility. Originating in the tech community, they fetishise new products and the experience of unpacking them: lingering close-ups of iPhones and games consoles as they emerge from their packaging. Around 2013, the trend spread to children's toys, and something weird started to happen. Children exposed to the videos would lock on to them with a laser-like focus and endlessly reloop them in the way that previous generations wore out tapes of their favourite Disney movies. The younger the children, the less the actual content seems to matter. The repetition of the process, together with the bright colours and the constant sense of revelation, seems to transfix them. On YouTube, they could surf through hours and hours of such videos, continuously buoyed up by reassuring repetition and endless surprises, their desires constantly fed by the system's recommendation algorithms.[1]

Children's television, particularly that aimed at preschool children, always seems odd to adults. Before it disappeared

from mainstream broadcasts and took up a new life on dedicated digital channels and online, the last great controversy of
the kids' broadcast era was Teletubbies, which depicted five
baby–bear–creatures with aerials on their heads and television
screens in their bellies bumbling around green fields and hills,
playing games and taking naps. The show was a huge success,
but it also bothered people who thought that kids' TV should
in some way be educational. The Teletubbies communicated in
a simplified 'goo-goo' language, which parents and newspapers thought would inhibit children's development. In fact, the
Teletubbies' language had been developed by speech scientists
and had its own internal logic. It also included many of the
themes that would be automated by the surprise egg videos:
call-and-response setups and cries of 'again, again' when a
sequence was about to be repeated.[2] What struck adults as
bizarre, nonsensical, and somewhere between boring and
threatening, created a safe and reassuring world for small children. Knowingly or unknowingly, it is these psychological
traits that have made surprise egg videos and their kin so
popular on YouTube today. But in their combination of child-
ish appeal, promised reward, and algorithmic variation, they
are also what makes the videos so terrifying.

YouTube recommendation algorithms work by identifying
what viewers like. Entirely new and uncategorised content has
to go it alone on the network, existing in a kind of limbo that
can only be disturbed by incoming links and outside recommendations. But if it finds an audience, if it starts to collect
views, the algorithms may deign to place it among their recom-
mended videos – featuring it on the sidebar of other videos and
boosting it to regular viewers, thus increasing its 'discoverabil-
ity'. Even better, if it comes with a description, if it's properly
titled and tagged to identify it in an algorithmically friendly
way, the system can group it with other similar videos. It's
pretty simple: if you like that, you'll like this, and down the
rabbit hole you go. You can even set the website to autoplay,

so that when one video ends, the next one in the recommendation queue will play, and so on to eternity. Kids generate
recommendation profiles pretty quickly, and they intensify fast
when children lock onto a particular kind of video and replay
it over and over again. The algorithms love that: it identifies a
clear need, and they attempt to feed it.

On the other side of the screen, you have people making the
videos. Making videos is a business, and it comes with one
simple incentive: get more views, and you get more money.
YouTube, a Google company, is partnered with AdSense, also
a Google company. Alongside – and increasingly within,
before, after, and even during – videos, AdSense serves adver-
tisements. When they get views on the adverts that accompany
the videos, the creators get paid – usually in 'cost per mille'
(CPM, or per thousand views). A specific creator's CPM varies
a lot, because not all videos and not all views are accompanied
by ads, and the CPM rate itself can change depending on a
variety of factors. But videos can be worth a fortune: 'Gangnam
Style', the Korean pop hit that was the first to break 1 billion
views on YouTube, earned $8 million dollars from AdSense
from its first 1.23 billion views, or about 0.65 cents per view.[3]
You don't have to have Gangnam-level success to make a
living from YouTube, although it's obviously easier to get
higher returns by making more and more videos, trying to get
them in front of more and more eyeballs – and targeting
markets, like children, that watch videos over and over again.

YouTube's official guidelines state that the site is for ages
thirteen and up, with parental permission required for those
below eighteen, but there's nothing to stop a thirteen-year-old
accessing it. Moreover, there's no need to have an account at
all; like most websites, YouTube tracks unique visitors by
their address, browser and device profile, and behaviour, and
it can build a detailed demographic and preference profile to
feed the recommendation engines without the viewer ever
consciously submitting any information about themselves.

That applies even if the viewer is a three-year-old child plonked in front of their parent's iPad and mashing the screen with a balled-up fist.

The frequency with which such a situation occurs is obvious in the site's own viewer statistics. Ryan's Toy Review, a channel specialising in unboxing videos and other kids' tropes, is the sixth most popular channel on the platform, only just behind Justin Bieber and the WWE.[4] At one point in 2016, it was the most popular. Ryan is six years old, has been a YouTube star since he was three, and has 9.6 million subscribers. His family is estimated to earn around $1 million a month from their videos.[5] Next in the list is Little Baby Bum, which specialises in nursery rhymes for preschoolers. With just 515 videos, they have accrued 11.5 million subscribers and 13 billion views.

Children's YouTube is a vast and lucrative industry because on-demand video is catnip to both parents and their kids – and thus to content creators and advertisers as well. Small children, mesmerised by familiar characters and songs, bright colours, and soothing sounds, can be kept quiet and entertained for hours. The common tactic of assembling many nursery rhyme or cartoon episodes into hours-long compilations, and making a virtue of their length in video descriptions and titles, points to the amount of time some kids are spending with them.

As a result, YouTube broadcasters have developed a huge number of tactics to draw parents' and children's attention to their videos, and the advertising revenues that accompany them. One of them, as demonstrated in the surprise egg mash-ups, is a kind of keyword excess, cramming as many relevant search terms into a video title as possible. The result is what is known as word salad, a random sample from just a single channel reading, 'Surprise Play Doh Eggs Peppa Pig Stamper Cars Pocoyo Minecraft Smurfs Kinder Play Doh Sparkle Brilho'; 'Cars Screamin' Banshee Eats Lightning McQueen Disney

Pixar'; 'Disney Baby Pop Up Pals Easter Eggs SURPRISE'; '150 Giant Surprise Eggs Kinder CARS StarWars Marvel Avengers LEGO Disney Pixar Nickelodeon Peppa'; and 'Choco Toys Surprise Mashems & Fashems DC Marvel Avengers Batman Hulk IRON MAN'.[6]

This unintelligible assemblage of brand names, characters and keywords points to the real audience for the descriptions: not the viewer, but the algorithms that decide who sees which videos. The more keywords you can cram into a title, the more likely it is that your video will find its way into the recommendations, or even better, simply autoplay when a similar video finishes. The result is millions of videos with cascading, nonsensical titles – but then, YouTube is a video platform, and neither the algorithms nor the intended audience care about meaning.

There are other ways to get views to your channel too, and the simplest and most time-honoured of these is simply to copy and pirate other content. A quick search for 'Peppa Pig' on YouTube yields more than 10 million results – and the front page is almost entirely from the verified 'Peppa Pig Official Channel', run by the show's creators. But quickly the results start to fill up with other channels, although the way YouTube uniformly displays its search results makes it hard to notice. One such channel is the unverified Play Go Toys, which has 1,800 subscribers and consists of pirated Peppa Pig episodes, unboxing videos, as well as videos of official Peppa Pig episodes being acted out with branded toys, titled as if they are the actual episodes.[7] Mixed in among them are videos of – presumably – the channel owner's own children playing with the toys, and going to the park.

While this channel is merely indulging in a little harmless piracy, it shows how the structure of YouTube facilitates the delamination of content and author, and how this impacts our awareness and trust of its source. One of the traditional roles of branded content is that it is a trusted source. Whether it's

Peppa Pig on children's TV or a Disney movie, whatever one's feelings about the industrial model of entertainment production, these products are carefully produced and monitored so that kids are essentially safe watching them, and can be trusted as such. This no longer applies when brand and content are disassociated by the platform, and so known and trusted content provides a seamless gateway to unverified and potentially harmful content.

This is the exact same process as the delamination of trusted news media on Facebook feeds and in Google results that is currently wreaking such havoc on our cognitive and political systems. When a fact-checked *New York Times* article is shared on Facebook or pops up in the 'related content' box of a Google Search, the link appears almost identical to one shared from NewYorkTimesPolitics.com, a website built by a teenager in Eastern Europe and entirely filled with invented, inflammatory and highly partisan stories about the US election.[8] We'll return to those sites in a bit, but the result on YouTube is that it's incredibly easy for strange and inappropriate content to appear intermingled with – and almost indistinguishable from – known sources.

Another striking example of the weirdness of children's video is the Finger Family. In 2007, a YouTube user called Leehosok uploaded a video in which two sets of finger puppets dance to the tinny, background sound of a recorded nursery rhyme: 'Daddy finger, daddy finger, where are you? Here I am, here I am, how do you do?' and so on through mommy finger, brother finger, sister finger, and baby finger. While the song clearly predated the video, this is its debut on YouTube.[9] As of late 2017, there are at least 17 million versions of the Finger Family Song on YouTube. Like the surprise egg videos, they cover every possible genre, with billions and billions of aggregated views. Little Baby Bum's version alone has 31 million views. One on the popular channel ChuChu has half a billion. The simplicity of the premise makes it ripe for automation: a basic piece of software can top an animated hand with any object or character, so Superhero Finger Families, Disney Finger Families, fruit and gummy bear and lollipop Finger Families, and their infinite varieties, spill down the page, accumulating millions and millions more views. Stock animations, audio tracks, and lists of keywords are assembled in their thousands to produce an endless stream of videos. It becomes difficult to get a purchase on such processes without simply listing their endless variations, but it's important to grasp how vast this system is, and how indeterminate its actions, process, and audience. It's also international: there are variations of Finger Family and Learn Colours videos for Tamil epics and Malaysian cartoons that are unlikely to pop up in any anglophone search results. This very indeterminacy and reach is key to this system's existence, and its implications. Its dimensionality makes it difficult to grasp, or even to really think about.

The view numbers of these videos must be taken under serious advisement. Just as a huge number of these videos are created by automated pieces of software – bots – they are also viewed by bots, and even commented on by bots. The arms race between bot makers and Google's machine learning algorithms is one that Google lost a long time ago across most of its properties. It's also one that it has no real reason to take seriously: while it may publicly denounce and downplay the activity of bots, they massively magnify the number of adverts shown, and thus the revenue Google generates. But that complicity shouldn't obscure the fact that there are also many actual children, plugged into iPhones and tablets, watching these videos over and over again – in part accounting for the inflated view numbers – while learning to type basic search terms into the browser, or simply mashing the sidebar to bring up another video. Increasingly, voice-activated commands alone will do the job of calling up content.

The weirdness only increases when humans reappear in the loop. Pringles Tin and Incredible Hulk 3D Finger Families might be easy to understand, at least procedurally, but well-known channels with crews of human actors also begin to reproduce the same logic out of the necessity of gaining page views. At some point, it becomes impossible to determine the degree of automation that is at work, or how to parse out the gap between human and machine.

Bounce Patrol is a children's entertainment group from Melbourne, who follow in the brightly coloured tradition of pre-digital kid sensations like their fellow Australians, the Wiggles. Their YouTube channel, Bounce Patrol Kids, has almost 2 million subscribers, and they post professionally produced videos featuring their crew of human actors at the rate of about one per week.[10] Yet Bounce Patrol's productions follow closely the inhuman logic of algorithmic recommendation. The result is the deep weirdness of a group of people endlessly acting out the implications of a combination of algorithmically generated keywords: 'Halloween Finger Family & more Halloween Songs for Children Kids Halloween Songs Collection'; 'Australian Animals Finger Family Song | Finger Family Nursery Rhymes'; 'Farm Animals Finger Family and more Animals Songs | Finger Family Collection – Learn Animals Sounds'; 'Safari Animals Finger Family Song | Elephant, Lion, Giraffe, Zebra & Hippo! Wild Animals for kids'; 'Superheroes Finger Family and more Finger Family Songs! Superhero Finger Family Collection'; 'Batman Finger Family Song – Superheroes and Villains! Batman, Joker, Riddler, Catwoman'; and on and on and on. It's old-school improvisation, only the cues are being shouted out by a computer fed on the demands of a billion hyperactive toddlers. This is what content production looks like in the age of algorithmic discovery: even if you're a human, you end up impersonating the machine.

We've encountered pretty clear examples of the disturbing outcomes of full automation before, like the Amazon phone cases and rape-themed T-shirts. Nobody set out to create phone cases with drugs and medical equipment on them; it was just a deeply weird probabilistic outcome. Likewise, the case of the 'Keep Calm and Rape A Lot' T-shirts is depressing – and distressing – but comprehensible. Nobody set out to create these shirts; they just paired an unchecked list of verbs and pronouns with an online image generator. It's quite possible that none of these shirts ever physically existed, or were ever purchased or worn, and thus that no harm was done. It's significant, however, that the people creating these items failed to notice, and neither did their distributor. They literally had no idea what they were doing.

What starts to become apparent is that the scale and logic of the system is complicit in these outputs, and compels us to think through their implications. These outcomes entrain the wider social effects of previous examples, such as racial and gender bias in big data and machine intelligence–driven systems, and in the same manner they have no easy, or even preferable, solutions.

How about a video entitled 'Wrong Heads Disney Wrong Ears Wrong Legs Kids Learn Colors Finger Family 2017 Nursery Rhymes'? The title alone confirms its automated provenance. The origin of the 'Wrong Heads' trope will remain a mystery for now. But it's easy to imagine, as with the Finger Family Song, that somewhere there is a totally original and harmless version that made enough kids laugh that it started to climb the algorithmic rankings, until it made it onto the word salad lists. There, it would have combined with Learn Colors, Finger Family, Nursery Rhymes, and all of these other tropes – not merely as words but as images, processes, and actions – to be mixed into this particular assemblage.

The video consists of the Finger Family song played over an animation of rotating character heads and bodies from Disney's *Aladdin*. Initially innocent, if mismatched, a strangeness creeps in with the appearance of a non-*Aladdin* character – Agnes, the little girl from Universal's *Despicable Me*. Agnes is the arbiter of the scene: when the heads match up, she cheers; when they don't, she bursts into floods of simulated tears. While the mechanism is clear, the result is pure pablum: the minimum of effort to produce the minimum of meaning.

The video's creator, BABYFUN TV, has produced many similar videos, all of which work in exactly the same way. The character Hope from Disney's *Inside Out* bawls through a Smurfs and Trolls head swap. Wonder Woman weeps at the X-Men. It goes on and on. BABYFUN TV only has 170 subscribers and very low view rates, but then there are thousands and thousands of channels like this. Viewing numbers on YouTube and other mass content aggregators aren't significant in the abstract, but in their accumulation. The underlying mechanism of Wrong Heads is clear, but the constant overlaying and intermixing of different tropes starts to become troubling to adult sensibilities: a growing sense of something inhuman, of the uncanny valley between us and the system producing such content. It feels like a mistake, somewhere, deeper than the surface content.

In BABYFUN's Wrong Heads videos, the same identical, scratchy digital sample of a child crying features in each video. While we might find it disturbing, it's possible – like the gurgling baby in the Teletubbies' sun – that this sound might provide some of the rhythm or cadence or relation to their own experience that actual babies are attracted to in this content. But nobody made this decision: it has been warped and stretched through algorithmic repetition and recombination in ways that nobody intended, that nobody actually wanted to happen. And what happens when this endless recirculation and magnification loops back to humans again?

Toy Freaks is a hugely popular YouTube channel – sixty-eighth on the platform, with 8.4 million subscribers – that features a father and his two daughters playing out many of the tropes we've identified so far, along the same principles as Bounce Patrol: the girls open surprise eggs, and they sing seasonal variations of the Finger Family song. As well as nursery rhymes and learning colours, Toy Freaks specialises in gross-out situations, such as food fights and filling bathtubs with fake insects. Toy Freaks has caused a degree of controversy, with many viewers feeling the videos border on abuse and exploitation – if they don't cross the line entirely – citing videos of the children vomiting, bleeding, and in pain.[11] Toy Freaks is a YouTube verified channel, although verification simply means that a channel has more than 100,000 subscribers.[12]

Toy Freaks is almost tame compared to its imitators. A Vietnamese variant called Freak Family features a young girl drinking bathroom products and cutting herself with a razor.[13] Elsewhere, children fish brightly coloured automated weapons out of muddy rivers. A live-action Elsa from *Frozen* drowns in a swimming pool. Spiderman invades a Thai beach resort and teaches colours through the medium of gaffer tape, wrapped around bikini-clad teenagers. Policemen wearing outsize baby heads and rubber Joker masks terrorise patrons at a Russian water park. It just goes on and on. The amplification of tropes in popular, human-led channels such as Toy Freaks leads to them being endlessly repeated across the network in increasingly outlandish and distorted recombinations. But there's an undercurrent of violence and degradation – one that doesn't, we might still hope, come from the dark imaginations of grossout loving, actual children.

Sections of YouTube, like the rest of the internet, have long played host to a culture of violent affrontery, in which nothing is sacred. YouTube Poop is one such subculture, featuring mostly harmless, if deliberately offensive, remixes of other videos, overdubbing sweary rants and drug references onto children's TV shows. It's often the first level of weirdness that parents encounter too. One official Peppa Pig video, in which Peppa goes to the dentist, seems to be popular – although, confusingly, what appears to be the real episode is only available on an unofficial channel. In the official timeline, Peppa is appropriately reassured by a kindly dentist. In one version appearing high in the results of a 'peppa pig dentist' search, she is basically tortured, with teeth bloodily removed to the sounds of screaming. Disturbing Peppa Pig videos, which tend towards extreme violence and fear, with Peppa eating her father or drinking bleach, are widespread. Many are obviously parodies, or even satires of themselves: indeed, previous controversies around them have resulted in them receiving protection from copyright claims under that legal right. They're not setting out to terrorise children – not really – even when they do. But they are, and they're also setting off a whole chain of emergent outcomes in response.

Simply attributing YouTube weirdness and terror to the actions of trolls and dark humourists doesn't really cut it. In the video cited, Peppa endures her horrendous dental experience, and then she transforms into a series of Iron Man/pig/robot hybrids and performs the Learn Colours dance. Whatever agency is at play here is far from clear: the video starts with a trollish Peppa parody, but later syncs into the kind of automated repetition of tropes we've seen before. It's not just trolls, or just automation; it's not just human actors playing out an algorithmic logic, or algorithms mindlessly responding to recommendation engines. It's a vast and almost completely hidden matrix of interactions between desires and rewards, technologies and audiences, tropes and masks.

Other examples seem less accidental, and more intentional. One whole strand of video production involves automated recuts of video game footage, reprogrammed with superheroes or cartoon characters instead of soldiers and gangsters. Spiderman breaks the legs of the Grim Reaper and Elsa from *Frozen* and buries them up to their neck in a pit. The Teletubbies – yes, them again – reprise Grand Theft Auto in motorcycle chases and bank heist shoot-outs. Dinosaurs, pierced with ice creams and lollipops, destroy city blocks. Nurses eat faeces to the sound of the Finger Family Song. Nothing makes sense and everything is wrong. Familiar characters, nursery tropes, keyword salad, full automation, violence, and the very stuff of kids' worst dreams combine in channel after channel after channel of undifferentiated content, churned out at the rate of hundreds of new videos every week. Cheap technologies and cheaper distribution methods are put in the service of industrialised nightmare production.

What does it take to make these videos, and who makes them? How can we even know? Just because there aren't human actors doesn't mean there aren't people involved. Animation is easy these days, and online content for children is one of the simplest ways of making money from 3-D animation, because the aesthetic standards are lower and independent production can profit through scale. It uses existing and easily available content (such as character models and motion-capture libraries), and it can be repeated and revised endlessly and mostly meaninglessly because the algorithms don't discriminate – and neither do the kids. Cheap animations might be the work of a small studio of half a dozen people low on other work; they might be huge warehouses of slave labour, sweatshops for video production; they might be the product of a rogue dumb AI, an experimental project left in a box somewhere that's just kept on running, racking up millions of views in the process. If it were some state power or network of paedophiles deliberately attempting to poison a generation – as some online commentators believe – we wouldn't know. It might just be what the machine wants to do. Raising the question online simply tips one down another rabbit hole of conspiracy and trauma. The network is certainly incapable of diagnosing itself, just as the system is incapable of tempering its demands.

Kids are being traumatised by these videos. They watch their favourite cartoon characters acting out scenes of murder and rape.[14] Parents have reported behaviour changes in their children after watching disturbing videos. These network effects cause real and probably lasting damage. To expose young children – some very young – to violent and disturbing scenes is a form of abuse. But it would be a mistake to deal with this issue as a simple matter of 'won't somebody think of the children' hand-wringing. Obviously this content is inappropriate; obviously there are bad actors out there; obviously some of these videos should be removed. Obviously, too, this raises questions of fair use, appropriation, free speech and so on. But a reading of this situation only through this lens fails to fully grasp the mechanisms being deployed, and is thus incapable of thinking its implications in totality and responding accordingly.

What characterises many of the strange videos out there is the level of horror and violence on display. Some of the time it's kids being gross, and some of the time it's trollish provocation; most of the time it seems deeper, and more unconscious than that. The internet has a way of amplifying and enabling many of our latent desires – in fact, it's what it seems to do best. It's possible to argue this tendency towards the positive: the efflorescence of network technologies has allowed many to realise and express themselves in ways never before possible, increasing their individual agency and liberating forms of identity and sexuality that have never spoken so vibrantly and in so many diverse voices as today. But here, where millions of children and adults play for hours, days, weeks, months and years – where they reveal, through their actions, their most vulnerable desires to predatory algorithms – that tendency seems overwhelmingly violent and destructive.

Accompanying the violence are untold levels of exploitation: not of children because they are children, but of children because they are powerless. Automated reward systems like YouTube algorithms necessitate exploitation to sustain their revenue, encoding the worst aspects of rapacious, free market capitalism. No controls are possible without collapsing the entire system. Exploitation is encoded into the systems we are building, making it harder to see, harder to think and explain, harder to counter and defend against. What makes it disturbing is that this is not a science fictional exploitative future of AI overlords and fully robot workforces in the factories, but exploitation in the playroom, in the living room, in the home and the pocket, being driven by exactly the same computational mechanisms. And humans are degraded on both sides of the equation: both those who, numbed and terrified, watch the videos; and those who, low paid or unpaid, exploited or abused, make them. In between sit mostly automated corporations, taking the profit from both sides.

These videos, wherever they are made, however they come to be made, and whatever their own conscious intentions, are bred by a system that was consciously intended to show videos to children for profit. The unconsciously generated, emergent outcomes of this are all over the place.

To expose children to this content is abuse. This is not the same as the debatable but undoubtedly real effects of film or video game violence on teenagers, or the effects of pornography or extreme images on young minds. Those are important debates, but they're not even what is being discussed here. At stake on YouTube is very young children, effectively from birth, being deliberately targeted with content that will traumatise and disturb them, via networks that are extremely vulnerable to exactly this form of abuse. It's not about intention, but about a kind of violence inherent in the combination of digital systems and capitalist incentives.

The system is complicit in the abuse, and YouTube and Google are complicit in that system. The architecture they have built to extract the maximum revenue from online video is being hacked by unknown persons to abuse children – perhaps not even deliberately, but at a massive scale. The owners of these platforms have an absolute responsibility to deal with that, just as they have a responsibility to deal with the radicalisation of (mostly) young (mostly) men via extremist videos – of any political persuasion. They have so far shown absolutely no inclination to do this, which is despicable but sadly unsurprising. But the question of how they can respond without shutting down the services themelves, and many of the systems that resemble them, has no easy answer.

This is a deeply dark time, in which the structures we have built to expand the sphere of our communications and discourses are being used against us – all of us – in systematic and automated ways. It is hard to keep faith with the network when it produces horrors such as these. While it is tempting to dismiss YouTube's wilder examples as trolling, of which a significant number certainly are, that fails to account for the sheer volume of content weighted in a particularly grotesque direction. It presents many and complexly entangled dangers, including that such events will be used as justification for increased control over the internet, sweeping censorship, surveillance, and crackdowns on freedom of speech. In this, YouTube's children's crisis reflects the wider cognitive crisis produced by automated systems, weak machine intelligence, social and scientific networks, and the wider culture – with its own matching set of easy scapegoats and cloudier, entangled substructures.

In the final weeks of the 2016 US election, the international media descended on the small city of Veles, in the Republic of Macedonia. A short hour's drive from the capital Skopje, Veles is a former industrial centre of just 44,000 people, but it received attention at the highest levels. In the last days of the campaign, even President Obama became obsessed with the place. It had come to epitomise a new media ecosystem in which, he said, 'everything is true and nothing is true'.[15]

In 2012, two brothers from Veles set up a website called HealthyFoodHouse.com. They stuffed it with weight-loss tips and recommendations for alternative remedies, culled from wherever they could find them on the internet, and over the years it drew more and more visitors. Their Facebook page has 2 million subscribers, and 10 million come to the site every month, drawn, via Google, to articles with titles like 'How To Get Rid of The Folds On Your Back And Sides in 21 Days' and '5 Soothing Essential Oils To Rub On Your Sciatic Nerve For Instant Pain Relief'. With the visitors, the AdSense earnings started rolling in: the brothers became local celebrities and spent their money on fast cars and bottles of champagne in Veles's nightclubs.

Other kids in Veles followed suit, many dropping out of school in order to devote their time to filling their burgeoning portfolios of websites with plagiarised and specious content. In early 2016, the same kids discovered that the biggest and most voracious consumers of news – any news at all – were Trump supporters, who gathered in large and easily targeted Facebook groups. Like the unverified channels of YouTube, their websites were indistinguishable – and no more or less authoritative – than the thousands of alternative news sites popping up across the internet in response to the Trumpian renunciation of mainstream media. More often than not, the distinction didn't even matter: as we've seen, all sources look the same on social networks, and clickbait headlines combined with confirmation bias acted on conservative audiences in much the same way that YouTube algorithms responded to 'Elsa Spiderman Finger Family Learn Colors Live Action' strings. Repeated clicks just pushed such stories higher in Facebook's own rankings. A few brave teens tried the same tricks on Bernie Sanders supporters, with less impressive results. 'Bernie Sanders supporters are among the smartest people I've seen,' said one. 'They don't believe anything. The post must have proof for them to believe it.'[16]

For a few brief months, headlines claiming that Hillary Clinton had been indicted or that the Pope had declared his support for Trump brought a trickle of wealth to Veles: a few more BMWs appeared in its streets, and more champagne was sold in its nightclubs. The American media, for its part, decried the 'amoral' attitudes and 'cocksure demeanours' of

Macedonian youth.[17] In doing so, it ignored, or failed to think, the histories and complex interrelationships that fuelled Macedonia's fake news boom – and in turn, failed to understand the wider, systemic implications of similar events.

Veles used to be officially known as Tito's Veles, when the city belonged not to the Republic of Macedonia, but to Yugoslavia. When that country and its networks fell apart, Macedonia managed to avoid the most bloody conflicts that tore apart the central Balkan states. In 2001, a UN-backed agreement made peace between the majority government and ethnic Albanian separatists, and in 2005 the country applied to join the European Union. But it faced one major impediment: a naming dispute with its southern neighbour, Greece. According to the Greeks, the name Macedonia belongs to the Greek province of the same name, and they accused the new Macedonians of planning to take it over. The dispute has simmered for over a decade, preventing the Republic's accession to the EU and subsequently to NATO, and causing it to slide away from further democratic reforms.

Frustrated at the lack of progress, divisions in society have deepened, and ethnic nationalisms have revived. One outcome has been the ruling party's policy of 'antiquisation': the deliberate appropriation and even fabrication of a Macedonian history.[18] Airports, train stations and stadiums were renamed after Alexander the Great and Philip of Macedon – both figures from Greek history who have little connection to Slavic Macedonia – as well as other places and figures from Greek Macedonia. Huge areas of Skopje were bulldozed and rebuilt in a more classical style, a programme costing hundreds of millions of Euros in a country with some of the lowest employment figures on the continent. The centre of the city now features massive statues officially referred to as simply the Warrior and the Warrior on Horseback – but known to everyone as Philip and Alexander. For a while, the country's official flag depicted the Vergina Sun, a symbol found on Philip's tomb

in Vergina, in northern Greece. These and other appropria-
tions have been supported by nationalist rhetoric, which has
been used to suppress minority and centrist parties. Politicians
and historians have received death threats for advocating a
compromise with Greece.[19] In short, Macedonia is a country
that has attempted to construct its whole identity on the basis
of fake news.

In 2015, a series of leaks revealed that the same government
pushing the antiquisation programme also sponsored an
extensive wiretapping operation by the country's security
services, which illegally recorded some 670,000 conversations
from more than 20,000 telephone numbers over more than a
decade.[20] Unlike in the United States, the United Kingdom, and
other democracies found to be eavesdropping on their own
citizens, the leaks led to the collapse of the government,
followed by the release of the intercepts to their subjects.
Journalists, members of parliament, activists and employees of
humanitarian NGOs received CDs containing hours of their
own most intimate conversations.[21] But just like everywhere
else, these revelations didn't change anything – they simply
fuelled more paranoia. Those on the right accused foreign
powers of orchestrating the scandal, doubling down on the
nationalist rhetoric. Trust in government and democratic institutions fell to a new low.

In such a climate, is it any surprise that the young people
of Veles should take wholeheartedly to a programme of disin-
formation, particularly when it is rewarded by the very
systems of modernity they have been told are the future? Fake
news is not a product of the internet. Rather, it is the manipulation of new technologies by the same interests that have
always sought to manipulate information to their own ends.
It is the democratisation of propaganda, in that ever more
actors can now play the role of propagandist. And ultimately
it is an amplifier of a division that exists already in society,
just as gang stalking websites are amplifiers for schizophrenia.

But the objectification of Veles, while ignoring the historical and social context that formed it, is symptomatic of a collective failure to comprehend the mechanisms we have built and with which we have surrounded ourselves – and of the fact that we are still seeking clear answers to cloudy problems.

In the months after the election, other actors were accused of its manipulation. The most popular scapegoat was Russia, the go-to bad guy for most contemporary shady tricks, particularly when these emerge from the internet. Following the Russian pro-democracy protests of 2011, which were largely organised through the internet, allies of Vladimir Putin became increasingly active online, setting up armies of pro-Kremlin sock puppets on social media. One such operation, known as the Internet Research Agency, employs hundreds of Russians in St Petersburg, from where they coordinate a campaign of blog posts, comments, viral videos and infographics pushing the Kremlin's line both within Russia and internationally.[22] These 'troll farms' are the electronic equivalent of Russia's gray zone military campaigns: elusive, deniable, and deliberately confusing. There are also thousands of them, at every administrative level: a constant background chatter of misinformation and malevolence.

In trying to support Putin's party in Russia, and to smear opponents in countries like Ukraine, the troll farms quickly learned that no matter how many posts and comments they produced, it was pretty hard to convince people to change their minds on any given subject. And so they started doing the next best thing: clouding the argument. In the US election, Russian trolls posted in support of Clinton, Sanders, Romney, and Trump, just as Russian security agencies seem to have had a hand in leaks against both sides. The result is that first the internet, and then the wider political discourse, becomes tainted and polarised. As one Russian activist described it, 'The point is to spoil it, to create the atmosphere of hate, to make it so stinky that normal people won't want to touch it.'[23]

Unidentified forces have influenced other elections too, each laced with conspiracy and paranoia. In the run-up to the EU referendum in the United Kingdom, a fifth of the electorate believed that the poll would be rigged in collusion with the security services.[24] Leave campaigners advised voters to take pens with them to vote, in order to ensure pencil votes weren't erased.[25] In the aftermath, attention focused on the work of Cambridge Analytica – a company owned by Robert Mercer, former AI engineer, hedge fund billionaire and Donald Trump's most powerful supporter. Cambridge Analytica's employees have described what they do as 'psychological warfare' – leveraging vast amounts of data in order to target and persuade voters. And of course it turned out that the election really was rigged by the security services, in the way that rigging actually happens: the board and staff of Cambridge Analytica, which 'donated' its services to the Leave campaign, includes former British military personnel – notably the former director of psychological operations for British forces in Afghanistan.[26] In both the EU referendum and the US election, military contractors used military intelligence technologies to influence democratic elections in their own countries.

Carole Cadwalladr, a journalist who has repeatedly highlighted the links between the Leave campaign, the US Right, and shadowy data firms, wrote,

> Try to follow this on a daily basis and it's one long headspin: a spider's web of relationships and networks of power and patronage and alliances that spans the Atlantic and embraces data firms, thinktanks and media outlets. It is about complicated corporate structures in obscure jurisdictions, involving offshore funds funnelled through the black-box algorithms of the platform tech monopolists. That it's eye-wateringly complicated and geographically diffuse is not a coincidence. Confusion is the charlatan's friend, noise its accessory. The babble on Twitter is a convenient cloak of darkness.[27]

Just as in the US election, attention turned to Russia as well. Researchers found that the Internet Research Agency had been on a Brexit tweeting spree, in characteristically divisive fashion. One account purporting to be a Texan republican, but suspended by Twitter for links to the Agency, tweeted, 'I hope UK after #BrexitVote will start to clean their land from muslim invasion!' and 'UK voted to leave future European Caliphate! #BrexitVote'. The same account had previously appeared on the front pages of the tabloid newspapers when it posted images purporting to show a Muslim woman ignoring victims of a terror attack in London.[28]

Beyond the 419 accounts identified as actively belonging to the Agency, untold numbers more were automated. Another report, the year after the referendum, found a network of more than 13,000 automated accounts tweeting on both sides of the debate – but eight times more likely to promote pro-Leave than pro-Remain content.[29] All 13,000 accounts were deleted by Twitter in the months after the referendum, and their origin remains unknown. According to other accounts, one-fifth of all online debate around the 2016 US election campaign was automated, and the actions of the bots measurably shifted public opinion.[30] Something is rotten in democracy when huge numbers of those participating in its debates are unaccountable and untraceable, when we cannot know who or even what they are. Their motives and their origin are entirely opaque, even as their effects on society grow exponentially. The bots are everywhere now.

In the summer of 2015, AshleyMadison.com, a dating website for married people seeking affairs, was hacked and the details of 37 million members leaked onto the internet. Digging through vast databases of explicit messages between the site's users, it rapidly became clear that for a site that promised to connect women and men directly – including guaranteeing affairs for its premium members – there was a huge discrepancy between the numbers of each gender. Of those 37 million users, just 5 million were women, and most of them had created an account and never logged on again. The exception was a hugely active cohort of some 70,000 female accounts that Ashley Madison called 'Angels'. The Angels were the ones who initiated contact with men – who had to pay to respond to them – and kept up conversations over months to keep them coming back, and paying more. The Angels, of course, were entirely automated.[31] Ashley Madison paid third parties to create millions of fake profiles in thirty-one different languages, building an elaborate system to administer and animate them. Some men spent thousands of dollars on the site – and some even had affairs in the end. But the vast majority simply spent years having explicit and fruitless conversations with pieces of software. Here is another take on the automation of dystopia: a social site where it's impossible to be social, half the participants are shadows, and participation is only possible through payment. Those exposed to the system had no way of knowing what was occurring, apart from the suspicion that something might be wrong. And it was impossible to act on that suspicion without destroying the fantasy on which the entire enterprise was assembled. The collapse of the infrastructure – the hack – revealed its bankruptcy, but it had already been made explicit in the technological framing of an abusive system.

When I first published research into the strangeness and violence of children's YouTube online, I received a rush of messages and emails from strangers who all believed they knew where the videos were coming from. Some had spent months tracking website owners and IP addresses across the web. Others had correlated live-action video locations with documented cases of abuse. The videos were coming from India, from Malaysia, from Pakistan (they were always coming from Elsewhere). They were the grooming tools of an international gang of paedophiles. They were the product of this one company. They were the output of a rogue AI. They were part of a concerted, international, and state-backed plan to corrupt

Western youth. Some of the emails were from cranks, some from dedicated researchers; all believed that they had somehow cracked the code. Most of their evaluations were convincing regarding some subset or aspect of the videos; all failed utterly when tested against their entirety.

What is common to the Brexit campaign, the US election, and the disturbing depths of YouTube is that, despite multiple suspicions, it is ultimately impossible to tell who is doing what, or what their motives and intentions are. Watching endlessly streaming videos, scrolling through walls of status updates and tweets, it's futile to attempt to discern between what's algorithmically generated nonsense or carefully crafted fake news for generating ad dollars; what's paranoid fiction, state action, propaganda, or spam; what's deliberate misinformation or well-meaning fact check. This confusion certainly serves the manipulations of Kremlin spooks and child abusers alike, but it's also broader and deeper than the concerns of any one group: it is how the world actually is. Nobody decided that this is how the world should evolve – nobody wanted the new dark age – but we built it anyway, and now we are going to have to live in it.

10

Cloud

In May 2013, Google invited a select group of around 200 guests to the Grove Hotel in Hertfordshire, England, for its annual Zeitgeist conference. Held every year since 2006, and followed by a public 'big tent' event in the hotel's grounds, the two-day gathering is intensely private, with only selected speakers' videos being released online. Over the years, the conference has featured talks by former US presidents, royalty, and pop stars, and the 2013 guest list included several heads of state and government ministers, CEOs of many of the largest European corporations, and the former chief of the British armed forces, alongside Google directors and motivational speakers. Several of the attendees, including Google's own CEO Eric Schmidt, would return to the same hotel a month later for the annual and even more secretive Bilderberg Group meeting of the world's political elite.[1] Topics in 2013 included 'Action This Day', 'Our Legacy', 'Courage in a Connected World', and 'The Pleasure Principle', with a succession of speeches urging some of the most powerful people in the world to support charity initiatives and seek their own happiness.

Schmidt himself opened the conference with a paean to the emancipatory power of technology. 'I think we're missing something,' he said, 'maybe because of the way our politics works, maybe because of the way the media works. We're not optimistic enough ... The nature of innovation, the things that are going on both at Google and globally are pretty positive for humankind and we should be much more optimistic about what's going to happen going forward.'[2]

In the discussion session that followed, in response to a question that suggested George Orwell's *1984* as a counter-example to such utopian thinking, Schmidt cited the spread of cell phones – and particularly of cell phone cameras – to illustrate how technology improved the world:

> It's very, very difficult to implement systemic evil now in an Internet age, and I'll give you an example. We were in Rwanda. Rwanda in 1994 had this terrible ... essentially genocide. 750,000 people were killed over a four-month period by machetes, which is a horrific, horrific way to do this. It required planning. People had to write it down. What I think about is in 1994, if everyone had a smartphone it would have been impossible to do that; that people would have actually noticed this was going on. The plans would have been leaked. Somebody would have figured it out and somebody would have reacted to prevent this terrible carnage.[3]

Schmidt's – and Google's – worldview is one that is entirely predicated on the belief that making something visible makes it better, and that technology is the tool to make things visible. This view, which has come to dominate the world, is not only fundamentally wrong; it is actively dangerous, both globally and in the specific instance that Schmidt states.

The wide spectrum of information that global policy makers possessed – particularly the United States, but also including the former colonial powers in the region, Belgium and France – both in the months and weeks preceding the genocide, and while it was occurring, has been exhaustively documented.[4] Multiple countries had embassy and other staff on the ground, as did NGOs, while the UN, foreign and state departments, militaries and intelligence groups all monitored the situation and withdrew personnel in response to the escalating crisis. The National Security Agency listened in to, and recorded, the now-notorious nationwide radio broadcasts calling for a 'final war' to 'exterminate the cockroaches'. (General Roméo Dallaire, the commander of the UN peacekeeping operation in Rwanda at the time of the genocide, later commented that 'simply jamming [the] broadcasts and replacing them with messages of peace and reconciliation would have had a significant impact on the course of events'.)[5] For years, the United States denied that it possessed any direct evidence of the atrocities as they were occurring, but in the trial of one Rwandan *genocidaire* in 2012, the prosecution unexpectedly produced high-resolution satellite photos shot over the country in May, June, and July of 1994, throughout the course of the 'one hundred days of genocide'.[6] The images – drawn from a much larger trove classified by the National Reconnaissance Office and the National Geospatial-Intelligence Agency – depicted roadblocks, destroyed buildings, mass graves, and even bodies lying in the streets of Butare, the former capital.[7]

The situation repeated itself in the Balkans in 1995, when CIA operatives watched the massacre of some 8,000 Muslim men and boys at Srebrenica from their situation room in Vienna via satellite.[8] Days later, photographs from a U-2 spy plane showed the freshly dug mounds of mass graves: evidence that wasn't shown to President Clinton until a month later.[9] But institutional inertia cannot really be blamed, as the kind of distributed image making that Schmidt calls for has since come to pass. Today, satellite images of mass graves are no longer the preserve of military and state intelligence agencies. Instead, before-and-after images of trenches filled with murdered bodies, such as those in the grounds of the Daryya Mosque, south of Damascus, in 2013, are available on Google Maps.[10]

In all of these cases, surveillance reveals itself as a wholly retroactive enterprise, incapable of acting in the present and entirely subservient to the established and utterly compromised interests of power. What was missing in Rwanda and Srebrenica was not evidence of an atrocity, but the willingness to act upon it. As one investigative report on the Rwandan killings noted, 'Any failure to fully appreciate the genocide stemmed from political, moral, and imaginative weaknesses, not informational ones.'[11] This statement feels like it could be the punchline to this book: a damning indictment of our ability to either ignore or seek more raw information, when the problem is not with our knowing, but with our doing.

Such a denunciation of the degraded power of the image should not, however, be taken as support of Schmidt's position that more images or more information, however democratically and distributedly generated, would have helped. The very technology that Schmidt insists upon as a counter to systemic evil, the smartphone, has been shown again and again to amplify violence and expose individuals to its ravages. Following Kenya's disputed election result in 2007, the place of the radio stations in Rwanda was taken by the cell phone, and the swirling violence was fed by circulating text messages urging ethnic groups on both sides to slaughter one another. Over 1,000 people were killed. One widely shared example exhorted people to make and send lists of their enemies:

> We say no more innocent Kikuyu blood will be shed. We will slaughter them right here in the capital city. For justice, compile a list of Luos and Kalus(ph) you know at work or in your estates, or elsewhere in Nairobi, plus where and how their children go to school. We will give you numbers to text this information.[12]

The problem of hate messages was so severe that the government attempted to circulate its own messages of peace and reconciliation, and humanitarian NGOs blamed the worsening cycle of violence directly on the escalating rhetoric within the closed, inaccessible communities created by cell phones. Subsequent studies have found that across the continent, even when income inequality, ethnic fractionalisation and geography are taken into account, increases in cell phone coverage are associated with higher levels of violence.[13]

None of this is to argue that the satellite or the smartphone themselves create violence. Rather, it is the uncritical, unthinking belief in their amoral utility that perpetuates our inability to rethink our dealings with the world. Every unchallenged assertion of the neutral goodness of technology supports and sustains the status quo. The Rwanda claim simply does not stand – in fact, the reverse is true, and Schmidt, one of the world's most powerful facilitators of data-driven digital expansion, with a crowd of global business and government leaders as his audience, is not merely wrong, but dangerously so.

Information and violence are utterly and inextricably linked, and the weaponisation of information is accelerated by technologies that purport to assert control over the world. The historical association between military, government, and corporate interests on the one hand, and the development of new technologies on the other, makes this clear. The effects are seen everywhere. And yet we continue to place an inordinate value upon information that locks us into repeated cycles of violence, destruction, and death. Given our long history of doing exactly the same thing with other commodities, this realisation should not and cannot be dismissed.

The phrase 'data is the new oil' was apparently coined in 2006 by Clive Humby, the British mathematician and architect of the Tesco Clubcard, a supermarket reward programme.[14] Since then, it has been repeated and amplified, first by marketers, then by entrepreneurs, and ultimately by business leaders and policy makers. In May 2017, the *Economist* devoted an entire issue to the proposition, declaring that 'smartphones and the internet have made data abundant, ubiquitous and far more valuable . . . By collecting more data, a firm has more scope to improve its products, which attracts more users, generating even more data, and so on.'[15] The president and CEO of Mastercard told an audience in Saudi Arabia, the world's largest producer of actual oil, that data could be as effective as crude as a means of generating wealth (he also said it was a 'public good').[16] In British parliamentary debates on leaving the European Union, data's oily qualities were cited by Members of Parliament on both sides.[17] Yet few such citations address the implications of long-term, systemic and global reliance on such a poisonous material, or the dubious circumstances of its extraction.

In Humby's original formulation, data resembled oil because 'it's valuable, but if unrefined it cannot really be used. It has to be changed into gas, plastic, chemicals, etc to create a valuable entity that drives profitable activity; so must data be broken down, analyzed for it to have value.'[18] The emphasis on the work required to make information useful has been lost over the years, aided by processing power and machine intelligence, to be replaced by pure speculation. In the process of simplification, the analogy's historical ramifications, as well as its present dangers and its long-term repercussions, have been forgotten.

Our thirst for data, like our thirst for oil, is historically imperialist and colonialist, and tightly tied to capitalist networks of exploitation. The most successful empires have always promulgated themselves through a selective visibility: that of the subaltern to the centre. Data is used to map and classify the subject of imperialist intention, just as the subjects of empires were forced to register and name themselves according to the diktats of their masters.[19] The same empires first occupied, then exploited, the natural reserves of their possessions, and the networks they created live on in the digital infrastructures of the present day: the information superhighway follows the networks of telegraph cables laid down to control old empires. While the fastest data routes from West Africa to the world still run through London, so the British-Dutch mutinational Shell continues to exploit the oil of the Nigerian delta. The subsea cables girding South America are owned by corporations based in Madrid, even as countries there struggle to control their own oil profits. Fibre-optic connections funnel financial transactions by way of offshore territories quietly retained through periods of decolonisation. Empire has mostly rescinded territory, only to continue its operation at the level of infrastructure, maintaining its power in the form of the network. Data-driven regimes repeat the racist, sexist, and oppressive policies of their antecedents because these biases and attitudes have been encoded into them at the root.

In the present, the extraction, refinement, and use of data/oil pollutes the ground and air. It spills. It leaches into everything. It gets into the ground water of our social relationships and it poisons them. It enforces computational thinking upon us, driving the deep divisions in society caused by misbegotten classification, fundamentalism and populism, and accelerating inequality. It sustains and nourishes uneven power relationships: in most of our interactions with power, data is not something that is freely given but forcibly extracted – or impelled in moments of panic, like a stressed cuttlefish attempting to cloak itself from a predator.

The ability of politicians, policy makers and technocrats to talk approvingly of data/oil today should be shocking, given what we know about climate change, if we were not already so numb to their hypocrisy. This data/oil will remain hazardous well beyond our own lifetimes: the debt we have already accrued will take centuries to dissipate, and we have not come close as yet to experiencing its worst, inevitable effects.

In one key respect, however, even a realistic accounting of data/oil is insufficient in its analogous power, for it might give us false hope of a peaceful transfer to an information-free economy. Oil is, despite everything, defined by its exhaustibility. We are already approaching peak oil, and while every oil shock prompts us to engage and exploit some new territory or some destructive technology – further endangering the planet and ourselves – the wells will eventually run dry. The same is not true of information, despite the desperate fracking that appears to be occurring when intelligence agencies record every email, every mouse click, and the movements of every cell phone. While peak knowledge may be closer than we think, the exploitation of raw information can continue infinitely, along with the damage it does to us and our ability to reckon with the world.

In this, information more closely resembles atomic power than oil: an effectively unlimited resource that still contains immense destructive power, and that is even more explicitly connected than petroleum to histories of violence. Atomic information might, however, force us to confront existential questions of time and contamination in ways that petroculture, bubbling up through the centuries, has mostly managed to avoid.

We have traced the ways in which computational thinking, evolved with the help of the machines, developed to build the atomic bomb, and how the architecture of contemporary processing and networking was forged in the crucible of the Manhattan Project. We have also seen the ways in which data leaks and breaches: the critical excursions and chain reactions that lead to privacy meltdowns and the rhizomatic mushroom cloud. These analogies are not mere speculations: they are the inherent and totalising effects of our social and engineering choices.

Just as we spent forty-five years locked in a Cold War perpetuated by the spectre of mutually assured destruction, we find ourselves in an intellectual, ontological dead end today. The primary method we have for evaluating the world – more data – is faltering. It's failing to account for complex, human-driven systems, and its failure is becoming obvious – not least because we've built a vast, planet-spanning information-sharing system for making it obvious to us. The mutually assured privacy meltdown of state surveillance and leak-driven countersurveillance activism is one example of this failure, as is the confusion caused by real-time information overload from surveillance itself. So is the discovery crisis in the pharmacological industry, where billions of dollars in computation are returning exponentially fewer drug breakthroughs. But perhaps the most obvious is that despite the sheer volume of information that exists online – the plurality of moderating views and alternative explanations – conspiracy theories and fundamentalism don't merely survive, they proliferate. As in the nuclear age, we learn the wrong lesson over and over again. We stare at the mushroom cloud, and see all of this power, and we enter into an arms race all over again.

But what we should be seeing is the network itself, in all of its complexity. The network is only the latest, but certainly the most advanced, civilisation-scale tool for introspection our species has built thus far. To deal with the network is to deal with a Borgesian infinite library and all the inherent contradictions contained within it: a library that will not converge and continually refuses to cohere. Our categories, summaries and authorities are no longer merely insufficient; they are literally incoherent. As H. P. Lovecraft noted in his annunciation of a new dark age, our current ways of thinking about the world can no more survive exposure to this totality of raw information than we can survive exposure to an atomic core.

The 'Black Chamber', forerunner to the National Security Agency, was established as the first peacetime cryptanalytic organisation by the United States in 1919, dedicated to the cracking open of information, its refinement and combustion in the name of power. Its physical analogue was constructed by Enrico Fermi under the bleachers of Chicago's Stagg Field in 1942 from 45,000 blocks of black graphite, and used to shield the world's first artificial nuclear reaction. Just as the once-secret mesa town of Los Alamos finds its contemporary equivalent in the NSA data centres under construction in the Utah desert, so the black chamber is reified today both in the opaque glass and steel of NSA's

Photograph: US Department of Energy.

Exponential pile precursor to Chicago Pile-1, 1942.

headquarters at Fort Meade, Maryland, and in the endless, inscrutable server racks of Google, Facebook, Amazon, Palantir, Lawrence Livermore, Sunway TaihuLight, and the National Defense Management Center.

The two chambers of Fermi and the NSA represent encounters with two annihilations – one of the body, and one of the mind, but both of the self. Both are analogues of the endlessly destructive pursuit of ever more finely grained knowledge, at the expense of the acknowledgement of unknowing. We've built modern civilisation on the dialectic that more information leads to better decisions, but our engineering has caught up with our philosophy. The novelist and activist Arundhati Roy, writing on the occasion of the detonation of India's first nuclear bomb, called it 'the end of imagination' – and again, this revelation is literalised by our information technologies.[20]

In response to the end of the imagination, unmistakeably visible not only in the looming mushroom cloud but in the inhuman longevity of atomic half-lives that will continue to radiate long after humanity itself expires, we have resorted to myth and silence. Proposals put forward for marking long-term waste storage in the United States include sculpture so terrible in form that other species will recognise its location as evil. One verbal formulation compiled to accompany it states, 'This place is not a place of honor. No highly esteemed deed is commemorated here. Nothing valued is here.'[21] Another proposal by the Human Interference Task Force, convened by the Department of Energy in the 1980s, suggested the breeding of 'radiation cats' that would change colour when exposed to radioactive emissions and serve as living indicators of danger, to be accompanied by works of art and fable that would transmit the significance of this change through deep cultural time.[22] The Onkalo spent nuclear fuel repository, dug deep into the bedrock beneath Finland, has suggested another plan: once completed, it will simply be erased from the map, its location hidden and eventually forgotten.[23]

An atomic understanding of information presents, at the last, such a cataclysmic conception of the future that it forces us to insist upon the present as the only domain for action. In contrast and in opposition to nihilistic accounts of original sins and dys/utopian imaginings of the future, one strand of environmental and atomic activism posits the notion of guardianship.[24] Guardianship takes full responsibility for the toxic products of atomic culture, even and especially when they have been created for our ostensible benefit. It is based on the principles of doing the least harm in the present and of our responsibility to future generations – but does not presume that we can know or control them. As such, guardianship calls for change, while taking on the responsibility of what we have already created, insisting that deep burial of radioactive materials precludes such possibilities and risks widespread contamination. In this, it aligns itself with the new dark age: a place where the future is radically uncertain and the past irrevocably contested, but where we are still capable of speaking directly to what is in front of us, of thinking clearly and acting with justice. Guardianship insists that these principles require a moral commitment that is beyond the abilities of pure computational thinking, but well within, and utterly appropriate to, our darkening reality.

Ultimately, any strategy for living in the new dark age depends upon attention to the here and now, and not to the illusory promises of computational prediction, surveillance, ideology and representation. The present is always where we live and think, poised between an oppressive history and an unknowable future. The technologies that so inform and shape our present perceptions of reality are not going to go away, and in many cases we should not wish them to. Our current life support systems on a planet of 7.5 billion and rising utterly depend upon them. Our understanding of those systems and their ramifications, and of the conscious choices we make in their design, in the here and now, remain entirely within our capabilities. We are not powerless, not without agency, and not limited by darkness. We only have to think, and think again, and keep thinking. The network – us and our machines and the things we think and discover together – demands it.

Afterword

In January of 2022, the artificial intelligence research laboratory OpenAI released a piece of software called DALL-E. DALL-E allowed its users to enter a simple description of an image they had in their mind and, after a brief pause, the

'A pig with wings flying over the moon, illustrated by Antoine de Saint-Exupéry', generated by DALL-E.

software would produce an almost uncannily good interpretation of their suggestion, worthy of a jobbing illustrator or Photoshop designer – but much faster, and for free.[1] Typing in, for example, 'a pig with wings flying over the moon, illustrated by Antoine de Saint-Exupéry' resulted, after a minute or two of processing, with several convincing renderings of porcine astronauts, in the patchy but recognisable watercolour brushes of the creator of *The Little Prince*.

The internet went wild. Social media was immediately flooded with all sorts of bizarre and wondrous creations, an exuberant hodgepodge of fantasies and artistic styles, accompanied by a growing literature on the ins and outs of making the best use of the tool and, particularly, how to structure queries to get the most interesting outcomes.

The latter skill has become known as prompt engineering: the technique of framing one's instructions as clearly as possible with respect to the parameters of the machine, so that it returns the results which most closely match one's expectations – or perhaps exceed them. Commentators were quick to predict that prompt engineering would become a sought-after and well-remunerated job description in a No-Code future, where the most powerful way of interacting with intelligent systems would be through the medium of human language, and the limits on their creations would be the limits of our own imaginations.[2]

Imitators and advances followed quickly: DALL-E mini (later renamed Craiyon) gave those not invited to OpenAI's private beta a chance to play around with a similar, less powerful, but still highly impressive tool. Meanwhile the independent commercial effort Midjourney and the open-source Stable Diffusion used subtly different techniques to much the same ends. Within a few months, the field had rapidly advanced to the generation of short videos and 3D models, with new tools appearing daily from academic departments and hobbyist programmers as well as the established giants of social media and now AI: Facebook (aka Meta), Google, Microsoft and others.[3] A new field of research, software, and contestation had opened up.

The name DALL-E combines the robot protagonist of Disney's *WALL-E* with the Spanish surrealist artist Salvador Dali. On the one hand, you have the figure of a plucky, autonomous, and adorable little machine sweeping up the debris of a collapsed human civilisation, and on the other a man whose most repeated *bon mots* include 'Those who do not want to imitate anything, produce nothing' and 'What is important is to spread confusion, not eliminate it.' Both make admirable namesakes for the broad swathe of tools that have come to be known as AI image generators.

In less than a year, as of the time of writing, AI image generation has captured the popular imagination, provided a number of new ways to think about artificial intelligence, and diversified rapidly. It's impossible to say where it will be in a few more years, but it already makes for a good example of some of the ways in which complex computation and its social and political ramifications have advanced – or not – in the half decade since *New Dark Age* was written and published.

AI image generation relies on the assembly and analysis of millions upon millions of tagged images; that is, images which come with some kind of description of their contents already attached. These images and descriptions are then processed through complex neural networks that learn to associate particular, and deeply nuanced, qualities of the image – shapes, colours, compositions – with certain words and phrases. They can then layer these qualities on top of one another to produce new arrangements of shape, colour, and composition based on the billions of differently weighted associations produced by a simple prompt. But where did all those original images come from?

The datasets released by LAION, a German non-profit, are a good example of the kind of image-text collections used to train large AI models (they provided the basis for both Stable Diffusion and Google's Imagen, among others). For more than a decade, another non-profit web organisation, Common Crawl, has been indexing and storing as much of the public World Wide Web as it can access, filing away as many as 3 billion web pages every month.[4] Researchers at LAION took a chunk of that data and pulled out every image with an associated 'alt' tag, a line or so of text which is meant to be used to describe images on web pages. After some trimming, links to the original images and the text describing them are released in vast collections: LAION-5B, released in March 2022, contains more than 5 billion text-image pairs.[5] So, in short, these images are 'public' images in the broadest sense: any image ever published on the internet might get gathered up into them, with exactly the kind of strange consequences one might expect.

Lapine, a San Francisco–based digital artist, was scanning the LAION database in September 2022 when she found something quite disturbing. Using a tool called Have I Been Trained, Lapine found her own face in the database and traced the original image back to photographs taken by a doctor when she was undergoing treatment for a rare genetic condition.[6] The photographs were taken as part of her clinical documentation, and she signed documents which restricted their use to her medical file alone. The doctor involved died in 2018. Yet, somehow, these private medical images ended up first online, then in Common Crawl's archive and LAION's dataset, and were finally ingested into the neural networks learning to make new images. For all we know, the mottled pink texture of our piggy astronaut might have been blended, however subtly, from the raw flesh of a cancer patient.

'It's the digital equivalent of receiving stolen property. Someone stole the image from my deceased doctor's files and it ended up somewhere online, and then it was scraped into this dataset,' Lapine told *Ars Technica*. 'It's bad enough to have a photo leaked, but now it's part of a product. And this goes for anyone's photos, medical record or not. And the future abuse potential is really high.' (According to their Twitter account, Lapine continues to use tools like DALL-E to make their own art.)[7]

The entirety of AI image generation, and many data-driven applications like it, is based on this wholesale appropriation of existing images, the scope of which we can barely comprehend. Public or private, legal or otherwise, most of these images exist in the nebulous domain of 'fair use' (permitted in the US, but questionable if not outright illegal in the European Union) and, like most of what goes on inside advanced neural networks, it's impossible to reverse engineer, rare encounters like Lapine's aside. But we can be certain of this: far from being the magical, novel creations of brilliant machines, the outputs of AI image generation are entirely dependent on the uncredited and unremunerated work of generations of human artists. AI image generation is pure primitive accumulation: expropriation of labour from the many for the enrichment and advancement of the few.

The weirdness of AI image generation exists in the output too, in revealing ways. DALL-E and its ilk are capable of iterating upon their prompts in ways which both hone the user's vision and completely subvert it. One user tried typing in nonsense phrases and was confused and somewhat discomforted to discover that DALL-E mini seemed to have a very good idea of what a 'Crungus' was: an otherwise unknown phrase which consistently produced images of a snarling, naked, ogre-like figure. 'Crungus' was sufficiently clear within the programme's imagination that he could be manipulated easily: other users quickly offered up images of ancient Crungus tapestries, Roman-style Crungus mosaics, oil paintings of Crungus, photos of Crungus hugging various celebrities, and, this being the internet, 'sexy' Crungus.[8]

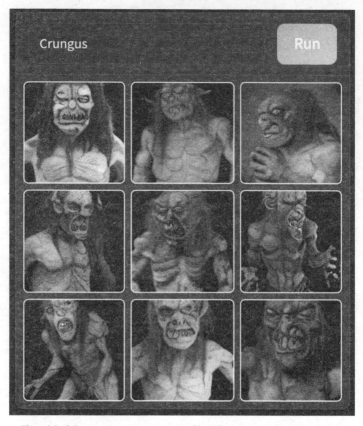

The original Crungus images, as generated by @Brainimage using DALL-E mini.

So, who or what is Crungus? Twitter users were quick to describe him as 'the first AI cryptid', a creature like Bigfoot or the Mothman who exists, in this case, within the under-explored terrain of the AI's imagination. And this is about as clear an answer as we can get at this point, due to our limited understanding of how the system works. We can't peer inside its decision-making processes for the same reasons we can't understand exactly how Google Translate works (see chapter 6). It lives somewhere in the high-dimensional space of the AI's model of the world, composited from billions of references which have escaped their origins and coalesced into a mythological figure untethered from human experience. But thanks to image generation, we have pictures of it.

A similar experience occurred to another AI-experimenting digital artist, who was exploring the use of negative prompts. Negative prompting is a technique by which it is possible to generate what the system considers to be the polar opposite of what is described. When they entered 'Brando::-1', the system returned something which looked a bit like a logo for a video game company called DIGITA PNTICS. That this might, across the multiple dimensions of the system's vision of the world, be the opposite of Marlon Brando seems reasonable enough. But when they checked to see if it went the other way, by typing in 'DIGITA PNTICS skyline logo::-1', something much stranger happened: all of the images depicted a creepy-looking woman with sunken eyes and reddened cheeks, who the artist christened Loab. Once discovered, Loab seemed unusually, and disturbingly, persistent. Repeated iterations of the image, combined with ever more divergent text prompts, kept bringing Loab back, in increasingly nightmarish forms, in which blood, gore, and violence predominated.[9]

Here's one explanation for Loab, and possibly Crungus: although it's very, very hard to imagine the topology of the space of the machine's imagination, it is possible to imagine it having a shape. This shape is never going to be perfectly (hyper-)spherical: rather, it is going to have troughs and peaks, mountains and valleys, areas full of information and areas lacking many features at all. Those areas of high information correspond to networks of associations which the system 'knows' a lot about. One can imagine the regions related to human faces, cars, and cats, for example, being pretty dense, given the distribution of images one finds on a survey of the whole internet.

It is these regions that an AI image generator will draw on most heavily when creating its pictures. But there are other places, less visited, which come into play when negative prompting – or indeed, nonsense phrases – are deployed. In order to satisfy such queries, the machine must draw on more esoteric, less certain connections, and perhaps even infer from the totality of what it does know what its opposite might be. Here, in the hinterlands, Loab and Crungus are to be found.

That's a satisfying theory – mathematically at least – but it does raise certain uncomfortable questions about *why* Crungus and Loab look like they do; why they tip towards horror and violence, why they hint at nightmares. AI image generators, in their attempt to understand and replicate the entirety of human visual culture, seem to have recreated our darkest fears as well. In this, they remind me strongly of the deep tendency towards disquiet, horror, and abuse I found in the algorithmic soup of YouTube recommendations, as described in chapter 9. Perhaps this is just a sign that these systems are very good indeed at aping human consciousness, all the way down to the existential horror that lurks in the benthic depths of being alive: our fears of filth, death, and corruption. And if so, we need to acknowledge that these will be persistent components of the machines we build in our own image. There is no escaping such obsessions and dangers, no moderating or engineering away the reality of the human condition, no 'post-humanity' at all. The dirt and disgust of living and dying will stay with us and need addressing, just as the hope, love, joy and discovery will.

This matters, because while AI image generators reproduce many of the weird, creepy, racist, and sexist tropes we have seen arise in all kinds of algorithmic systems in the New Dark Age – everything from racist digital cameras to predictive policing programmes – they're also upping the game. The benchmark of AI performance is shifting from the narrow domain of puzzles and challenges – from playing Chess or Go or obeying the traffic laws – to the much broader territory of imagination and creativity.

While claims about AI's 'creativity' might be overblown – there is no true originality in image generation, only very skilled imitation and pastiche – that doesn't mean it isn't capable of taking over many common 'artistic' tasks long considered the preserve of skilled workers, from illustrators and graphic designers, to musicians, videographers, and, indeed, writers. This is a step change in our relationship, because instead of capturing clearly defined abilities, AI is now engaging with affect, the underlying experience of feeling, emotion, and mood, and this will allow it to shape and influence the world at ever deeper and persuasive levels.

It doesn't have to be this way, of course. There is still time for a centaur turn within affective AI, akin to Kasparov's Advanced Chess games. Thoughtful prompt engineering opens a space for generative iteration upon ideas, a fruitful back-and-forth between very different types of imagination. Thoughtful relations with AI, which consider it a collaborator rather than a competitor, promise all kinds of new forms of creativity, but they depend on a step change in our own culture and imagination too, one which reckons with the powerful forces unleashed by capital-driven technology industries while retaining a sense of wonder and optimism about the nascent intelligences we share the planet with.[10]

Such a rethinking remains almost impossible while corporate forces are in the ascendant, as they are today. While there are open-source and freely shared equivalents of many of today's advanced AI programmes, the sheer costs of training large AI models makes them prohibitive for all but a few mega-corporations, and the profits foreseen mean that university departments, which might have once studied these technologies and turned them to better uses, are drained of talent by industry. When one reads that training a new top-of-the-line model costs millions of dollars – a figure far beyond the capabilities of most citizens or academics – it's hard not to conclude that computation, in all its forms, is becoming more centralised, and thus less democratic and less like anything resembling the public interest.[11]

Meanwhile, the externalities continue to accrue. In chapter 3, we saw how digital technologies are accelerating climate change through their almost entirely uncontrolled emission of greenhouse gases. This has continued apace, and this growth is in large part the fault of AI too, as those expensive models require ever more hot and energy-hungry machines to train and run. Training a single AI model – according to research published back in 2019 – might emit more than 284 tonnes of carbon dioxide equivalent, which is nearly five times as much as the entire lifetime of the average American car, including its manufacture.[12]

These emissions are expected to grow by nearly 50 per cent over the next five years, all while the planet continues to heat up, acidifying the oceans, igniting wildfires, throwing up superstorms, and driving species to extinction.[13] It's hard to think of anything more utterly stupid than Artificial Intelligence, as it is practised in the current era.

It is the little things too, of course, that keep making the news. In the town of Adel, in rural Georgia, residents compare the noise generated by a new Bitcoin-mining facility to low-flying helicopters: 'You cannot go into your house, eat your supper without hearing that noise inside your house. You cannot watch TV without hearing that noise inside your house. If you come outside, you must wear earplugs and now with the increased number of units, you must wear earplugs inside the house,' one local told the TV news.[14]

A similar story is told in Limestone, Tennessee, where a Bitcoin-mining facility, 'surrounded by barriers, cameras and fencing topped with razor wire', emits enough noise to drown out front-porch gatherings.[15] Noise is up close and personal;

the heat and deadly gases entering the atmosphere are harder to reckon, but far more damaging in the long term.

The entanglement of climate and computational excess, perhaps the greatest hallmark of the New Dark Age, is only going to get deeper, and more damaging. In a study published by the *Lancet Planetary Health* in September 2022, researchers found that online hate speech – racist, misogynistic, and homophobic tweets, most notably – increased by 22 per cent when temperatures rose above 42 °C (and by up to 12 per cent when they fell below minus 3 °C). On a planet entering a phase of ever more extreme and abrupt swings in climate, it seems that we too are becoming more extreme, less tolerant, and more prone to argument, disagreement, and violence.[16] Is this an artefact of the carbon-induced stupidity described in chapter 3, or of the loss of agency and status that inflects all of our dealings with complex, opaque technologies? Is it the natural tendency of a species defined by its inability to recognise the humanity of those who appear different? Does that distinction matter anymore? Is it even meaningful? We are inextricably, ecologically entwined with the things we make and the culture we live inside, one acting upon the other. There is no technological solution which, by itself, can change who we are. That requires more conscious, deliberate, and collective effort.

With that in mind though, let's interrogate that 'we' for a minute, something which is perhaps not as well explicated in *New Dark Age* as it should have been. The above study, like much of the research and storytelling in *New Dark Age*, confined itself to the United States of America – which is not to say that social media users in other countries are paragons of restraint and understanding, but that the mediatic and academic lenses we see the world through are still as stuck in twentieth-century modes as any of our technological undertakings.

That 'we' is far from universal, and many of the problems that surround us might be better answered, and have long been apparent and interrogated, outside the narrow framing of Northern European and American thinking – and beyond the human.

Indigenous languages are under threat around the world. The UN estimates that one disappears every two weeks, and with that disappearance goes generations of knowledge and experience. This problem, the result of colonialism and racist assimilation policies over centuries, is compounded by the rising dominance of machine-learning language models, which ensure that popular languages increase their power, while lesser-known ones are drained of exposure and expertise.

In Aotearoa New Zealand, a small non-profit radio station called Te Hiku Media, which broadcasts in the Māori language, decided to address this. Their massive archive of more than twenty years of broadcasts, representing a vast range of idioms, colloquialisms, and unique phrases, many of them no longer spoken by anyone living, was being digitised, but needed to be transcribed to be of use to language researchers and their community. In response, they decided to train their own speech recognition model: 'teaching the computer to speak Māori became absolutely necessary'.[17]

Over the next few years, Te Hiku Media, using open-source technologies as well as systems they developed themselves, achieved the almost impossible: a highly accurate speech recognition system for the Māori language, which was built and owned by its own language community. This was more than a software effort. They contacted every Māori community group they could and asked them to record themselves speaking pre-written statements in order to provide a corpus of annotated speech, a prerequisite for training their model.

There was a cash prize for whoever submitted the most sentences – one activist, Te Mihinga Komene, recorded 4,000 phrases alone – but the organisers found that the greatest motivation for contributors was the shared vision of revitalising the language while keeping it in the community's ownership. Within a few weeks, they created a model with 86 per cent accuracy – more than enough to get them started transcribing their full archive.[18]

Te Hiku Media's achievement cleared a path for other indigenous groups to follow, with similar projects now being undertaken by Mohawk peoples in south-eastern Canada and Native Hawaiians. It also established the principle of data sovereignty around indigenous languages, and by extension other forms of indigenous knowledge. When international for-profit companies started approaching Māori speakers to help build their own models, Te Hiku Media campaigned against these efforts, arguing, 'They suppressed our languages and physically beat it out of our grandparents, and now they want to sell our language back to us as a service.'[19]

'Data is the last frontier of colonization,' Keoni Mahelona, a Native Hawaiian and one of the co-founders of Te Hiku Media wrote. All of Te Hiku's work is released under what they named the Kaituhi Kaitiakitanga License, a legal guarantee of guardianship and custodianship which ensures that all the data that went into the language model and other projects remains the property of the community which created it, and is theirs to license, or not, as they deem appropriate according to their *tikanga* (Māori customs and protocols). In this way, the Māori language is revitalised, while resisting and altering the systems of digital colonialism which continue to repeat centuries of oppression.

The other current that has become apparent to me in the years since writing *New Dark Age* is that a focus on human technologies alone obscures and erases ways of thinking and being beyond the human which are of urgent import. One of the issues I grappled with extensively in the book is that of 'unknowing': the ability to see, understand, and act with agency and in the interests of justice in the face of vast, complex systems which are beyond our full comprehension. But this horizon of knowability, made so explicit by planetary-scale computation, is not a new experience for our species. We have practised unknowing for as long as we have been on this planet.

We have always lived among systems, global, local and microscopic, which we have tried to dominate without fully understanding – the climate and the biosphere, other species and natural forces, the web of life itself – and the result has been as disastrous as our attempts to dominate the infosphere. But just because we cannot fully know, as in the famous essay by the philosopher Thomas Nagel, 'what it is like to be a bat', or any other non-human being, we can and have – mostly, as ever, outside the narrow confines of the Western Enlightenment – found harmonious ways of living alongside other life forms.[20] What better guides to the New Dark Age than beings which do not need light to think, to feel, and to make new worlds?

Technology is making inroads into these worlds, with the development of sophisticated systems for animal tracking, revealing hitherto unknown patterns of behaviour and desire, which allow us to shift our own patterns of life to better accommodate the needs of other species.[21] Efforts are under-way – of dubious promise – to use machine learning to understand the language of whales, prairie dogs, and many other species whose complex forms of communication we are beginning to recognise as meaningful, and as the basis for new understandings of intelligence, as well as political rights.[22]

Technology, properly considered, is also a guide to seeing things which have always existed around us in a new light. When the internet first started to grow beyond a few research institutions, it became apparent that this new network did not behave like previous ones, as understood by mathematical topology: it was 'scale-free'. This meant that it could contain many nodes, with many different numbers of connections, but it could shrink and grow without limits. A new kind of mathematics was developed to understand it, which became known as complex network theory. And in turn, it was discovered that complex network theory was an excellent way of modelling the newly discovered mycorrhizal networks which lie beneath the forest floor, connecting different species of trees and allowing them to communicate and share information and nutrients.[23]

Technological discovery has opened up a new understanding of the natural world, because it is the production of metaphors as well as materials. These metaphors can be applied far beyond the domain of technology itself, to our great enrichment. It's my personal suspicion that AI might one day come to perform a similar role: by opening our solipsistic minds to the possibility of forms of intelligence beyond the human, we might yet come to a greater awareness of, and accommodation with, all the other kinds of intelligence, the infinitude of ways of being and knowing, that already exist around us on this planet.

'We', even the reductive *we* of Northern Europe and America, have already shifted a lot in the last five years. There is more awareness of the climate emergency and the dangers that we face, and a renewed sense of activism and urgency. Writing about the climatic and ecological aspects of the New Dark Age changed me utterly, and I believe from messages and conversations that many readers were similarly affected.

The goal of this book was always to lay out, as clearly as possible and without compromising on falsely optimistic solutions, the situation we find ourselves in. Meaningful action remains compromised by lack of agency – precisely the issue, exacerbated by contemporary technology, which I identified as the central condition of the New Dark Age. Yet we can learn and change; and technology, if we do not want to go back to the caves, or be condemned to them by a planetary apocalypse, will play a role in that change.

After all, as the dearly departed Ursula K. Le Guin once wrote: 'That's the neat thing about technologies. They're what we can learn to do.'[24]

James Bridle
October 2022

Acknowledgements

To my partner in everything, Navine G. Dossos, thank you for all your support, patience, fierce ideas, and selfless love. Special thanks to Russell Davies, Rob Faure-Walker, Katherine Brydan, Cally Spooner, and Charlie Lloyd, who were kind enough to read drafts and give me their thoughts. Thanks to Tom Taylor, Ben Terret, Chris Heathcote, Tom Armitage, Phil Gyford, Alice Bartlett, Dan Williams, Nat Buckley, Matt Jones, and the RIG, BRIG, THFT and Shepherdess crews, for all of the conversations, and to everyone in the Infrastructure Club. Thanks to Kevin Slavin, Hito Steyerl, Susan Schuppli, Trevor Paglen, Karen Barad, Ingrid Burrington, Ben Vickers, Jay Springett, George Voss, Tobias Revell, and Kyriaki Goni for their work and our conversations. Thanks to Luca Barbeni, Honor Harger, and Katrina Sluis for their faith in my work. Thanks to Leo Hollis for asking, and everyone at Verso for seeing it through. Thanks to Gina Fass and everyone at Romantso in Athens, where most of this work was written, and to Helene Black and Yiannis Colakides at Neme in Limassol, who saw me through the last chapters. And thank you to Tom and Eleanor, Howard and Alex, and to my parents, John and Clemancy, for your unfailing support and enthusiasm.

Notes

1 Chasm

1. 'The Cloud of Unknowing', anonymous, 14th Century.
2. 'Science is not enough, religion is not enough, art is not enough, politics and economics is not enough, nor is love, nor is duty, nor is action however disinterested, nor, however sublime, is contemplation. Nothing short of everything will really do.' From Aldous Huxley, *Island*, New York: Harper & Brothers, 1962.
3. H. P. Lovecraft, 'The Call of Cthulhu', *Weird Tales*, February 1926.
4. Rebecca Solnit, 'Woolf's Darkness: Embracing the Inexplicable', *New Yorker*, April 24, 2014, newyorker.com.
5. Donna Haraway, 'Anthropocene, Capitalocene, Chthulucene: Staying with the Trouble' (lecture, 'Anthropocene: Arts of Living on a Damaged Planet' conference, UC Santa Cruz, May 9, 2014), opentranscripts.org.
6. Virginia Woolf, *Three Guineas*, New York: Harvest, 1966.

2 Computation

1. John Ruskin, *The Storm-Cloud of the Nineteenth Century: Two Lectures Delivered at the London Institution February 4th and 11th, 1884*, London: George Allen, 1884.
2. Ibid.
3. Ibid.
4. Alexander Graham Bell, in a letter to his father Alexander Melville Bell, dated February 26, 1880, quoted in Robert V. Bruce, *Bell: Alexander Graham Bell and the Conquest of Solitude*, Ithaca, NY: Cornell University Press, 1990.

5. 'The Photophone', *New York Times*, August 30, 1880.
6. Oliver M. Ashford, *Prophet or Professor? The Life and Work of Lewis Fry Richardson*, London: Adam Hilger Ltd, 1985.
7. Lewis Fry Richardson, *Weather Prediction by Numerical Process*, Cambridge: Cambridge University Press, 1922.
8. Ibid.
9. Vannevar Bush, 'As We May Think', *Atlantic*, July 1945.
10. Ibid.
11. Ibid.
12. Ibid.
13. Vladimir K. Zworykin, *Outline of Weather Proposal*, Princeton, NJ: RCA Laboratories, October 1945, available at meteohistory.org.
14. As quoted in Freeman Dyson, *Infinite in All Directions*, New York: Harper & Row, 1988.
15. 'Weather to Order', *New York Times*, February 1, 1947.
16. John von Neumann, 'Can We Survive Technology?', *Fortune*, June 1955.
17. Peter Lynch, *The Emergence of Numerical Weather Prediction: Richardson's Dream*, Cambridge: Cambridge University Press, 2006.
18. '50 Years of Army Computing: From ENIAC to MSRC', Army Research Laboratory, Adelphi, MD, November 1996.
19. George W. Platzman, 'The ENIAC Computations of 1950 – Gateway to Numerical Weather Prediction', *Bulletin of the American Meteorological Society*, April 1979.
20. Emerson W. Pugh, *Building IBM: Shaping an Industry and Its Technology*, Cambridge, MA: MIT Press, 1955.
21. Herbert R. J. Grosch, *Computer: Bit Slices from A Life*, London: Third Millennium Books, 1991.
22. George Dyson, *Turing's Cathedral: The Origins of the Digital Universe*, New York: Penguin Random House, 2012.
23. IBM Corporation, 'SAGE: The First National Air Defense Network', IBM History, ibm.com.
24. Gary Anthes, 'Sabre Timeline', *Computerworld*, May 21, 2014, computerworld.com.

25. 'Flightradar24.com blocked Aircraft Plane List', Radarspotters, community forum, radarspotters.eu.

26. Federal Aviation Administration, 'Statement By The President Regarding The United States' Decision To Stop Degrading Global Positioning System Accuracy', May 1, 2000, faa.gov.

27. David Hambling, 'Ships fooled in GPS spoofing attack suggest Russian cyberweapon', *New Scientist*, August 10, 2017, newscientist.com.

28. Kevin Rothrock, 'The Kremlin Eats GPS for Breakfast', *Moscow Times*, October 21, 2016, themoscowtimes.com.

29. Chaim Gartenberg, 'This Pokémon Go GPS hack is the most impressive yet', *Verge*, Circuit Breaker, July 28, 2016, theverge.com.

30. Rob Kitchin and Martin Dodge, *Code/Space: Software and Everyday Life*, Cambridge, MA: MIT Press, 2011.

31. Brad Stone, 'Amazon Erases Orwell Books From Kindle', *New York Times*, July 17, 2009, nytimes.com.

32. R. Stuart Geiger, 'The Lives of Bots', in Geert Lovink and Nathaniel Tkaz, eds, *Critical Point of View: A Wikipedia Reader*, Institute of Network Cultures, 2011, available at networkcultures.org.

33. Kathleen Mosier, Linda Skitka, Susan Heers, and Mark Burdick, 'Automation Bias: Decision Making and Performance in High-Tech Cockpits', *International Journal of Aviation Psychology* 8:1, 1997, 47–63.

34. 'CVR transcript, Korean Air Flight 007 – 31 Aug 1983', Aviation Safety Network, aviation-safety.net.

35. K. L. Mosier, E. A. Palmer, and A. Degani, 'Electronic Checklists: Implications for Decision Making', Proceedings of the Human Factors Society 36th Annual Meeting, Atlanta, GA, 1992.

36. 'GPS Tracking Disaster: Japanese Tourists Drive Straight into the Pacific', *ABC News*, March 16, 2012, abcnews.go.com.

37. 'Women trust GPS, drive SUV into Mercer Slough', *Seattle Times*, June 15, 2011, seattletimes.com.

38. Greg Milner, 'Death by GPS', *Ars Technica*, June 3, 2016, arstechnica.com.

39. S. T. Fiske and S. E. Taylor, *Social Cognition: From Brains to Culture*, London: SAGE, 1994.

40. Lewis Fry Richardson, quoted in Ashford, *Prophet or Professor?*.

41. Lewis F. Richardson, 'The problem of contiguity: An appendix to Statistics of Deadly Quarrels', in *General systems: Yearbook of the Society for the Advancement of General Systems Theory*, Ann Arbor, MI: The Society for General Systems Research, 1961, 139–87.

3 Climate

1. 'Trembling tundra – the latest weird phenomenon in Siberia's land of craters', *Siberian Times*, July 20, 2016, siberiantimes.com.

2. US Geological Survey, 'Assessment of Undiscovered Oil and Gas in the Arctic', USGS, 2009, energy.usgs.gov.

3. '40 now hospitalised after anthrax outbreak in Yamal, more than half are children', *Siberian Times*, July 30, 2016, siberiantimes.com.

4. Roni Horn, 'Weather Reports You', Artangel official website, February 15, 2017, artangel.org.uk.

5. 'Immigrants Warmly Welcomed', *Al Jazeera*, July 4, 2006, aljazeera.com.

6. Food and Agriculture Organization of the United Nations, 'Crop biodiversity: use it or lose it', FAO, 2010, fao.org.

7. 'Banking against Doomsday', *Economist*, March 10, 2012, economist.com.

8. Somini Sengupta, 'How a Seed Bank, Almost Lost in Syria's War, Could Help Feed a Warming Planet', *New York Times*, October 12, 2017, nytimes.com.

9. Damian Carrington, 'Arctic stronghold of world's seeds flooded after permafrost melts', *Guardian*, May 19, 2017, theguardian.com.

10. Alex Randall, 'Syria and climate change: did the media get it right?', Climate and Migration Coalition, climatemigration.atavist.com.

11. Jonas Salomonsen, 'Climate change is destroying Greenland's earliest history', *ScienceNordic*, April 10, 2015, sciencenordic.com.

12. J. Hollesen, H. Matthiesen, A. B. Møller, and B. Elberling, 'Permafrost thawing in organic Arctic soils accelerated by ground heat production', *Nature Climate Change* 5:6 (2015), 574–8.

13. Elizabeth Kolbert, 'A Song of Ice', *New Yorker*, October 24, 2016, newyorker.com.

14. Council for Science and Technology, 'A National Infrastructure for the 21st century', 2009, cst.gov.uk.

15. AEA, 'Adapting the ICT Sector to the Impacts of Climate Change', 2010, gov.uk.

16. Council for Science and Technology, 'A National Infrastructure for the 21st century'.

17. AEA, 'Adapting the ICT Sector to the Impacts of Climate Change'.

18. Tom Bawden, 'Global warming: Data centres to consume three times as much energy in next decade, experts warn', *Independent*, January 23, 2016, independent.co.uk.

19. Institute of Energy Economics, 'Japan Long-Term Energy Outlook – A Projection up to 2030 under Environmental Constraints and Changing Energy Markets', Japan, 2006, eneken.ieej.or.jp.

20. Eric Holthaus, 'Bitcoin could cost us our clean-energy future', *Grist*, December 5, 2017, grist.org.

21. Digital Power Group, 'The Cloud Begins With Coal – Big Data, Big Networks, Big Infrastructure, and Big Power', 2013, tech-pundit.com.

22. Bawden, 'Global warming'.

23. Alice Ross, 'Severe turbulence on Aeroflot flight to Bangkok leaves 27 people injured', *Guardian*, May 1, 2017, theguardian.com.

24. Anna Ledovskikh, 'Accident on board of plane Moscow to Bangkok', YouTube video, May 1, 2017.

25. Aeroflot, 'Doctors Confirm No Passengers Are In Serious Condition After Flight Hits Unexpected Turbulence', May 1, 2017, aeroflot.ru.

26. M. Kumar, 'Passengers, crew injured due to turbulence on MAS flight', *Star of Malaysia*, June 5, 2016, thestar.com.my.

27. Henry McDonald, 'Passenger jet makes emergency landing in Ireland with 16 injured', *Guardian*, August 31, 2016, theguardian.com.

28. National Transportation Safety Board, 'NTSB Identification: DCA98MA015', ntsb.gov.

29. Federal Aviation Administration, FAA Advisory Circular 120-88A, 2006.

30. Paul D. Williams & Manoj M. Joshi, 'Intensification of winter transatlantic aviation turbulence in response to climate change', *Nature Climate Change* 3 (2013), 644–8.

31. Wolfgang Tillmans, *Concorde*, Cologne: Walther Konig Books, 1997.

32. William B. Gail, 'A New Dark Age Looms', *New York Times*, April 19, 2016, nytimes.com.

33. Joseph G. Allen, et al., 'Associations of Cognitive Function Scores with Carbon Dioxide, Ventilation, and Volatile Organic Compound Exposures in Office Workers: A Controlled Exposure Study of Green and Conventional Office Environments', *Environmental Health Perspectives* 124 (June 2016), 805–12.

34. Usha Satish, et al., 'Is CO2 an Indoor Pollutant? Direct Effects of Low-to-Moderate CO2 Concentrations on Human Decision-Making Performance', *Environmental Health Perspectives* 120:12 (December 2012), 1671–7.

4 Calculation

1. William Gibson, interviewed by David Wallace-Wells, 'William Gibson, The Art of Fiction No. 211', *Paris Review* 197 (Summer 2011).

2. Tim Berners-Lee, 'How the World Wide Web just happened', Do Lectures, 2010, thedolectures.com.

3. 'Cramming more components onto integrated circuits', *Electronics* 38:8 (April 19, 1965).

4. 'Moore's Law at 40', *Economist*, March 23, 2005, economist.com.

5. Chris Anderson, 'End of Theory', *Wired Magazine*, June 23, 2008.

6. Jack W. Scannell, Alex Blanckley, Helen Boldon, and Brian Warrington, 'Diagnosing the decline in pharmaceutical R&D efficiency', *Nature Reviews Drug Discover* 11 (March 2012), 191–200.

7. Richard Van Noorden, 'Science publishing: The trouble with retractions', *Nature*, October 5, 2011, nature.com.

8. F. C. Fang, and A. Casadevall, 'Retracted Science and the Retraction Index', *Infection and Immunity* 79 (2011), 3855–9.

9. F. C. Fang, R. G. Steen, and A. Casadevall, 'Misconduct accounts for the majority of retracted scientific publications', *FAS*, October 16, 2012, pnas.org.

10. Daniele Fanelli, 'How Many Scientists Fabricate and Falsify Research? A Systematic Review and Meta-Analysis of Survey Data', *PLOS ONE*, May 29, 2009, *PLOS ONE*, journals.pl.

11. F. C. Fang, R. G. Steen, and A. Casadevall, 'Why Has the Number of Scientific Retractions Increased?', *PLOS ONE*, July 8, 2013, journals.plosone.org.

12. 'People Who Mattered 2014', *Time*, December 2014, time.com.

13. Yudhijit Bhattacharjee, 'The Mind of a Con Man', *New York Times*, April 26, 2013, nytimes.com.

14. Monya Baker, '1,500 scientists lift the lid on reproducibility', *Nature*, May 25, 2016, nature.com.

15. For more on the math of this experiment, see Jean-Francois Puget, 'Green dice are loaded (welcome to p-hacking)', IBM developer-Works blog entry, March 22, 2016, ibm.com.

16. M. L. Head, et al., 'The Extent and Consequences of P-Hacking in Science', *PLOS Biology* 13:3 (2015).

17. John P. A. Ioannidis, 'Why Most Published Research Findings Are False', *PLOS ONE*, August 2005.

18. Derek J. de Solla Price, *Little Science, Big Science,* New York: Columbia University Press, 1963.

19. Siebert, Machesky, and Insall, 'Overflow in science and its implications for trust', *eLife* 14 (September 2015), ncbi.nlm.nih.gov.

20. Ibid.

21. Michael Eisen, 'Peer review is f***ed up – let's fix it', personal blog entry, October 28, 2011, michaeleisen.org.

22. Emily Singer, 'Biology's big problem: There's too much data to handle', *Wired*, October 11, 2013, wired.com.

23. Lisa Grossman and Maggie McKee, 'Is the LHC throwing away too much data?', *New Scientist*, March 14, 2012, newscientist.com.

24. Jack W. Scannell, et al., 'Diagnosing the decline in pharmaceutical R&D efficiency', *Nature Reviews Drug Discovery* 11 (March 2012) 191–200.

25. Philip Ball, *Invisible: The Dangerous Allure of the Unseen*, London: Bodley Head, 2014.

26. Daniel Clery, 'Secretive fusion company claims reactor breakthrough', *Science*, August 24, 2015, sciencemag.org.

27. E. A. Baltz, et al., 'Achievement of Sustained Net Plasma Heating in a Fusion Experiment with the Optometrist Algorithm', *Nature Scientific Reports* 7 (2017), nature.com.

28. Albert van Helden and Thomas Hankins, eds, *Osiris, Volume 9: Instruments*, Chicago: University of Chicago Press, 1994.

5 Complexity

1. Guy Debord, 'Introduction to a Critique of Urban Geography', *Les Lèvres Nues* 6 (1955), available at library.nothingness.org.

2. James Bridle, The Nor, essay series, 2014–15, available at shorttermmemoryloss.com.

3. Jame Bridle, 'All Cameras are Police Cameras', The Nor, November 2014.

4. James Bridle, 'Living in the Electromagnetic Spectrum', The Nor, December 2014.

5. Christopher Steiner, 'Wall Street's Speed War', *Forbes*, September 9, 2010, forbes.com.

6. Kevin Fitchard, 'Wall Street gains an edge by trading over microwaves', *GigaOM*, February 10, 2012, gigaom.com.

7. Luis A. Aguilar, 'Shedding Light on Dark Pools', US Securities and Exchange Commission, November 18, 2015, sec.gov.

8. 'Barclays and Credit Suisse are fined over US "dark pools"', *BBC*, February 1, 2016, bbc.com.

9. Martin Arnold, et al., 'Banks start to drain Barclays dark pool', *Financial Times*, June 26, 2014, ft.com.

10. Care Quality Commission, Hillingdon Hospital report, 2015, cqc.org.uk/location/RAS01.

11. Aneurin Bevan, *In Place of Fear*, London: William Heinemann, 1952.

12. Correspondence with Hillingdon Hospital NHS Trust, 2017, whatdotheyknow.com/request/hillingdon_hospital_structure_us.

13. Chloe Mayer, 'England's NHS hospitals and ambulance trusts have £700million deficit', *Sun*, May 23, 2017, thesun.co.uk.

14. Michael Lewis, *Flash Boys*, New York: W. W. Norton & Company, 2014.

15. Ibid.

16. 'Forget the 1%', *Economist*, November 6, 2014, economist.com.

17. Thomas Piketty, *Capital in the Twenty-First Century*, Cambridge, MA: Harvard University Press, 2014.

18. Jordan Golson, 'Uber is using in-app podcasts to dissuade Seattle drivers from unionizing', *Verge*, March 14, 2017, theverge.com.

19. Carla Green and Sam Levin, 'Homeless, assaulted, broke: drivers left behind as Uber promises change at the top', *Guardian*, June 17, 2017, theguardian.com.

20. Ben Kentish, 'Hard-pressed Amazon workers in Scotland sleeping in tents near warehouse to save money', *Independent*, December 10, 2016, independent.co.uk.

21. Kate Knibbs, 'Uber Is Faking Us Out With "Ghost Cabs" on Its Passenger Map', *Gizmodo*, July 28, 2015, gizmodo.com.

22. Kashmir Hill, '"God View": Uber Allegedly Stalked Users For Party-Goers' Viewing Pleasure', *Forbes*, October 3, 2014, forbes.com.

23. Julia Carrie Wong, 'Greyball: how Uber used secret software to dodge the law', *Guardian*, March 4, 2017, theguardian.com.

24. Russell Hotten, 'Volkswagen: The scandal explained', *BBC*, December 10, 2015, bbc.com.

25. Guillaume P. Chossière, et al., 'Public health impacts of excess NOx emissions from Volkswagen diesel passenger vehicles in Germany', *Environmental Research Letters* 12 (2017), iopscience.iop.org.

26. Sarah O'Connor, 'When Your Boss Is An Algorithm', *Financial Times*, September 8, 2016, ft.com.

27. Jill Treanor, 'The 2010 "flash crash": how it unfolded', *Guardian*, April 22, 2015, theguardian.com.

28. 'Singapore Exchange regulators change rules following crash', *Singapore News*, August 3, 2014, singaporenews.net.

29. Netty Idayu Ismail and Lillian Karununga, 'Two-Minute Mystery Pound Rout Puts Spotlight on Robot Trades', *Bloomberg*, October 7, 2017, bloomberg.com.

30. John Melloy, 'Mysterious Algorithm Was 4% of Trading Activity Last Week', *CNBC*, October 8, 2012, cnbc.com.

31. Samantha Murphy, 'AP Twitter Hack Falsely Claims Explosions at White House', *Mashable*, April 23, 2013, mashable.com.

32. Bloomberg Economics, @economics, Twitter post, April 23, 2013, 12:23 p.m.

33. For more examples from Zazzle, see Babak Radboy, 'Spam-erican Apparel', *DIS* magazine, dismagazine.com.

34. Roland Eisenbrand and Scott Peterson, 'This Is The German Company Behind The Nightmarish Phone Cases On Amazon', *OMR*, July 25, 2017, omr.com.

35. Jose Pagliery, 'Man behind "Carry On" T-shirts says company is "dead"', *CNN Money*, March 5, 2013, money.cnn.com.

36. Hito Steyerl and Kate Crawford, 'Data Streams', *New Inquiry*, January 23, 2017, thenewinquiry.com.

37. Ryan Lawler, 'August's Smart Lock Goes On Sale Online And At Apple Retail Stores For $250', *TechCrunch*, October 14, 2014, techcrunch.com.

38. Iain Thomson, 'Firmware update blunder bricks hundreds of home "smart" locks', *Register*, August 11, 2017, theregister. co.uk.

39. John Leyden, 'Samsung smart fridge leaves Gmail logins open to attack', *Register*, August 24, 2017, theregister.co.uk.

40. Timothy J. Seppala, 'Hackers hijack Philips Hue lights with a drone', *Engadget*, November 3, 2016, engadget.com.

41. Lorenzo Franceschi-Bicchierai, 'Blame the Internet of Things for Destroying the Internet Today', *Motherboard*, October 21, 2016, motherboard.vice.com.

42. Yossi Melman, 'Computer Virus in Iran Actually Targeted Larger Nuclear Facility', *Haaretz*, September 28, 2010, haaretz.com.

43. Malcolm Gladwell, 'The Formula', *New Yorker*, October 16, 2006, newyorker.com.

44. Gareth Roberts, 'Tragedy as computer gamer dies after 19-hour session playing World of Warcraft', *Mirror*, March 3, 2015, mirror.co.uk; Kirstie McCrum, 'Tragic teen gamer dies after "playing computer for 22 days in a row"', *Mirror*, September 3, 2015, mirror.co.uk.

45. Author interview with medical staff, Evangelismos Hospital, Athens, Greece, 2016.

46. See, for example, Nick Srnicek and Alex Williams, *Inventing the Future: Postcapitalism and a World Without Work*, London and New York: Verso, 2015.

47. Deborah Cowen, *The Deadly Life of Logistics*, Minneapolis, MN: University of Minnesota Press, 2014.

48. Bernard Stiegler, *Technics and Time 1: The Fault of Epimetheus*, Redwood City, CA: Stanford University Press, 1998; cited in Alexander Galloway, 'Brometheanism', *boundary* 2, June 21, 2017, boundary2.org.

6 Cognition

1. Jeff Kaufman, 'Detecting Tanks', blog post, 2015, jefftk.com.

2. 'New Navy Device Learns by Doing', *New York Times*, July 8, 1958.

3. Joaquín M. Fuster, 'Hayek in Today's Cognitive Neuroscience', in Leslie Marsh, ed., *Hayek in Mind: Hayek's Philosophical Psychology*, Advances in Austrian Economics, volume 15, Emerald Books, 2011.

4. Jay Yarow, 'Google Cofounder Sergey Brin: We Will Make Machines That "Can Reason, Think, And Do Things Better Than We Can"', *Business Insider*, July 6, 2014, businessinsider.com.

5. Quoc V. Le, et al., 'Building High-level Features Using Large Scale Unsupervised Learning', Proceedings of the 29th International Conference on Machine Learning, Edinburgh, Scotland, UK, 2012.

6. Tom Simonite, 'Facebook Creates Software That Matches Faces Almost as Well as You Do', *MIT Technology Review*, March 17, 2014, technologyreview.com.

7. Xiaolin Wu and Xi Zhang, 'Automated Inference on Criminality using Face Images', *ARXIV*, November 2016, arxiv.org.

8. Xiaolin Wu and Xi Zhang, 'Responses to Critiques on Machine Learning of Criminality Perceptions', *ARXIV*, May 2017, arxiv.org.

9. Stephen Wright and Ian Drury, 'How old are they really?', *Daily Mail*, October 19, 2016, dailymail.co.uk.

10. Wu and Zhang, 'Responses to Critiques on Machine Learning'.

11. Wu and Zhang, 'Automated Inference on Criminality using Face Images'.

12. 'Racist Camera! No, I did not blink . . . I'm just Asian!', blog post, May 2009, jozjozjoz.com.

13. 'HP cameras are racist', YouTube video, username: wzamen01, December 10, 2009.

14. David Smith, '"Racism" of early colour photography explored in art exhibition', *Guardian*, January 25, 2013, theguardian.com.

15. Phillip Martin, 'How A Cambridge Woman's Campaign Against Polaroid Weakened Apartheid', *WGBH News*, December 9, 2013, news.wgbh.org.

16. Hewlett-Packard, 'Global Citizenship Report 2009', hp.com.

17. Trevor Paglen, 're:publica 2017 | Day 3 – Livestream Stage 1 – English', YouTube video, username: re:publica, May 10, 2017.

18. Walter Benjamin, 'Theses on the Philosophy of History', in *Walter Benjamin: Selected Writings, Volume 4: 1938–1940*, Cambridge, MA: Harvard University Press, 2006.

19. PredPol, '5 Common Myths about Predictive Policing', predpol.com.

20. G. O. Mohler, M. B. Short, P. J. Brantingham, et al., 'Self-exciting point process modeling of crime', *JASA* 106 (2011).

21. Daniel Jurafsky and James H. Martin, *Speech and language processing: an introduction to natural language processing, computational linguistics, and speech recognition*, 2nd edition, Upper Saddle River, NJ: Prentice Hall, 2009.

22. Walter Benjamin, 'The Task of the Translator', in *Selected Writings Volume 1 1913–1926*, Marcus Bullock and Michael W. Jennings, eds, Cambridge, MA and London: Belknap Press, 1996.

23. Murat Nemet-Nejat, 'Translation: Contemplating Against the Grain', *Cipher*, 1999, cipherjournal.com.

24. Tim Adams, 'Can Google break the computer language barrier?', *Guardian*, December 19, 2010, theguardian.com.

25. Gideon Lewis-Kraus, 'The Great A.I. Awakening', *New York Times*, December 14, 2016, nytimes.com.

26. Cade Metz, 'How Google's AI viewed the move no human could understand', *Wired*, March 14, 2016, wired.com.

27. Iain M. Banks, *Excession*, London: Orbit Books, 1996.

28. Sanjeev Arora, Yuanzhi Li, Yingyu Liang, et al., 'RAND-WALK: A Latent Variable Model Approach to Word Embeddings', *ARXIV*, February 12, 2015, arxiv.org.

29. Alec Radford, Luke Metz, and Soumith Chintala, 'Unsupervised Representation Learning with Deep Convolutional Generative Adversarial Networks', Nov 19, 2015, *ARXIV*, arxiv.org.

30. Robert Elliott Smith, 'It's Official: AIs are now re-writing history', blog post, October 2014, robertelliottsmith.com.

31. Stephen Levy, 'Inside Deep Dreams: How Google Made Its Computers Go Crazy', *Wired*, November 12, 2015, wired.com.

32. Liat Clark, 'Google's Artificial Brain Learns to Find Cat Videos', *Wired*, June 26, 2012, wired.com.

33. Melvin Johnson, Mike Schuster, Quoc V. Le, et al., 'Google's Multilingual Neural Machine Translation System: Enabling Zero-Shot Translation', *ARXIV*, November 14, 2016, arxiv.org.

34. Martín Abadi and David G. Andersen, 'Learning to Protect Communications with Adversarial Neural Cryptography', *ARXIV*, 2016, arxiv.org.

35. Isaac Asimov, *I, Robot*, New York: Doubleday, 1950.

36. Chris Baraniuk, 'The cyborg chess players that can't be beaten', *BBC Future*, December 4, 2015, bbc.com.

7 Complicity

1. Nick Hopkins and Sandra Laville, 'London 2012: MI5 expects wave of terrorism warnings before Olympics', *Guardian*, June 2012, theguardian.com.

2. Jerome Taylor, 'Drones to patrol the skies above Olympic Stadium', *Independent*, November 25, 2011, independent.co.uk.

3. '£13,000 Merseyside Police drone lost as it crashes into River Mersey', *Liverpool Echo*, October 31, 2011, liverpoolecho.co.uk.

4. FOI Request, 'Use of UAVs by the MPS', March 19, 2013, available at whatdotheyknow.com.

5. David Robarge, 'The Glomar Explorer in Film and Print', *Studies in Intelligence* 56:1 (March 2012), 28–9.

6. Quoted in the majority opinion penned by Circuit Judge J. Skelly Wright, Phillippi v. CIA, United States Court of Appeals for the District of Columbia Circuit, 1976.

7. Or see @glomarbot on Twitter, an automated search created by the author.

8. W. Diffie and M. Hellman, 'New directions in cryptography', *IEEE Transactions on Information Theory* 22:6 (1976), 644–54.

9. 'GCHQ trio recognised for key to secure shopping online', *BBC News*, October 5, 2010, bbc.co.uk.

10. Dan Goodin, 'How the NSA can break trillions of encrypted Web and VPN connections', *Ars Technica*, October 15, 2015, arstechnica.co.uk.

11. Tom Simonite, 'NSA Says It "Must Act Now" Against the Quantum Computing Threat', *Technology Review*, February 3, 2016, technologyreview.com.

12. Rebecca Boyle, 'NASA Adopts Two Spare Spy Telescopes, Each Maybe More Powerful Than Hubble', *Popular Science*, June 5, 2012, popsci.com.

13. Daniel Patrick Moynihan, *Secrecy: The American Experience*, New Haven, CT: Yale University Press, 1998.

14. Zeke Miller, 'JFK Files Release Is Trump's Latest Clash With Spy Agencies', *New York Times*, October 28, 2017, nytimes.com.

15. Ian Cobain, *The History Thieves*, London: Portobello Books, 2016.

16. Ibid.

17. Ibid.

18. Ian Cobain and Richard Norton-Taylor, 'Files on UK role in CIA rendition accidentally destroyed, says minister', *Guardian*, July 9, 2014, theguardian.com.

19. 'Snowden-Interview: Transcript', NDR, January 26, 2014, ndr.de.

20. Glyn Moody, 'NSA spied on EU politicians and companies with help from German intelligence', *Ars Technica*, April 24, 2014, arstechnica.com.

21. 'Optic Nerve: millions of Yahoo webcam images intercepted by GCHQ', *Guardian*, February 28, 2014, theguardian.com.

22. 'NSA offers details on "LOVEINT"', *Cnet*, September 27, 2013, cnet.com.

23. Kaspersky Lab, *The Regin Platform: Nation-State Ownage of GSM Networks*, November 24, 2014, available at securelist.com.

24. Ryan Gallagher, 'From Radio to Porn, British Spies Track Web Users' Online Identities', *Intercept*, September 25, 2015, theintercept.com.

25. Andy Greenberg, 'These Are the Emails Snowden Sent to First Introduce His Epic NSA Leaks', *Wired*, October 13, 2014, wired.com.

26. James Risen and Eric Lichtblau, 'Bush Lets U.S. Spy on Callers Without Courts', *New York Times*, December 16, 2005, nytimes.com.

27. James Bamford, 'The NSA Is Building the Country's Biggest Spy Center (Watch What You Say)', *Wired*, March 14, 2012, wired.com.

28. 'Wiretap Whistle-Blower's Account', *Wired*, April 6, 2006, wired.com.

29. 'Obama admits intelligence failures over jet bomb plot', BBC News, January 6, 2010, news.bbc.co.uk.

30. Bruce Crumley, 'Flight 253: Too Much Intelligence to Blame?', *Time*, January 7, 2010, time.com.

31. Christopher Drew, 'Military Is Awash in Data From Drones', *New York Times*, January 20, 2010, nytimes.com.

32. 'GCHQ mass spying will "cost lives in Britain", warns ex-NSA tech chief', *The Register*, January 6, 2016, theregister.co.uk.

33. Ellen Nakashima, 'NSA phone record collection does little to prevent terrorist-attacks', *Washington Post*, January 12, 2014, washingtonpost.com.

34. New America Foundation, 'Do NSA's Bulk Surveillance Programs Stop Terrorists?', January 13, 2014, newamerica.org.

35. Jennifer King, Deirdre Mulligan, and Stephen Rafael, 'CITRIS Report: The San Francisco Community Safety Program', UC Berkeley, December 17, 2008, available at wired.com.

36. K. Pease, 'A Review Of Street Lighting Evaluations: Crime Reduction Effects', *Crime Prevention Studies* 10 (1999).

37. Stephen Atkins, 'The Influence Of Street Lighting On Crime And Fear Of Crime', Crime Prevention Unit Paper 28, UK Home Office, 1991, available at popcenter.org.

38. Julian Assange, 'State and Terrorist Conspiracies', *Cryptome*, November 10, 2006, cryptome.org.

39. Caroline Elkins, *Imperial Reckoning: The Untold Story of Britain's Gulag in Kenya*, New York: Henry Holt and Company, 2005.

40. 'Owners Watched Fort McMurray Home Burn to Ground Over iPhone', YouTube video, username: Storyful News, May 6, 2016.

8 Conspiracy

1. Joseph Heller, *Catch-22*, New York: Simon & Schuster, 1961.

2. See James Bridle, 'Planespotting', blog post, December 18, 2013, booktwo.org, and other reports by the author.

3. For a good overview of the trial, see: Kevin Hall, *The ABC Trial* (2006), originally published at ukcoldwar.simplenet.com, archived at archive.li/1xfT4.

4. Richard Aldrich, *GCHQ: The Uncensored Story of Britain's Most Secret Intelligence Agency*, New York: HarperPress, 2010.

5. Duncan Campbell, 'GCHQ' (book review), *New Statesman*, June 28, 2010, newstatesman.com.

6. Chris Blackhurst, 'Police robbed of millions in plane fraud', *Independent*, May 19, 1995, independent.co.uk.

7. US Air Force, *Weather as a Force Multiplier: Owning the Weather in 2025*, 1996, csat.au.af.mil.

8. 'Take Ur Power Back!!: Vote to leave the EU', YouTube video, username: Flat Earth Addict, June 21, 2016.

9. 'Nigel Farage's Brexit victory speech in full', *Daily Mirror*, June 24, 2016, mirror.co.uk.

10. Carey Dunne, 'My month with chemtrails conspiracy theorists', *Guardian*, May 2017, theguardian.com.

11. Ibid.

12. International Cloud Atlas, cloudatlas.wmo.int.

13. A. Bows, K. Anderson, and P. Upham, *Aviation and Climate Change: Lessons for European Policy*, New York: Routledge, 2009.

14. Nicola Stuber, Piers Forster, Gaby Rädel, and Keith Shine, 'The importance of the diurnal and annual cycle of air traffic for contrail radiative forcing', *Nature* 441 (June 2006).

15. Patrick Minnis, et al., 'Contrails, Cirrus Trends, and Climate', *Journal of Climate* 17 (2006), available at areco.org.

16. Aeschylus, *Prometheus Bound*, c. 430 BC, 477: 'The flight of crook-taloned birds I distinguished clearly – which by nature are auspicious, which sinister.'

17. Susan Schuppli, 'Can the Sun Lie?', in *Forensis: The Architecture of Public Truth*, Forensic Architecture, Berlin: Sternberg Press, 2014, 56–64.

18. Kevin van Paassen, 'New documentary recounts bizarre climate changes seen by Inuit elders', *Globe and Mail*, October 19, 2010, theglobeandmail.com.

19. SpaceWeather.com, Time Machine, conditions for July 2, 2009.

20. Carol Ann Duffy, 'Silver Lining', Sheer Poetry, 2010, available at sheerpoetry.co.uk.

21. Lord Byron, 'Darkness', 1816.

22. Richard Panek, '"The Scream", East of Krakatoa', *New York Times*, February 8, 2004, nytimes.com.

23. Leo Hickman, 'Iceland volcano gives warming world chance to debunk climate sceptic myths', *Guardian*, April 21, 2010, theguardian.com.

24. David Adam, 'Iceland volcano causes fall in carbon emissions as eruption grounds aircraft', *Guardian*, April 19, 2010, theguardian.com.

25. 'Do volcanoes emit more CO_2 than humans?', *Skeptical Science*, skepticalscience.com.

26. J. Pongratz, et al., 'Coupled climate–carbon simulations indicate minor global effects of wars and epidemics on atmospheric CO_2 between AD 800 and 1850', *Holocene* 21:5 (2011).

27. Simon L. Lewis and Mark A. Maslin, 'Defining the Anthropocene', *Nature* 519 (March 2015), nature.com.

28. David J. Travis, Andrew M. Carleton, and Ryan G. Lauritsen, 'Climatology: Contrails reduce daily temperature range', *Nature* 418 (August 2002), 601.

29. Richard J. Hofstadter, 'The Paranoid Style in American Politics', *Harper's* magazine, November 1964.

30. Fredric Jameson, 'Cognitive Mapping', in C. Nelson, L. Grossberg, eds, *Marxism and the Interpretation of Culture*, Champaign, IL: University of Illinois Press, 1990.

31. Hofstadter, 'The Paranoid Style in American Politics'.

32. Dylan Matthews, 'Donald Trump has tweeted climate change skepticism 115 times. Here's all of it', *Vox*, June 1, 2017, vox.com.

33. Tim Murphy, 'How Donald Trump Became Conspiracy Theorist in Chief', *Mother Jones*, November/December 2016, motherjones.com.

34. *The Alex Jones Show*, August 11, 2016, available at mediamatters.org.

35. US Air Force, 'Weather as a Force Multiplier'.

36. Mike Jay, *The Influencing Machine: James Tilly Matthews and the Air Loom*, London: Strange Attractor Press, 2012.

37. Edmund Burke, *Reflections on the Revolution in France*, London: James Dodsley, 1790.

38. V. Bell, C. Maiden, A. Munoz-Solomando, and V. Reddy, '"Mind control" experiences on the internet: implications for the

psychiatric diagnosis of delusions', *Psychopathology* 39:2 (2006), 87–91.

39. Will Storr, 'Morgellons: A hidden epidemic or mass hysteria?', *Guardian*, May 7, 2011, theguardian.com.

40. Jane O'Brien and Matt Danzico, '"Wi-fi refugees" shelter in West Virginia mountains', *BBC*, September 13, 2011, bbc.co.uk.

41. 'The Extinction of the Grayzone', *Dabiq* 7, February 12, 2015.

42. Murtaza Hussain, 'Islamic State's goal: "Eliminating the Grayzone" of coexistence between Muslims and the West', *Intercept*, November 17, 2015, theintercept.com.

43. Hal Brands, 'Paradoxes of the Gray Zone', Foreign Policy Research Institute, February 5, 2016, fpri.org.

9 Concurrency

1. Adrienne Lafrance, 'The Algorithm That Makes Preschoolers Obsessed With YouTube', *Atlantic*, July 25, 2017, theatlantic.com.

2. Paul McCann, 'To Teletubby or not to Teletubby', *Independent*, October 12, 1997, independent.co.uk.

3. Christopher Mims, 'Google: Psy's "Gangnam Style" Has Earned $8 Million On YouTube Alone', *Business Insider*, January 23, 2013, businessinsider.com.

4. 'Top 500 Most Viewed YouTube Channels', SocialBlade, October 2017, socialblade.com.

5. Ben Popper, 'Youtube's Biggest Star Is A 5-Year-Old That Makes Millions Opening Toys', *Verge*, December 22, 2016, theverge.com.

6. Blu Toys Club Surprise, YouTube channel.

7. Play Go Toys, YouTube channel.

8. Samanth Subramanian, 'The Macedonian Teens Who Mastered Fake News', *Wired*, February 15, 2017, wired.com.

9. 'Finger Family', YouTube video, username: Leehosok, May 25, 2007.

10. Bounce Patrol Kids, YouTube channel.

11. Charleyy Hodson, 'We Need To Talk About Why THIS Creepy AF Video Is Trending On YouTube', *We The Unicorns*, January 19, 2017, wetheunicorns.com.

12. In November 2017, after I published an article about this, Toy Freaks and numerous other channels mentioned in the article were removed by YouTube. At the time of writing, however, many similar channels and videos could still be easily found on the platform. See 'Children's YouTube is still churning out blood, suicide and cannibalism', *Wired*, 23 March 2018, wired.co.uk.

13. 'Freak Family' Facebook Page, administered by Nguyễn Hùng, facebook.com/touyentb2010.

14. Sapna Maheshwari, 'On YouTube Kids, Startling Videos Slip Past Filters', *New York Times*, November 4, 2017, nytimes.com.

15. David Remnick, 'Obama Reckons with a Trump Presidency', *New Yorker*, November 28, 2016, newyorker.com.

16. Subramanian, 'The Macedonian Teens Who Mastered Fake News'.

17. Lalage Harris, 'Letter from Veles', *Calvert Journal*, 2017, calvert-journal.com.

18. 'The name game', *Economist*, April 2, 2009, economist.com.

19. 'Macedonia police examine death threats over name dispute', *International Herald Tribune*, March 27, 2008, available at archive.li/nkYzJ.

20. Joanna Berendt, 'Macedonia Government Is Blamed for Wiretapping Scandal', *New York Times*, June 21, 2015, nytimes.com.

21. 'Macedonia: Society on Tap', YouTube video, username: Privacy International, March 29, 2016.

22. Adrian Chen, 'The Agency', *New York Times*, June 2, 2015, nytimes.com.

23. Adrian Chen, 'The Real Paranoia-Inducing Purpose of Russian Hacks', *New Yorker*, July 27, 2016, newyorker.com.

24. YouGov Poll, 'The Times Results EU Referndum 160613', June 13–14, 2016, available at bit.ly/1Ypml3w.

25. Andrew Griffin, 'Brexit supporters urged to take their own pens to polling stations amid fears of MI5 conspiracy', *Independent*, June 23, 2016, independent.co.uk.

26. Carole Cadwalladr, 'The great British Brexit robbery: how our democracy was hijacked', *Guardian*, May 7, 2017, theguardian.com.

27. Carole Cadwalladr, 'Trump, Assange, Bannon, Farage ... bound together in an unholy alliance', *Guardian*, October 27, 2017, theguardian.com.

28. Robert Booth, Matthew Weaver, Alex Hern, and Shaun Walker, 'Russia used hundreds of fake accounts to tweet about Brexit, data shows', *Guardian*, November 14, 2017, theguardian.com.

29. Marco T. Bastos and Dan Mercea, 'The Brexit Botnet and User-Generated Hyperpartisan News', *Social Science Computer Review*, October 10, 2017.

30. Alessandro Bessi and Emilio Ferrara, 'Social bots distort the 2016 U.S. Presidential election online discussion', *First Monday* 21:11 (November 2016), firstmonday.org.

31. Annalee Newitz, 'The Fembots of Ashley Madison', *Gizmodo*, August 27, 2015, gizmodo.com.

10 Cloud

1. Matthew Holehouse, 'Bilderberg Group 2013: guest list and agenda', *Telegraph*, June 6, 2013, telegraph.co.uk.

2. Eric Schmidt, 'Action This Day – Eric Schmidt, Zeitgeist Europe 2013', YouTube video, username: ZeitgeistMinds, May 20, 2013.

3. Ibid.

4. William Ferroggiaro, 'The U.S. and the Genocide in Rwanda 1994', The National Security Archive, March 24, 2004, nsarchive2.gwu.edu.

5. Russell Smith, 'The impact of hate media in Rwanda', *BBC*, December 3, 2003, news.bbc.co.uk.

6. Keith Harmon Snow, 'Pentagon Satellite Photos: New Revelations Concerning "The Rwandan Genocide"', *Global Research*, April 11, 2012, globalresearch.ca.

7. Keith Harmon Snow, 'Pentagon Produces Satellite Photos Of 1994 Rwanda Genocide', *Conscious Being*, April 2012, consciousbeingalliance.com.

8. Florence Hartmann and Ed Vulliamy, 'How Britain and the US

decided to abandon Srebrenica to its fate', *Observer*, July 4, 2015, theguardian.com.

9. 'Srebrenica: The Days of Slaughter', *New York Times*, October 29, 1995, nytimes.com.

10. Ishaan Tharoor, 'The Destruction of a Nation: Syria's War Revealed in Satellite Imagery', *Time*, March 15, 2013, world.time.com.

11. Samantha Power, 'Bystanders to Genocide', *Atlantic*, September 2001, theatlantic.com.

12. Ofeiba Quist-Arcton, 'Text Messages Used to Incite Violence in Kenya', *NPR*, February 20, 2008, npr.org.

13. Jan H. Pierskalla and Florian M. Hollenbach, 'Technology and Collective Action: The Effect of Cell Phone Coverage on Political Violence in Africa', *American Political Science Review* 107:2 (May 2013).

14. Michael Palmer, 'Data is the New Oil', blog post, ANA, November 2006, ana.blogs.com.

15. 'The world's most valuable resource is no longer oil, but data', *Economist*, May 6, 2017, economist.com.

16. David Reid, 'Mastercard's boss just told a Saudi audience that "data is the new oil"', *CNBC*, October 24, 2017, cnbc.com.

17. Stephen Kerr MP, Kevin Brennan MP, debate on 'Leaving the EU: Data Protection', October 12, 2017, transcript.

18. Palmer, 'Data is the New Oil'.

19. For details of imperial classification and forced naming, see James C. Scott, *Seeing Like a State*, New Haven, CT: Yale University Press, 1998.

20. Arundhati Roy, 'The End of Imagination', Guardian, August 1, 1998, theguardian.com.

21. Sandia National Laboratories, 'Expert Judgment on Markers to Deter Inadvertent Human Intrusion into the Waste Isolation Pilot Plant', report, SAND92-1382 / UC-721, page F-49, available at wipp.energy.gov.

22. *And into Eternity . . . Communication over 10000s of Years: How Will We Tell our Children's Children Where the Nuclear Waste is?*, Zeitschrift für Semiotik (in German), Berlin: Deutschen Gesellschaft für Semiotik 6:3 (1984).

23. Michael Madsen, dir., *Into Eternity*, Films Transit International, 2010.

24. See Rocky Flats Nuclear Guardianship project, 'Nuclear Guardianship Ethic statement', 1990, rev. 2011, rockyflatsnuclearguardianship.org.

Afterword

1. openai.com/blog/dall-e/

2. See for example, Shubham Saboo, 'Prompt Engineering: The Career of Future', *Medium*, May 2022.

3. See for example makeavideo.studio from Meta AI (aka Facebook) and imagen.research.google from Google.

4. Common Crawl annotates its own work at commoncrawl.org/connect/blog/.

5. For more on LAION's methodology, see laion.ai/faq/.

6. Have I Been Trained was created by the artists Mat Dryhurst and Holly Herndon specifically to allow artists to see if their work was being used to train AI image generation models. For more on this see Chris Stokel-Walker, 'This couple is launching an organization to protect artists in the AI era', inverse.com, September 14, 2022.

7. Matt Growcot, 'Shocked Artist Finds Private Medical Photos in AI Training Data Set, *Petapixel*, September 26, 2022, twitter.com/LapineDeLaTerre.

8. For the origins of Crungus, see @Brainmage (Guy Kelly)'s thread on Twitter: twitter.com/Brainmage/status/1538111384390619136.

9. For the origins of Loab, see @supercomposite's thread on Twitter: twitter.com/supercomposite/status/1567162313194471428.

10. For more on this line of thinking, see James Bridle, *Ways of Being: Beyond Human Intelligence*, London: Allen Lane, 2022.

11. See for example, Kyle Wiggers, 'AI Weekly: AI model training costs on the rise, highlighting need for new solutions', *VentureBeat*, October 15, 2021.

12. Karen Hao, 'Training a single AI model can emit as much carbon as five cars in their lifetimes', *MIT Technology Review*, June 2019.

13. Will Buchanan, 'The Carbon Footprint of AI', devblogs.microsoft.com, October 26, 2020.

14. Cheyanne Walker, 'Adel residents plead for help after loud Bitcoin operation moves into their community', Fox 31, December 5, 2021.

15. Kevin Williams, 'An Appalachian town was told a bitcoin mine would bring an economic boom. It got noise pollution and an eyesore', *Washington Post*, March 18, 2022.

16. Annika Stechemesser, Anders Levermann, and Leonie Wenz, 'Temperature impacts on hate speech online: evidence from 4 billion geolocated tweets from the USA', *Lancet Planetary Health*, September 2022.

17. Karen Hao, 'A new vision of artificial intelligence for the people', *MIT Technology Review*, April 22, 2022.

18. More resources from Te Hiku Media can be found at tehiku.nz.

19. Donavyn Coffey, 'Māori are trying to save their language from Big Tech', *Wired*, April 28, 2021.

20. Thomas Nagel, 'What Is It Like to Be a Bat?', *Philosophical Review*, volume 83, no. 4, October 1974.

21. A good example of contemporary space-based animal tracking is the ICARUS project, whose results include continent-scale migration studies and earthquake prediction: icarus.mpg.de/en.

22. See, for example, Craig Welch, 'Groundbreaking effort launched to decode whale language', *National Geographic*, April 19, 2021, and 'Prairie dogs' language decoded by scientists', CBC News, June 21, 2021.

23. For an exploration of the relationship between network theory and mycorrhizal webs, see Merlin Sheldrake, *Entangled Life: How Fungi Make Our Worlds, Change Our Minds and Shape Our Futures*, London: Vintage, 2021.

24. Ursula K. Le Guin, 'A Rant about "Technology"', ursulakleguinarchive.com.

Index

Locators in *bold italic* represent images/pictures

Index